# Women and Work

The age of post-feminism?

*Edited by*
LIZ SPERLING
MAIREAD OWEN

*Technical Editor*
Liz James

# Ashgate

Aldershot • Burlington USA • Singapore • Sydney

Published by
Ashgate Publishing Ltd
Gower House
Croft Road
Aldershot
Hants GU11 3HR
England

Ashgate Publishing Company
131 Main Street
Burlington
Vermont 05401
USA

Ashgate website: http://www.ashgate.com

**British Library Cataloguing in Publication Data**
Women and work : the age of post-feminism?
  1.Women - Employment
  I.Sperling, Liz II.Owen, Mairead
  331.4

**Library of Congress Control Number:** 00-132581


ISBN  1 84014 950 7

Printed in Great Britain by
Antony Rowe Ltd, Chippenham, Wiltshire

# Contents

# List of Figures

# List of Tables

# List of Contributors

**Jean Burrell** and **Hilary Rollin** had been colleagues in the School of Languages at Oxford Brookes University for several years before they discovered they had both studied Spanish at the same small London University college. Jean now lectures in French language and French women's writing and Hilary is a lecturer in the expanding Spanish department. They have recently collaborated on several conference papers and articles on their research project on women's employment, particularly in the hospitality industry, in four European countries. Hilary has also presented papers and articles focusing on the Spanish situation. With Jean Monnet Fund support, they and their colleagues have developed an undergraduate course looking at women's employment in Europe.

**Joanne Cook** is a researcher on an EU(TSER) funded project on labour market participation and social exclusion. She is also currently completing her PhD, which examines the restructuring of social rights, using case studies of UK flexible employment and welfare benefits policies. Her recent work includes the re-structuring of citizenship, flexible employment and welfare benefits policies in the UK and gendered political economy.

**Gillian A. Dunne** is a Senior Research Fellow at the LSE Gender Institute. Her research at Cambridge University and at LSE explores the relationship between gender and sexuality. In comparative studies which focus on 'non-heterosexual' experience of work and family life, she is interested in illuminating the role of institutional heterosexuality for reproducing gender inequality. She has recently completed a study on gay fatherhood, and is currently working on transitions to adulthood from the perspectives of young lesbian and gay people. Her books include, *Lesbian Lifestyles: Women's Work and the Politics of Sexuality* and *Living 'Difference'?: Lesbian Experience of Work and Family-life*.

**Catherine Fletcher** is based in the Faculty of Languages and European Studies at the University of the West of England. Her current research is on equal opportunities in training, focusing specifically on the insurance industry.

**Andrea Lee** is a Senior Lecturer in Human Resource Management in the Department of Management at the University of Central Lancashire. Her teaching and research interests cover equality issues, gender and work. The material for this chapter was drawn from her MPhil research which examined the implementation of an equal opportunity policy within a local authority.

**Mairead Owen** is a Senior Lecturer in Women's Studies at Liverpool John Moores University. Her first degree was in Sociology and her PhD at Liverpool University was jointly supervised by the Department of English and that of Communication Studies. This 'eclectic' background continues in her teaching and research, with work on women and equal opportunities, women and the media, feminist pedagogy and gender and ageing. Her publications include chapters and articles on teaching and learning in Women's Studies and on women's reading of popular fiction, while her present research focuses on issues around women and the body, and the social construction of older age.

**Nicola Piper** is a Research Fellow at the Nordic Institute of Asian Studies in Copenhagen. She obtained her MA in Japanese Studies and PhD in Sociological Studies, both from the University of Sheffield (UK). She taught for three years at the School of East Asian Studies at Sheffield. Her research interests are in various aspects of international labour migration, and she has published a book on immigrants' citizenship in Britain and Germany, as well as a number of articles on female labour migrants in Japan. Her current research project deals with gender, war crimes and the issue of compensation in Japan and Germany. She is also co-editor of a forthcoming book on gender, work and globalisation.

**Liz Sperling** is Senior Lecturer in Politics at Liverpool John Moores University. She is currently writing a book on women, political philosophy and politics. Her past work includes research into the Europeanisation of local government, women's policy networks and women's political representation on Quangos.

**Lesley Twomey** has been Head of Spanish at the University of Northumbria at Newcastle since 1997. Her PhD, completed in 1995, is on 'The Immaculate Conception in Fifteenth Century Castilian and Catalan Poetry: A Comparative Thematic Study'. She has continued to research in the field of fifteenth century literature. In addition, Lesley maintains research on working women in Spain and has presented papers and articles in this area. She has edited a book on *Faith and Fanaticism: Religious Fervour* in Early Modern Spain, and is currently editing a comparative study of women's lives, entitled *Women Face the New Millenium.*

**Linda Walsh** and **Liz James** are colleagues at Liverpool John Moores University. Linda mainly teaches microeconomics, financial and industrial economics, and economic methods. Her research interests are in the area of Eastern Europe and accession to the European Union. She has recently contributed two shared chapters to M. Mannin (ed.) (1999) *Pushing Back the Boundaries.* Liz has a PhD in Interdisciplinary Women's Studies from the University of Warwick. Her research interests include working-class women's writing.

# Acknowledgements

We would like to thank John Vogler and the Research Committee of the School of Social Sciences at Liverpool John Moores University for the financial support they gave as we approached the submission deadline. Without this we would not have been able to afford the most valuable member of our team, Liz James. It is Liz who ensured that our deadlines were kept, has done justice to our work in her meticulous production of the chapters and who basically ensured that the book ever reached its final stages.

# 1 Introduction: Women and Work in the Age of Post-feminism

LIZ SPERLING

This book considers the position of women and work in the modern economy. From the legislative effects on 'freeing' women to work and initiatives to attain status as equals within the workforce, to the choices that women make in relation to paid employment, it is possible to measure the extent to which we live in a post-feminist era.[1] The concept of 'post-feminism' is not one that I would choose to posit. It is, however, an idea that has been bandied about as a result of the measurable increase of women's visibility in the public sphere. The argument that opportunities exist for women to grab, and the consequent focus on the individual for failure to progress in whatever field, is attractive to those attempting solidarity or sympathy with 'disadvantaged' groups such as women electors, employees and consumers, whilst simultaneously clinging to power. The fact that more opportunities for women do exist in paid employment, which empowers women in other activities (Blumberg, 1995:5), is undeniable. How far such opportunities have created an epoch of equalitarianism is open to question.

**The Women Have Arrived!**

The mid- to late 1990s, in Britain, have been heralded as the 'age of women' by journalists, employers and researchers who have become aware of the presence of large numbers of women in paid employment (Carvel, 1996; Younger and Warrington, 1996). The trends, according to such intrepid commentators, are set to continue as more girls and young women are successful in public examinations. For example, since 1993 in the United Kingdom (UK), girls have generally outstripped the performance of boys at GCSE and A level (*Times Education Supplement*, 6.9.1996 and 13.9.1996; EOC, 1994 and 1998). Whilst the education of women globally may not present quite as promising a picture as that of the UK and other developed countries, certainly educational opportunities for women throughout the world are improving (Joekes, 1987:16; Blumberg, 1995:7; United Nations, 1995a:7;

1

Seager, 1997:9). Moreover, as modes of work change universally, women are more likely to fit the model of 'worker', based on the traditional patterns of women in work (United Nations, 1995a:49). For example, in developed countries as work becomes increasingly less secure, manifested by the increase in part-time and temporary contracts, employers' identification of women as primary carers, who desire 'pin-money', becomes obvious. Such workers' 'flexibility' in terms of conditions of work is heaven-sent in a free-market economy. Similarly in developing countries, poverty and the detrimental effects of, for example, structural adjustment programmes, which often have a greater impact on women provide rich pickings from among women for employers in a global economy (United Nations, 1992:95; International Labour Office, 1995:3; United Nations, 1996). Thus, the United Nations (UN) Platform for Action notes

> due to, *inter alia,* difficult economic situations and a lack of bargaining power resulting from gender inequality, many women have been forced to accept low pay and poor working conditions and thus have often become *preferred workers* (1996:94, my emphasis),

and the report of the Secretary General to the United Nations states that 'the majority of newly created jobs have tended to be atypical. As it turns out, these atypical employment patterns correlate with the feminisation of the labour force' (United Nations, 1995b:182).

Naturally, it is not difficult to challenge the concept of the 'age of women'. While more women may, indeed, be entering the workforce, and the conditions of work favour the 'ideal type' of married mother working for extra household income, the reality of women and work does not present a picture of social and economic advantage. As Seager notes, 'women's participation as workers in this new world economy is not an unalloyed sign of progress' (1997:9). This is not to fall into the trap of essentialism. Examples of highly 'successful' women, such as Nicola Horlick, 35-year old mother of five children, who managed pension funds for Morgan Grenfell, for a salary of around £1m a year, and Marjorie Scardino, first woman to run a FTSE 100 company in the UK, serve to illustrate that not all women are oppressed by organisations or circumstances.[2] Moreover, in striving to render all women equal in their disadvantage, we may deny the possibility of achieving success in developing equality of opportunity. Women's inequalities in work, and in society generally, are not just seen in relation to men but between women themselves. This does not just concern pay and conditions: the 'good' and 'honest' woman worker is not one who works in the sex industry; lesbians may face discrimination in work, or in finding work, when they declare their sexuality; the opportunities for better educated women and presumably those from more affluent or 'cultured' backgrounds differ from those of unqualified, unskilled women; the commitment of women with children, especially lone parents, may be questioned at interview or in post; and women from different ethnic backgrounds may suffer the prejudices of both racism and sexism in the workplace, or the queues to it. It may be argued that such disadvantage is peculiar to Western experience. This will be true to some extent. However, UN surveys (1991; 1995a) demonstrate the universality of women's disadvantage in the workforce, citing themes familiar to Western researchers: men's domination of trade unions, reluctance to train and hire women, the potential for women to demand equality legislation for things like maternity or parental leave, and the general perception of women that suggests it is best to give them marginal jobs (United Nations, 1991:88). Moreover, research in this book indicates the international phenomenon of discrimination between women. Whilst being aware of the differences of women, for this volume we are concerned with issues of commonality between them.

**New Economy: New Opportunity**

The expansion of the female labour-force is a global phenomenon (Mitter, 1986; United Nations, 1992; Blumberg et al., 1995; OECD, 1996). Indeed, many analyses note that the changing global economy is directly responsible for women's increased, and men's declining, proportion of the workforce (ILO/INSTRAW, 1985:21; Mitter, 1986:14; OECD, 1996:186 Table A). This may be especially noticeable, although not necessarily more prevalent, in developing countries with the growth in industrialisation and the international search for cheap labour (ILO/INSTRAW, 1985:21; Pettman, 1996:163; Steans, 1998:134). It is here that more women are moving into the public sphere from, for example, family farms (ILO/INSTRAW, 1985:23). Unfortunately, increased opportunities for women in the workforce have not alleviated the differential between the types of jobs that women and men do, and the remuneration received for work (ILO, 1995:3; Joekes, 1987:18-19). The Second Review and Appraisal of Nairobi Forward-looking Strategies for the Advancement of Women notes that

> while trade expansion led to an increase in the supply of jobs for women, the quality of those jobs was often poor and they were insecure, paid only a

fraction of the male wage for the same job and lacked social protection (United Nations, 1995b:36-37).

Indeed, a major characteristic of the emergent global economy is the creation of what Moghadam quotes as 'global assembly line' (1995:20; see also Pettman, 1996; Mies, 1998). In this model, developed countries control production of goods which is transferred to the cheaper labour markets at the periphery, that is, to the developing nations. In fact, many indebted governments of the Third World have set up Export Production Zones (EPZs) where factories, staffed predominantly by poorly paid and otherwise exploited women, specifically produce goods for the global market (Steans, 1998:136). Thus the nineteenth century Western tableau, inscribed with capitalist industrialists using women as low paid, insecure industrial workers operating in often unsafe conditions (Miles, 1989), becomes the global norm. While women in developed countries may be perceived as benefiting from belonging to the 'core' nations, and certainly better off economically than their 'sisters' in the Third World, the shift from manufacturing to service industries has destabilised the tenured job market.

It may not seem so paradoxical, then, that despite the increase of women in the labour force throughout the world, female unemployment is also prevalent. The rightward shift towards market practices in the developed countries has resulted in the contraction of manufacturing industries and the public sector, in contrast to the simultaneous expansion of private sector employment (United Nations, 1995a:52-53; ILO, 1995:3). These first two sectors traditionally favoured women workers. Thus, for example, in OECD countries the growth in the service sector is peopled mainly by women working on non-standard contracts; part-time, temporary and fixed-term (OECD, 1994:111). Coupled with what the UN calls 'the re-employment challenge' in which 'women experience greater difficulties than men in finding re-employment' as a result of the decreasing public sector and continuing discrimination, patterns of female unemployment should not be surprising (United Nations, 1995a:52). Of course, unemployment in developing countries does not necessarily compare easily to that in developed market economies. However, structural adjustment programmes, in which loans may be acquired on working towards and meeting progressively strict conditions imposed by the IMF (Steans, 1998:142), and which rely on export-led economic growth together with cuts in public expenditure, have an uneven impact on women which are familiar to the West. For example, cuts in public expenditure result in loss of welfare jobs and services, both of which affect women as workers and as providers of primary care in health and social welfare services (Tickner, 1991:196). Moreover, the UN notes that in nations where agricultural, self-employed and home work still prevail, female unemployment may be grossly underrepresented in official statistics (United Nations, 1995a:53), a phenomenon quantified by the ILO (1999:para 18) which stated that the inclusion in national accounts of women's work in the informal economy would add 25 per cent to GNP.

A clear connection exists here in consideration of another recognisable global phenomenon, that of the extra burden that working women carry. Thus, in both developed and developing countries, women undertake the majority of household and caring duties (United Nations, 1991:101-102), and in developing countries women are also responsible for much unpaid, subsistence work such as growing and processing food for home and market (United Nations, 1995c:51; Mitter, 1986:142). While men may contribute to unpaid domestic work, they do not do so in proportion to their status as 'partner' in the household. The situation of women is made worse by structural adjustment programmes in which export drives pass much control over agricultural production to mechanisation and to men. This not only serves to undermine women's subsistence farming, with its resultant consequences for domestic food production, but it forces women into yet greater reliance on the informal economy, homeworking and making 'luxury' goods for First World markets, prostitution and everyday survival services for their families (Pettman, 1996; Mies, 1998). Thus, it appears that familiar patterns of un/employment based on traditional perceptions of gender and work appear not to have been greatly affected by the opportunities afforded women in the new global economy.

**Equal Opportunities in the New Labour Market**

Attempts to increase equal opportunities through legislation are not necessarily universal. Western Europe and the United States (US) may have well entrenched, if not well implemented, equality legislation. Despite such initiatives as the European Union's (EU) series of Medium Term Action Programmes which recognise the constraints of the private sphere on women's equal opportunities in work,[3] equality legislation *per se* operates in the public sphere alone, albeit acknowledging that working mothers require maternity and childcare provision of some sort and, more recently, joint parental leave. A further point at issue is that of how equality legislation and initiatives suit developing countries where women comprise up to 40 per cent of unpaid subsistence food growers on family farms and an indeterminate proportion of the informal, unregulated and largely undocumented economy, including such occupations as prostitution (United Nations, 1991:90 and 93-94; United Nations, 1995a:58; Moghadam, 1995:21). Even in developed countries, the increase in the informal sector (Blumberg et al., 1995) further decreases the force of equality legislation. Thus, legislation often can do little to ensure integral or comprehensive equality of opportunity in employment markets.

Equal opportunities has been described by some as a 'feminist fallacy' (Quest, 1992). Whereas the increasing rhetoric of the market economy relies on concepts such as choice, equality of opportunity, and individual empowerment, collectivised equal opportunities denies such achievement. Indeed, McElroy states that, 'the preferential treatment of women in employment is nothing less than a frontal attack on the rights of the individual and the free market' (1992:113). Certainly, Western feminism may not be appropriate to women in developing countries. Indeed, feminism may seem 'inappropriate' to many women throughout the world. However, it surely cannot be claimed that the free market is non-discriminating in terms of gender. The historical patterns of gender segregation of occupations, status and pay manifestly point to the failure of the market to ensure liberty and equality of opportunity between the sexes in global employment markets and between the gendered workforces of developed and developing states. The gendered global assembly line increasingly assumes the hierarchical nature of domestic capitalist production relations played out between rich and poor countries. Moreover, the fact that historically, in developing and, increasingly, in developed countries, women's wages are an essential part, and often the whole, of household income (OECD, 1995:19),[4] would logically assume a more balanced workforce than is apparent from labour statistics (ILO/United Nations, 1985; United Nations, 1991; ILO, 1999:para 17). Critics of legislation to improve conditions for women in work allege that it is the increasing number of women workers that has driven down the price of their labour (Papps, 1992), an idea analysed by Linda Walsh and Liz James in this volume. Conversely, the historical and continuing overwhelming number of men in the labour force seems to have kept their wages universally higher than women's (United Nations, 1995a:73-74). As David (1986) implies in her analysis of the family and New Right ideology, markets can only function on the basis of women's work in the home and other unpaid economic activity.

The work of the UN to audit and address the issue of women's disadvantaged position in general, and in work specifically, is an example and acknowledgement of the fact that 'natural' forces do not engender equality, or equality of opportunity, and that changes in markets globally overtly affect women differentially. For example, rationalisation of working practices and organisational structures may lead to higher paid workers, usually men, being most badly affected. While this may result in more jobs becoming available for women, it also perpetuates their economic disadvantage in terms of pay and working conditions (United Nations, 1995:x-xi).[5] Moreover, equal opportunities legislation is an attempt to redress a socio-economic and political imbalance created from the pursuit of self-interest. However, such legislation, whatever the diverse motivations of the initiators and instigators, has to operate within existing and developing frameworks.[6]

In this respect, Joanne Cook (ch.2) considers the concept of increased flexible working within the EU, a system relatively advanced in terms of equality legislation. Here, the growth of 'atypical' work is seen to fall outside the parameters of the legislative framework. Hence, the part-time retail workers and homeworkers in the manufacturing sector of Cook's study, mainly women, have unequal access to legal processes set up to ensure employment rights. The concentration of women in insecure, non-unionised jobs, often undertaken in isolation from other workers, ensures that women are unaware of their rights, and that the risk of attempting legal action in the case of discriminatory employment practices minimises use of available channels of redress. Moreover, Cook, like Nicola Piper (ch.9), brings into question the definition of 'worker' in relation to employment rights. Where legislation applies to those in formal paid employment, it may increasingly encompass fewer workers as flexibility creates more self-employed, sub-contracted and homeworkers.

Of course, where equal opportunities legislation exists, the potential for differing interpretations and levels of implementation is evident. While Cook's study indicates that member states of the EU can play with words to affect the parameters of legislation and those who may claim redress,[7] Hilary Rollin and Jean Burrell (ch.3), and Catherine Fletcher (ch.4), in their comparative studies of EU member states, consider how different traditions of work, as well as the state's attitude to women in work and equality issues, account for differential female employment patterns. For example, as globalised patterns of female employment become increasingly evident in the EU, the suspicion in Spain accruing to part-time work, together with an historical dearth of nursery school provision, means that the increase of women in the labour force has outpaced demand for female labour. In France and the UK, on the other hand, temporary fixed term and/or part-time contracts have been taken up with gusto, although with some provisos based on better protective legislation for part-time workers in France which make it less economical to employ large numbers of part-time, usually female, workers.

It was only with the election of a Labour government in 1997 that the UK acceded to such initiatives as the minimum wage and the Social Chapter of the Maastricht Treaty. This contrasts with the historical situation of countries like France and Spain which are apparently much more willing to accept policies that aim to promote equality of opportunity for women in the workforce. Rollin and Burrell's description of the initiatives undertaken by governments in both countries appears encouraging, especially in light of the increase of female employment in states that encompass 'atypical' work patterns in employment legislation. However, the less advantaged position of working women compared to men is still evident and the advent of European equality directives, while being necessary has not proved sufficient to ensure equal employment practice, or the downgrading associated with feminisation of work.

Fletcher (ch.4) considers the implementation of equal opportunities policies in relation to training, and therefore advancement of women, in the service sector, taking the insurance industry as the focus of a comparative study between France and Britain. Again, differing levels of commitment to the concept as well as the practice of equal opportunities result in general disparities between the states. However, the individualisation of work within a market economy is evident within this study, indicating a potential for increased opportunities for women as 'groups' with special needs became a thing of the past. But this does not actually result in a more equalitarian basis for progress and advancement in the industry where vertical and horizontal segregation is still rife, the existence of equal opportunities legislation arguably relieving employers of the responsibility for monitoring and evaluating gender progress in organisations.

## Choice is a Many Splendoured Thing

Alongside the growth in equal opportunities initiatives in the West, the encroachment of free market ideas with the promise of increased choice has continued. Here the spectre of flexibility is again evident as workers are able to move in and out of jobs, have the opportunity to change their careers, and even move in and out of work as education and training become available throughout life. Naturally, 'choice' is a many-faceted concept: for many women choice may be whether to accept working in a framework and environment geared to male employment patterns or suffer poverty. As the UN describes it, more women than men choose 'low pay over no pay' (United Nations, 1995:xi). Moreover, choice is relative as traditionally the greater earning capacity of men may determine 'choice' in two-parent households with men as breadwinners and women as supplementary earners.[8] In other words, choices are made from an unequal base determined by differing power positions resulting from assumptions of gender roles.

Walsh and James's economic analysis (ch.6) considers the role of women's choices in relation to work and pay. Here we can see that while models and theories may assume choice, thereby imbuing women with responsibility for their economic status, external factors, such as employers' attitudes to women and the historically gendered division of labour, influence market processes. Thus, while it may be asserted that market conditions empower all individuals and allow women the choice to juggle employment and private responsibilities, it is more likely that markets are a mechanism for maintaining traditional interests that created, and perpetuate, gender differentials in the workplace.

Gillian Dunne (ch.7) introduces an interesting twist in the concept of economic choice, that of quality of life over standard of living. New Right political and economic theories and policies appear to conflate the two ideas assuming that maximising individual or family self-interest is dependent on increased wealth.[9] Thus, Harman's assertion that working men are dissatisfied with the division between their public and domestic lives, wanting to spend more time with their children, is significant but irrelevant as male employment is a wealth creator both within the family and the state. Indeed, Dunne's study indicates the dilemma of choice in which historical employment patterns perpetuate, and are perpetuated by, traditional gendered relations. In lesbian families where 'gender difference' is not a factor determining employment and domestic choices, indeed where a template for allocation of tasks does not exist, substantially different employment and lifestyle choices often emerge. Such choices may well correlate with Walsh and James's 'assertion' that women choose low pay. Indeed, where both partners have similar investments in employment and in family, the choice to forego 'wealth' for the opportunity to share child-rearing and increase quality of life is evident. Moreover, the opportunity that the changing economy provides for choice of home-based and self-employment appears to suit Dunne's analysis. However, Dunne acknowledges that her study mainly incorporates women from a relatively privileged, highly educated sector, mainly in professional occupations, a sector that the new economy benefits more than others. This is not to limit the contribution of the study to the parameters of lesbian households. Rather, as Dunne notes (p.130), the model portrayed in the household profiles and in the employment patterns chosen by lesbian couples with dependent children is one that could be applied much more broadly.

**Women Workers in the Age of Women**

As mentioned, Western economies often incorporate equality legislation, and many developed and developing countries are signatories to the Convention on the Elimination of All Forms of Discrimination against Women (CEDAW), adopted by the General Assembly of the United Nations in 1979. Of course, such measures do not assure women of equal treatment in employment or equal pay. Thus, of the 134 signatories to the Convention many have failed to adjust 'national laws, administrative practices or other public policies according to their obligations under the Convention' (United Nations, 1995b:6), and few states, if any, have achieved equality, or equality of opportunity, for women in the workforce.

Andrea Lee (ch.5) considers the experience of women where equality legislation exists and is meant to ensure equality of opportunity and of experience of women. Her study is of a traditionally male-dominated area of work in the UK, the Fire Service, where it becomes obvious that deeply entrenched attitudes and language have a significant effect on how quickly and how well equality measures can be instituted. This chapter introduces issues often invisible in the decision-making and implementation process: organisational culture, differential assumptions of equal opportunities and the defining parameters of different types of work. For example, where a job may be perceived as 'defining' sexuality, as fire-fighting defines masculinity (p.78), the intrusion of 'others' may be vehemently, if subtly, obstructed. Thus, equal opportunities, rather than being a positive and progressive concept, may be perceived as a threat to established behaviours and practices. In this case, it becomes an exercise in what Halford (1989:29) calls 'deliberate ineffectiveness'. Lee also indicates the problem of in/visibility of women in male-dominated occupations, where visibility highlights difference but invisibility hides and denies the unequal status of women in employment structures developed by, and for, men. Thus equal opportunity policy itself becomes part of the apparatus for denial of its objectives.

In Lesley Twomey's work (ch.8) the failure of equality legislation in post-Franco Spain is described in the context of traditional perceptions of women in relation to work. Certainly, women's rights in law are relatively recent, Franco's regime having denied equality before the law until 1970 when women were first allowed equal access to education (p.135). It was not until the post-Franco socialist government instigated a series of equality laws, presumably enhanced partly by Spain's membership of the EU, that women's entry to the workforce and into representative positions advanced. Twomey uses literature as a channel to analyse the underlying causes of continuity in the subjugation of women workers in Spain. In her analysis of the novel *Amado Amo* by Rosa Montero, a description of women's lack of equal opportunities in an economy that has seen rapid growth of women in the workforce is given. Thus the historical, stereotypical portrait of women as a symbol of men's success, women as victims of corporate power relationships, and women as unseen and powerless corporate actors, is exhibited. The portrayal of women as peripheral actors in organisations is utilised not to perpetuate the 'norm', but as a warning to avoid complacency in the presence of legislation that is supposed to ensure equality of opportunity.

Usually it is assumed that women are mostly disadvantaged in relation to men in work. This may be a function of a fairly stable geographical status of the majority of workers. However, migrant women workers may often suffer the added injustices of racial discrimination. The UN (1995a:67) notes the feminisation of labour migration as changes in the global economy differentially affect women, and feminist analysts of the International Political Economy (IPE) further emphasise the rise in the trafficking of women as the effects of the new global economy increase (Enloe, 1989; Pettman, 1996:170). The lack of support networks and concentration of women migrant workers in insecure, unregulated and low status jobs is noted, as is the increasing move of such women into the sex industry. Nicola Piper's work (ch.9) considers such circumstances in Japan where traditional definitions of 'work' and of female and male roles prevail. Thus, men work and Japanese women provide heirs, while migrant sex workers are merely 'sex objects' and not workers (p.155). A strong element of racism is also present in that Japanese wives have no 'duty' to provide men with sexual gratification beyond propagation requirements, thus a market is created for sexual services. This is mainly filled by migrant women who are subject to strict immigration laws that prevent them from taking up work other than in the 'entertainment' industry. Seager (1997:65) states that 35,000 women 'entertainers' from the Philippines and Thailand enter Japan annually. Coupled with institutionalised discriminatory practices that favour the migration of women from certain countries over others, giving them greater protection, the scene is set for certain groups of migrant women workers to be super-exploited as a result of almost total invisibility before the law.

**Legislative Dilemma: Equal Opportunity in a Global Economy?**

As with any writers, women can only build on their experiences and attempt to ratiocinate to the general population. This obviously causes problems as women who have different experiences feel ignored, betrayed, and possibly further exploited by people/sisters who should know better! The experience of female academics in American or European universities cannot equate with that of women agricultural workers in developing countries; the experiences of agricultural workers in Africa or Asia do not necessarily concur, let alone equate, with those of sex-workers in Pacific Rim countries, and so on. It is only by spreading the knowledge of women's different experiences that we can learn of each others' plight and maybe assist each other in remedying exploitation that is common, to different degrees, in all areas of work and all regions. Thus, personal experience as well as individual study becomes part of the universal collage of women workers' experience.

While most of the chapters herein are concerned with situations in which equality legislation exists but is not working comprehensively, the issues analysed may be globally applicable. What they illustrate is that endeavours to improve the situation of women in work as they are affected by new economic practices and requirements may be thwarted by various, sometimes innocently, unacknowledged institutionalised attitudes and practices. For example, historical patterns in organisational behaviours, definitions of such 'obvious' concepts as work and worker, the gendered, often hidden, symbolism of work in relation to esteem, as well as overt sexism, may individually or collectively obstruct the achievement of full implementation of legislation. All these barriers are exportable to developing economies in which women's presence in the workforce is increasing. Moreover, the question of whether it is fully in employers' interests to equalise the workforce has to be asked. Equality of opportunity for women may be a sound political objective but continuing exploitation of women in work suggests that it may not be a sound economic one, thus leading to a possible explanation, suggested by Mairead Owen (ch.10), that capitalism overtly prefers women as its staple base.

Contemporary studies show that changes in economic markets globally have a significant effect on women in the labour force. Some of these changes, such as increased educational and job opportunities, may be beneficial to women. However, even with such benefit, the gender gap between male and female workers, and differences between female workers in many cases, persist. Thus, against a background of economic progress for women, the contributions to this book confirm that we have yet to reach a state of 'post-feminism', a concept presumably intended by its proponents to indicate achievement of nirvana in terms of equality.

**Notes**

[1] The book is the result of a conference on 'Women and Equality: Rhetoric and Reality' held at Liverpool John Moores University on 6th July 1996. The theme was not one of post-feminism and authors were not required to write in this framework. Rather, post-feminism is a slant on the work given by the editors based on the popular idea that all women have to do is grasp the nettle if they are genuine in their desire to achieve equal status with men.

[2] Of course, it is possible that such women have had a longer and more arduous journey in achieving their position and status, and may still not have obtained equal remuneration to their male equivalents.

[3] The Medium Term Action Programmes began in the 1980s after a markedly increased number of women MEPs were elected following the 1979 introduction of direct elections to the European Parliament (Vallance and Davies, 1986). Although the EU had considerable equality legislation in place at that time, the new women MEPs were responsible for highlighting the failure of its implementation and for considering the remedy to this situation. The Programmes have become progressively more broadly focused acknowledging the integration of public and private issues in achieving equality for women and men in the workplace. Thus the Fourth Medium Term Action Programme 1996-2000 is concerned with 'mainstreaming', ensuring its consistency with special measures for women and men in sex-segregated areas of work, and with increasing the representation of women at all levels of decision making.

[4] The UN survey of women in the world indicates a world-wide growth in women-headed households. Of these, between 25-50 per cent are headed by elderly women, the rest consisting of single women or women with children and dependants (1991:18).

[5] The gendered effects of economic restructuring differ between regions. For example, the UN study shows that women in the transition economies fare worse than men (1995a:x). The latter tend to be employed in new industries and, as the support systems common to former Communist states are eliminated, paid employment for women with family responsibilities becomes more difficult.

[6] The concept of 'mainstreaming' has become a core concept for policy making in recent years in both the European Commission and, consequently, member states of the EU. While such a concept should be welcomed for placing women firmly and comprehensively on policy agendas, there is a danger that women will again have to conform to the 'norm' if they are to be 'mainstreamed' and that full implementation of mainstreaming would require too great a transition for existing structures and procedures to manage.

[7] Interpretation of legislation by the use of words and concepts that limit the potential of particular groups to utilise the provisions of the Act may, of course, be informed by acceptance of traditional patterns and attitudes.

[8] This is increasingly changing as new work practices favour women's flexibility and cheapness over male working traditions and expense.

[9] This does not assume equality of course.  Indeed inequality is a natural condition of political and economic society (Hayek, 1979; Levitas, 1986).

# 2 Citizenship and Flexible Employment: Homeworkers' and Part-time Workers' Access to Social Rights in the UK

JOANNE COOK

## Introduction[1]

Flexible employment practices are now broadly accepted as a feature of contemporary labour markets. Over the last decade a wealth of research has been carried out investigating processes of labour market flexibilisation, and debates have emerged about the best way of regulating this new employment. The European Union (EU) has been a focal point for many of these debates and has undergone a combined process of encouraging the growth of flexible employment, while also developing new employment rights such as those contained in the Social Chapter of the Maastricht Treaty. The restructuring of work has brought with it profound and far-reaching implications for the nature and content of social rights, and has thus formed a central issue of concern for the many citizenship writers. This chapter argues that gendered citizenship provides a useful framework for evaluating flexible employment and uncovering its negative implications. It will be argued that there is a need to place research on the gendered nature of flexible employment directly within a gendered citizenship framework in order to understand fully the implications of the growth of this employment.

The focus of this chapter is on the gap between formal employment rights and their realisation in practice. Formal structures are only part of the picture, in that it is necessary to examine the effects that the implementation of policy has on the ability of citizens to translate formal rights into substantive rights in order to realise social rights. Therefore, from a gendered citizenship perspective it is insufficient to simply outline entitlement to social rights without also investigating the role that inequalities of gender, race and class have on the realisation of these rights in practice. This framework will be adopted to uncover the importance of analysing social agency as well as structure.[2] The development of this approach is underpinned by three main arguments. Firstly, it is suggested that social agency has an impact on the development of flexible employment rights. Secondly, because social agency is gendered and the power of social groups is unequal, the rights developed frequently do not incorporate the needs of numerical flexible workers. This concept refers here to employment practices which make it easier for employers to adjust the number of workers they employ to correspond with demand (Dex and McCulloch, 1995). Thirdly, once employment rights are translated into law, the ability to access them is not gender neutral as they are implemented on top of pre-existing gender inequalities in the public and private spheres.

Once the inadequacies of flexible employment rights are revealed, it becomes increasingly difficult to view the growth of flexible work as wholly beneficial. Despite the wealth of literature on gender in this area, mainstream approaches to citizenship need to be more inclusive of gender differences and more attention needs to be paid to examining flexibility from the perspectives of the social groups located in this employment. It is necessary to understand that flexible employment impacts differently on particular social groups, which raises questions about the merits of embracing this employment, for as long as this work remains insufficiently regulated. In this sense gendered citizenship proves useful because it identifies the inadequacies of theory, policy and legislation, all of which situate flexibility as gender, race and class neutral.

Approaching an examination of flexible employment from a social rights perspective is in turn useful, since it provides a valuable basis for evaluating flexible employment, as access to rights is an important indicator of the conditions and benefits of employment. Loss of the right to appeal against unfair dismissal, for example, may seriously undermine an employee's ability to challenge unfair treatment. As a result, flexible employment may develop in a way that disproportionately advantages employers and disadvantages employees.

The empirical focus of this chapter will be upon the implementation in the United Kingdom of the Equal Opportunities Directives on equal pay and equal treatment for part-time workers.[3] It will concentrate specifically on the structural barriers that homeworkers in manufacturing and part-time workers in the retail sector experience in utilising their rights and influencing their development. Particular attention will be paid to issues of resources and representation, the argument being that trade unions are important in enabling flexible workers to access employment rights. This chapter focuses on one particular aspect of flexible employment, namely, numerical flexibility. Homework and part-time work constitute ideal test cases and have been selected because they are characteristic of numerical flexibility in respect of type of contract, hours and job insecurity. The empirical discussion is drawn from existing literature, and interviews conducted in 1996 to 1997 with trade unions at local, national and EU levels, the National Groups for Homeworkers (NGH), the European Commission, EU lobby groups, European Employers Association (UNICE), and the UK Permanent Representative to the EU (UKREP).

The following section will discuss the expansion of flexible employment, identifying it as a gendered construct. It is followed by a brief outline of the EU's approach to flexibility, the problems with the transposition of EU policy and the legal rights under investigation in this chapter. Then two ways in which the gendered citizenship approach can contribute to an inclusive analysis of flexible employment are considered. Firstly, the gap between formal and substantive rights will be examined within the context of gender inequalities in the public and private spheres. This framework is then applied to the barriers that home- and part-time workers experience in accessing employment rights. Secondly, as citizenship rights are understood as developing through a process of struggle by the exercise of social agency, this framework is utilised to investigate the resources available to home- and part-time workers to act as agents in realising flexible employment rights and in influencing the future development of those rights. Finally, the advantages of applying a gendered citizenship framework to flexible employment will be summarised and some brief recommendations made.

**Flexible Employment**

Reviews of both contemporary theory and policy reveal an abundance of references to processes of employment change which embody, facilitate and legitimise greater levels of flexibility. There is no unified view of flexibility, but there does appear to be a general consensus that economic and social restructuring is taking place (Jessop, 1994; Amin, 1994; Crouch, 1995; Jeffreys, 1995; Esping-Andersen, 1990; Commission of the European Communities, 1993). Establishing a working definition of flexible employment is, therefore, a necessary starting point. Flexibility is defined here as a process of economic restructuring which is driven by technological change, an intensification of international competition and the greater interconnectedness of the international economy. The consequences for employment regimes include a drive towards a greater variability of skills, hours and contracts in the labour market, and in some sectors a downward pressure on rights, wages, skills and conditions.

Two forms of flexibility have been identified in relation to employment: the numerical, already described, and the functional, which is the ability of firms to transfer labour between tasks and break down job demarcations. This chapter is concerned specifically with two types of numerical flexibility: contractual flexibility and place of work flexibility. From the perspective of workers there are both positive and negative forms of flexibility, which relate to questions of who defines it, in whose interests it operates, and what are the skills and negotiating power possessed by workers to achieve favourable terms and conditions. The enthusiasm for numerically flexible jobs in Britain has overwhelmingly led to the creation of low-paid, low-status employment in which workers' rights have been insufficiently protected (Dex and McCulloch, 1995:6; Walby, 1997:75). The majority of homework and part-time work falls into this category of numerical flexibility. This reflects the relatively weak bargaining stance of these workers and their low levels of unionisation making it difficult for employment rights to be claimed. Home- and part-time work, therefore, constitute a strong basis for evaluating the growth of negative flexible employment.

It is by no means inevitable that the embracing of flexible work practices should create poor quality jobs. Flexible employment could potentially be more beneficial to workers if it received equal rights with full-time employment. Trade unions have been lobbying for equal rights for flexible workers on the basis that failure to do so hinders women's participation in the labour market, producing a system whereby women are disproportionately excluded from employment rights due to their high levels of participation in flexible employment. To some degree this has been successful. The Employment Relations Act and the Labour Government's agreement to implement the EU Social Rights Directives, including the Part-time Workers Directive, will hopefully take us nearer to this objective (HMSO, 1999). However as these lobby groups stress, the propensity of women to choose part-time and other forms of flexible employment relates to the failure of EU and national policies to reconcile work and family for both women and men. Until policies are developed to address this issue head-on, gender equality within the labour market will remain some distance away.

Flexible employment is undoubtedly on the increase. Between 1984 and 1997 part-time employment increased by 25.8 per cent in the UK. In 1997 there were 6.7 million part-time workers in the UK, more than one in four of those in work in 1997 worked part-time (27.1 per cent) (Social Trends, 1998:80). In the EU as a whole the number of part-time workers in 1994 was 20 per cent higher than in 1987 (Commission of the European Communities, 1995:2). The gender composition of part-time and home-based work is quite dramatic in illustrating that the flexible workforce is profoundly gendered and racialised. For example, women constitute 94 per cent of homeworkers, 47 per cent of whom are from ethnic minority backgrounds (Huws, 1994:4). Additionally, 81.5 per cent of part-time employees in the retail sector are women (USDAW, 1994:10). Male part-time work was more common in the retail sector where over a quarter (27 per cent) of male part-time workers are located (Neathey and Hurstfield, 1995:5). Recently the level of male part-time employment has risen, and between 1984-1997 the number of male part-time workers more than doubled,[4] while the number of women part-time workers increased during the same period by nearly one quarter[5] (Social Trends, 1998:80). However, women still make up the overwhelming majority of part-time workers. Therefore, any examination of flexible employment and protective rights must recognise that flexibility impacts differently on particular social groups.[6] Ethnic minority and working-class women are more likely to be found in low-skilled, low status flexible work, traditionally viewed as predominantly women's work. This work is overwhelmingly non-unionised and inadequately regulated. As a result of inadequate regulation and the two-year qualifying period for statutory employment rights (now amended to one year), basic employment rights such as written contracts, the right to claim unfair dismissal, sick pay and redundancy compensation are either partial or completely absent. From this perspective, it becomes increasingly difficult to view the embrace of flexible job growth as a positive development. To summarise, the main issues that need to be addressed from a gendered perspective are: what types of flexible employment are being encouraged, how effectively is this employment being regulated, and how do embedded gender inequalities impact upon the usability of EU flexible employment rights.

*The EU's Approach to Flexibility*

EU economic policy on flexible employment is designed to increase job-intensive growth. The minimisation of non-wage costs and statutory charges is encouraged in order to provide fiscal incentives to employers to create low skilled (flexible) jobs (Commission of the European Communities, 1993:143). In many respects the EU's emphasis on deregulation of labour markets is centred around the interests of employers rather than employees and holds direct implications for the growth of part-time, temporary and home-based employment. Although the Labour Government has begun to implement the Part-time Workers Directive, it will be some time before the effects are seen in practice. Thus the present structure of employment in the UK continues to reflect the legacy of the previous Conservative Government's deregulationist policies. Consequently, many flexible workers, such as homeworkers, receive little or no access to statutory employment rights. Further, despite the onslaught of new legislation, some gaps in implementation will continue, since many of the barriers to realising employment rights set out in the following sections will remain. Because of this, attempts have been made at the EU level to regulate flexible employment and reduce its negative aspects.

The EU recognises that new forms of regulation are needed to ensure that low-skilled workers do not bear the costs of flexibility through the creation of a working poor. This process of according flexible work equal rights with 'core' employment is designed to encourage flexible work practices, while ensuring that full-time jobs are not simply turned into part-time jobs as a cost-cutting exercise. As Walby argues, in the long-term EU equal opportunities legislation has the potential to undermine the UK's low-wage flexible work strategy (Walby, 1999). Accordingly, the EU has embarked on a process of developing legislation to regulate and protect flexible work. Since the introduction of the Social Protocol to the Maastricht Treaty in 1992, negotiations between the social partners have been ongoing to develop agreements on specific types of flexible work. The agreement on part-time work emerged out of this process in 1997. However, both existing and new Directives are subject to the principle of subsidiarity, which provides considerable scope for member states to interpret EU policy and legislation in ways compatible with their own particular paths to flexibility (Office for Official Publications of the European Communities, 1992). The precise nature of implementation is left to member states, and the EU's role is one of ensuring cohesion rather than harmonisation. This is particularly important when considering the fact that most of the social regulations take the form of Directives which member states have to incorporate into national legislation. Scope clearly exists for diluting the spirit of the Directives, and even for non-implementation (Steiner and Woods, 1996).

The obstacles to effective implementation of Equal Opportunities Directives caused by the emergence of flexible employment rights at EU level and their mediation of rights formulation and implementation in the member states, have been extensively considered by Hoskyns (1996) and Ostner and Lewis (1995) in respect of Germany and Ireland. Hoskyns found that one of the aims of the processes at national level seems to have been 'to make sure that changes induced by the EC did not move policy too far from what were perceived to be the country's basic norms and values' (Hoskyns, 1996:123). In addition, Ostner and Lewis found that national interpretation and implementation of Equal Opportunities Directives were deeply hindered by national social policy regimes acting as gatekeepers, 'favouring policies compatible with culturally transmitted assumptions and tenets about gender roles' (Ostner and Lewis, 1995:193). This research suggests that national objectives pose substantial barriers to the effective implementation of Equal Opportunities Directives. The UK is no exception to this, the previous Conservative Government having opposed implementation of Equal Opportunities Directives until judicial review forced this in 1995.[7]

Proposals for an Atypical Workers Directive have been blocked for some time by the UK.[8] Discussion on fixed term and temporary work was dropped from the social partners' negotiations because agreement was proving too difficult to reach. However, as more common ground existed between the partners on the appropriate means to regulate part-time employment (DGV, ETUC interviews, 1996), an agreement was eventually achieved on part-time work through the social partners' negotiations under the Maastricht Protocol. The other areas of flexible work are still pending agreement. This reflects the marginalisation of people in other forms of flexible employment such as fixed-term and homeworkers. The agreement on part-time work, which will be implemented in the UK as part of the government's Employment Relations Act, will not take effect for some time and the outcome of its implementation will not surface for some years. Therefore, in these circumstances Equal Opportunities Directives provide an important source for flexible employment rights because, at the time of writing, no other EU legislation exists which can compel the UK to accord equal rights to flexible workers. It was the use of these Directives that forced the 1995 Amendment to the Employment Protection (Consolidation) Act. This amendment removed the eight and sixteen hours thresholds, which excluded part-time workers from statutory employment rights accorded to full-time employees.[9] Second, although not specifically intended to regulate flexible employment, Equal Opportunities Directives provide a good instrument for examining inclusion into employment rights since women are over-represented in low skilled and insecure flexible employment. The encouragement of this type of job growth has very specific consequences for women's equal access to rights. As we shall see in the next section, it follows that any problems women might encounter in accessing these rights will also extend to EU legislation aimed at regulating flexible employment. It is also suggested that the development of rights is not a one-way process. It is essential to examine the power of excluded groups to negotiate their inclusion. Before we can do this, however, we first need to establish why citizenship provides a useful framework.

**Gendered Citizenship, Structural Constraints and Substantive Rights**

Many citizenship theorists have analysed the development of socio-legal rights within the EU and attributed positive value to these developments (Meehan, 1993; Roche, 1992; Close, 1995; Walby, 1997). The evolution of EU citizenship rights has been received favourably within the UK amongst academics and rights activists given the back-drop of the constant erosion of citizenship rights that took place during four terms of Conservative government between 1979 and 1997.[10] However, the UK's position is an ambiguous one. Further investigation is needed to evaluate the impact of EU flexible employment rights in the workplace before these rights can be assumed to be fully effective. Using a gendered citizenship framework in this exercise is beneficial for the following two reasons. Firstly, it uncovers the need to go beyond the formal allocation of rights to account for the structural barriers which inhibit the realisation of employment rights (Barbalet, 1988; Close, 1995; Lister, 1995; Yuval-Davies, 1992; Phillips, 1991). In particular, it emphasises the importance of focusing on the public-private divide as a way of uncovering gender inequalities in accessing rights and developing more inclusive citizenship. Secondly, it understands citizenship rights as evolving from a process of struggle through the exercise of social agency, in that citizenship develops through processes of political struggle, negotiation and, depending on the outcome, either the repression of demands or inclusion into citizenship rights. The value of examining substantive inclusion into employment rights is now applied to the difficulties of regulating numerically flexible employment.

*Formal Inclusion/Substantive Exclusion*

As already identified, central to critical perspectives on citizenship is the assumption that there is a need to go beyond the formal allocation of rights to enable us to account for the barriers to realising rights and participating as full citizens. Close (1995) clearly illustrates this point. He argues that a fully inclusive notion of citizenship is not possible without addressing inequalities of power, resources and access and their interaction with an individual's or group's ability to realise full citizenship. Furthermore, Close draws on Barbalet's work to point out that formal myths of equality before the law actually reinforce informal inequalities resulting from the unequal distribution of power and resources throughout society (Barbalet cited in Close, 1995:1-8 and 56-67). For example, if flexible employment practices are encouraged, based on the inaccurate assumption that such employment is protected, then the exclusion of these workers from full citizenship is likely to be further reinforced.

The significance of inadequate legal rights is further enhanced by gendered citizenship's critique of false universalism. A gendered citizenship analysis illuminates the exclusionary tensions within citizenship whereby rights and obligations, that formally appear as universal, are structured in a manner that is inherently unequal. Understanding the impact that difference may have on individuals' experiences of, and access to, citizenship has been highlighted by gender- and race-centred theories for some time now, so much so, in fact, that explanations of how relations of gender, race and class interact and affect an individual's or group's ability to access rights is fundamental to our understanding of contemporary citizenship (Yuval-Davies, 1992; Phillips, 1993; Pixley, 1993; Lister, 1995 and 1997; Pateman, 1988b). Therefore, a gendered citizenship framework questions what barriers homeworkers and part-time workers experience in claiming employment rights rather than simply assuming that everyone has equal access to rights. Furthermore, this framework reveals the existence of layer upon layer of structural barriers to the realisation of employment rights, questioning how these relate to gender inequalities present in the public and private spheres.

The effectiveness of EU legislation designed to regulate flexible employment is fundamental to the working conditions of home- and part-time workers and their participation as full citizens. Consequently it is important to examine access to these employment rights in the workplace, rather than assuming that flexible work is protected, and encouraging its growth on this basis. This is a consideration that is frequently absent from non-gendered debates on flexible employment. At a theoretical level the complexities of regulating flexible work are frequently absent. As a result, the gendered inequalities which permeate flexible work are overlooked or underplayed (Jessop, 1994; Crouch, 1995; Grahl and Teague, 1995; Streek, 1995). In contrast, by understanding that citizenship outcomes interact with structural inequalities, gendered citizenship's logical starting point is to examine the nature of flexible work in practice. From this perspective, access to flexible employment rights must first be examined before claims can be made about the value of embracing flexible job growth. Therefore, the initial step is to identify the structural barriers which make it problematic for home- and part-time workers to transform formal rights into substantive rights. These constraints will be examined under the following themes: the inadequacy of formal rights and the impact of the public-private dichotomy.

*Legal Barriers to the Realisation of Employment Rights*

Many barriers exist to part-time and homeworkers accessing employment rights. They range from formal legal barriers, such as inadequate incorporation of Directives into national law, through to the practical problems caused by the uncertainty and complexity of EU law. This whole scenario is exacerbated by the limited power of the European Court of Justice (ECJ) to ensure the compliance of member states to EU law, which in turn has resulted in the development of a whole history of European case law based on direct and indirect effect.[11] As a result, inadequate implementation poses severe problems for the ability of workers in the private sector to claim EU employment rights. The degree to which employment rights are extended and compliance ensured will depend upon the particular path to flexible employment favoured by the member state. In the UK the implications for homeworkers and some part-time workers are immense because implementation is uneven and, in some workplaces, non-existent.

One example of uneven implementation is demonstrated by the way that Equal Opportunities Directives have been translated into UK law. This raises serious questions about the adequacy of equal opportunities legislation to meet the needs of homeworkers. A fundamental problem homeworkers have in claiming statutory employment rights is that the domestic legislation specifies that rights are extended to 'employees'. In the UK, homeworkers' employment status is technically that of 'self-employed', which means that employee rights are not automatically applicable. The EU legislation should theoretically overcome this problem because it uses the term 'worker'. However, homeworkers are private sector employees, which means that they cannot draw directly on EU Directives.[12] This is because Directives bind nation states directly, but they have to be incorporated into national law in order to bind employers. Therefore, employees in the private sector are still largely reliant on this incorporation into national law. Consequently, a huge barrier of proving employment status in employment tribunals continues to exist before any claims can be made about exclusion from statutory employment rights. Proving the employment status of homeworkers is made still more difficult as the majority do not have a written contract. Furthermore, legal obstacles are exacerbated by the tribunal process where decisions tend to be non-binding. As a result, a successful decision in favour of the homeworker does not lead automatically to the extension of these rights to other homeworkers employed by the same company.[13]

The Labour Government has made some concessions on this issue, since the NGH has been extremely active in lobbying for the new employment rights to be applied to homeworkers. For example, the national minimum wage applies to all those who work for another person, not just those employed under a contract of employment. Further, the Labour Government has stated in the 'Fairness at Work' White Paper that a similar approach will be taken for the Working Time Directive and all existing employment rights legislation. This offers new opportunities for homeworkers and their representatives to push for their inclusion into employment rights. However, the outcome is unlikely to be straightforward. There are far too few inspectors to cope with the scale of work involved in ensuring that these regulations are adhered to. Nevertheless, the application of employment legislation to all those who work for another person represents a breakthrough in the sense that there is now a much clearer legal base regarding the entitlement of homeworkers to employment rights.

A further layer of problems is posed by the UK National Insurance threshold. Many trade unions have stressed the barriers posed by the current threshold which, at the time of writing, is set at £64 a week. This is a significant factor which excludes many part-time and homeworkers from qualifying for welfare rights acquired through the payment of full National Insurance contributions, that is, basic state retirement pension, statutory maternity pay, statutory sick pay and contribution-based unemployment benefits. For example, the 1994 Labour Force Survey found that 2.2 million part-time workers earned less than the National Insurance threshold (TUC, 1995:1). National Insurance thresholds are not unique to the UK, but the UK levels are unusually high in a relatively low-wage economy. One official from the Union of Shop Distribution and Allied Workers (USDAW) expressed the view that the National Insurance threshold had effectively replaced the old eight and sixteen hours thresholds as the prime mechanism for excluding part-time workers from equal in-work benefits to those received by full-time workers. At the EU level, thresholds have been the subject of several cases brought to the ECJ. The decisions have been uneven. ECJ rulings on so-called 'gender neutral' policies have generally reflected an inability or unwillingness on the part of the ECJ to intervene in social security issues, preferring to emphasise the right of the member states to determine their own social policies.[14] Activist groups, trade unions and the Directorate General Five (DGV) Equal Opportunities Unit are working to close this gap. However, it falls into an extremely problematic area of social policy where EU competency remains underdeveloped and so the EU is likely to remain reluctant to intervene on this issue.

Adding to these concerns, National Insurance thresholds policy in the UK appears to have gone in the opposite direction. As part of the Labour Government's strategy of creating work incentives and making work pay, it has raised the lower earnings limit for employers' contributions to £81 a week and proposes to do the same eventually for employees (HM Treasury, 1998). This will actually increase the numbers of, predominantly women, part-time workers who fall outside of the National Insurance system. This is an issue which has raised concerns amongst some sectors of the trade union movement, who are keen to ensure that extensions to the lower earnings limit do not exacerbate the exclusion of part-time workers from welfare-based rights. At the time of writing, the outcome of this policy remains ambiguous.

*Relationship between the Private Sphere and Structural Inequality in the Public Sphere*

Feminist academics have emphasised the role that the public-private divide has played in constraining women's access to citizenship rights compared to their male counterparts (Pateman, 1988; Phillips, 1991). Focusing on the public-private dichotomy highlights two important issues. First, rights allocated in the public sphere may not be directly accessible by those women whose activities are not concentrated around this sphere. For example, since many employment-based rights are 'acquired', it is problematic for women who have intermittent employment to build up entitlement to these rights (Cook, 1997:268; Walby, 1997:20; Huws, 1997). Second, by focusing on the public-private divide we recognise that the nature of women's labour market participation reflects gender inequalities which permeate both the household and the labour market (Walby, 1986; Beechey and Perkins, 1987; Ginn et al., 1996; Phizacklea and Wolkowitz, 1995). Gender regimes bring about the overrepresentation of women in specific types of jobs.[15] Thus the position of many women in the labour market reflects both their role in the private sphere as carers, and structures of labour market segregation, which in turn tend to legitimise their location in low status, low-paid and non-unionised employment. These are types of employment where rights are difficult to access and also where numerical flexibility has become pervasive (Mitter, 1986; Phizacklea and Wolkowitz, 1995). In the context of employment rights such inequalities reveal the deep-rooted structural constraints impeding part-time and homeworkers' access to employment rights. These constraints can be seen particularly in relation to homework which lies in an ambiguous position between the two spheres. Many of the difficulties homeworkers face in claiming employment rights and getting their interests represented reflect the way that work in the household is perceived by society as a whole. This effectively renders homework invisible to the public sphere of employment regulations and even leads to a perception that it is not real work (Phizacklea and Wolkowitz, 1995:14-28).

In this context the problems that some women encounter in accessing rights located in the public sphere are of particular relevance. Homeworkers experience obstacles to claiming public sphere employment rights because their location in the private sphere leads to isolation and a denial that they are employees at all. For many employers, homeworkers offer a cheap source of labour, something which is clearly visible in the rates of pay that these workers receive, even in relation to public sphere workers who perform the same job. This is illustrated by a survey of homeworkers in Coventry undertaken by Phizacklea and Wolkowitz (1995). They found that in the West Midlands, in 1990, the average hourly earnings for home-based manual work were between £1.26-£1.31 per hour, compared with the average for women's earnings in manual employment outside of the home of some £3.23 per hour (Phizacklea and Wolkowitz, 1995:54). Public sphere employment rights are difficult to extend to the private sphere where formal structures of regulations are hard to enforce. In many respects some areas of women's labour are seen as cheap, numerically flexible and therefore devalued, unorganised and more open to flexible employment practices. This suggests that effective flexible employment legislation and policy needs to take into account the inherent inequalities in the public and private spheres and the emergent structural barriers to accessing rights. This issue is frequently absent from mainstream flexibility debates but becomes evident from a gendered political economy perspective. Until these issues are taken on board there will continue to be a gap between formal and substantive rights.

## Gendered Citizenship and Social Agency

Examining structural barriers to realising employment rights is an important way of developing a more inclusive analysis of flexible employment. However, this needs to be integrated with an analysis of the difficulties flexible workers encounter in negotiating their inclusion into employment rights, and in influencing employment policy at national and EU levels. Implicit within gendered approaches to citizenship is the notion that the development of rights should be placed within the context of social and political struggle. Citizenship has developed as a result of the exercise of agency, it is not merely something which is handed down by a paternalistic state (Barbalet, 1988; Williams, 1994; Lister, 1997). Furthermore, the language of citizenship has proved a useful, albeit limited, tool to excluded social groups seeking inclusion into social rights (Phillips, 1991; Lister, 1997). Lister, when drawing upon the concept of human agency to understand processes of inclusion and exclusion within citizenship, argues that it should be analysed as a dynamic process in which rights are not fixed. Thus, citizenship rights are constantly evolving, shaped by political struggles which seek to defend, reinterpret and extend them (Lister, 1997).

By adopting this approach to citizenship the importance of understanding the development of rights in an historical context becomes clear, highlighting that rights have always developed as a two-way process of structural accommodation and social struggle. Therefore, central to an understanding of the development of citizenship and the regulation of flexible employment is a recognition that 'structure is not to be equated with constraint, but is always both constraining and enabling' (Giddens, 1984:25). In this sense the analysis of structural constraints needs to be combined with a discussion of the ability of social groups to overcome these constraints.[16] As Lister points out:

> People can be, at the same time, both the subordinate objects of hierarchical power relations and subjects who are agents in their own lives, capable of exercising power in the generative sense of self-actualisation (Lister, 1997:40).

From this interpretation of citizenship, it is evident that an analysis of the emerging political economy of flexibility is incomplete without an understanding of the power of social groups to impact upon these changes. This principle is demonstrated by Hoskyns' research on the influence of the women's movement on the evolution of EU social policy. She provides an invaluable insight into how social groups can influence policy-making at the EU level. In addition, by drawing our attention to the constraints these groups face, she also demonstrates the limitations of this influence on EU women's policy. The ability of social groups to get their interests met at the EU level is limited because they have to work within the constraints of EU and member states' policy agendas. For example, the Women's Unit in the Commission has found it difficult to develop polices on ethnic minority women or poor women because these categories are hardly recognised as a concern by the EU. This is reflected in the scope of EU women's policy, in that the women who benefit the most from this policy are those whose main disadvantage stems from their gender (Hoskyns, 1996:199). This framework is now applied to examine the development of EU flexible employment policy and the representation of low-skilled flexible workers.

*Social Agency and the EU Policy-Making Process*

While social agency has an impact on EU policy making, certain groups lack the power and resources to influence employment policy. This may result either in a partial representation of their interests, or in some cases their complete absence from policy-making agendas. The structural exclusion of flexible workers relates to problems with the EU decision-making process and to the barriers faced by these groups at the grassroots level. Several studies have demonstrated that EU lobbying favours elite groups and organisations. The Commission often uses expert networks, trade union officials and established women's organisations, such as the European Women's Lobby (EWL), to advise on the development of its proposals. However, the resources required to organise transnationally often exclude smaller grassroots pressure groups.[17]  As a result, there is a distinct lack of grassroots organisations with a physical presence in Brussels. The EWL, the Anti-Poverty Network and the Network for the Unemployed, alongside the trade union movement, remain amongst the few EU-based organisations through which grassroots groups can voice their interests. Many of the groups interviewed for this research had very little access to EU policy networks. For both homeworkers and part-time workers the trade union movement provides the main source of representation. This lack of access is exacerbated by the difficulties that trade unions experience in representing flexible workers.

The issue of unequal social agency is reflected at the national level in terms of the insecure nature of flexible work and issues of trade union representation. A relationship can be identified between the existence of structural constraints and the exclusion of flexible workers from the resources needed to exert social agency. In the UK there are several barriers which make it difficult for home- and part-time workers to act as agents and negotiate inclusion into employment rights. One such structural constraint is that of the location. Most homeworkers and some part-time workers are located in non-regulated sectors of employment, poorly accessed by trade unions, leaving it largely to the discretion of employers to implement employment rights. Union representation remains a big problem for these workers. With Equal Opportunities Directives it is the responsibility of the member states to raise awareness of these rights amongst workers. In reality this is left to the unions, who themselves face barriers to accessing both members and non-members. For example, with the introduction of flexible working patterns, trade unions are finding it increasingly difficult to access workers due to shorter shift patterns that have no tea breaks.  In addition, factors such as the de-recognition of trade unions in the UK have exacerbated recruitment problems, although it is hoped that this will be eased by the establishment of a right to union recognition which is soon to be made law. However, at present the lack of awareness of EU employment rights continues to pose considerable barriers, with many flexible workers remaining unaware of their employment rights entitlement.  Furthermore, homeworkers and, to a lesser degree, part-time workers are unlikely to risk claiming employment rights because they may face dismissal.  Many sectors of flexible employment are insecure and temporary, leaving workers in no position to negotiate their inclusion into rights.  It follows, therefore, that without the support of a trade union these flexible workers are likely to continue to be excluded from employment rights.[18]

The aforementioned problem of location means that if homeworkers are not located on the shop floor, it is unlikely that traditional trade union recruitment practices are going to reach them.  However, on closer examination the absence of representation uncovers far more deep-rooted obstacles to the unions' ability to represent homeworkers and many part-time workers.  Analysis of trade unions as patriarchal structures has been well documented (Walby, 1986; Cockburn, 1996).  In part, the inability of trade unions to represent home- and part-time workers reflects the intrinsic gender inequalities within the internal structures of unions, while other obstacles to unionising flexible workers relate to issues surrounding flexible work itself. While there has been some opening up of access for women within trade unions, traditional approaches to industrial relations do not meet the needs of many women flexible workers.  For example, until recently the unions did not see recruiting numerical flexible workers as a priority.  These problems of representation are not only a result of gendered structures within trade unions, they also relate to the general problems that unions have experienced in coming to terms with forms of flexible working.  Ideological obstacles exist, given the understandable reluctance within the movement to legitimise forms of flexible employment, which actually undermine principles surrounding rights to secure and reasonable working conditions.[19]  However, this is little consolation for the women located in these sectors of employment.  In the case of part-time work, pressure from the Women's Officers within the Trades Union Congress, combined with the realisation that flexible working is here to stay, has led the movement to make a decisive shift in terms of recognising the need to unionise and protect these workers.  This is symbolised by the 1994 to 1996 TUC campaign on part-time work, which sought to raise awareness in the trade union movement of the need to be more pro-active about recruiting part-time workers and draw upon the new legislation on part-time work in their negotiations with employers. However, the comprehensive inclusion of part-time workers into the trade union movement is still a long way off. For example, in Neathey and Hurstfield's study, in one retail firm, almost nine in ten workers were part-time yet they formed less than 50 per cent of the union membership. This firm had particularly high levels of union members who worked part-time compared to the other retail firms studied (Neathey and Hurstfield, 1995:192). Overall the density of part-time workers in a trade union is usually half that of full-time workers (Bird and Corcoran, 1995).

In the case of homeworkers, trade unions have been particularly slow to adapt. The hidden nature of this employment makes it extremely difficult to recruit these workers. Additional obstacles arise from the fact that there is no economic incentive for unions to target numerical flexible workers, and as homeworkers tend to be frequently in and out of employment, very little revenue can be raised from union subscriptions. In a climate where trade unions are feeling the financial squeeze, this is bound to act as a disincentive. Conversely, the cost of union subscriptions to a homeworker who earns, on average, £46 for a 36-hour week acts as a disincentive for them to join (Huws, 1994:15), a disincentive equally applicable to part-time workers. However, financial disincentives are only part of the picture. The culture of trade unions poses immense barriers to the inclusion of flexible workers, and their inability to relate to and protect these workers exacerbates this vicious circle. Still, it is unwise to assume that the trade union movement can afford to avoid confronting the issue of flexible working indefinitely. Trade unions are beginning to acknowledge that their long-term survival is embedded in their capacity to come to terms with, and adapt to, flexible working. As one of the National Officers with the GMB stated in interview, 'The trade unions who integrate the needs of flexible workers, such as homeworkers, will be the successful trade unions of the future'. However, these adjustments have been slow to evolve and many ideological, structural and cultural changes will need to take place if trade unions are to be properly inclusive of numerical flexible workers.

## Conclusion

A gendered citizenship framework has highlighted many of the gaps which exist between formal EU rights and rights as they exist within the UK. This chapter has illustrated the importance of focusing on the specific circumstances of flexible workers and the difficulties they encounter in accessing employment rights. Consequently, it raises important questions, from various perspectives, about the desirability of embracing flexible employment growth while much of this work remains unregulated. The analysis of structural barriers to the realisation of employment rights has been accompanied by an examination of social agency which has highlighted several issues. First, existing employment rights do not take account of specific needs of flexible workers, leaving much of this employment insufficiently protected. Second, the relative absence of trade union representation means that these workers lack the enabling resources to negotiate inclusion into formal employment rights. Full inclusion into trade unions is one way of alleviating these problems but the inability of the trade union movement to relate to the needs of these workers remains a barrier. Third, lack of union representation places severe constraints upon the ability of flexible workers to influence the future development of employment rights at the national and EU levels. Consequently, workplace, national and EU gaps are present which restrict the ability of flexible workers to exercise agency either to realise existing employment rights on the one hand, or to influence the development of more inclusive employment rights on the other.

Gendered citizenship's dual focus on structural constraints and the impact of unequal social agency demonstrates how a more inclusive analysis of flexible employment might be developed. The significance of understanding that structural barriers to employment rights are entwined with processes of social agency is illustrated by the judicial review which forced the Amendment to the Employment Act in 1995. This indicates that the struggle to claim formal EU employment rights can lead to the development of the necessary agency to push for more inclusive employment rights and on this basis their importance should not be underestimated. In this sense, flexible employment rights are both subject to limitations while at the same time they offer new opportunities to diminish exclusion from these rights. The barriers to accessing employment rights, aided by the Labour Government's approach to labour market regulation, are slowly being dismantled for some flexible workers and, in the long term, political struggle may extend these rights to other flexible workers. This will only be fully effective, though, if the more embedded gender inequalities regarding representation and social attitudes towards part-time work and homeworking are also changed. The employment relations legislation still falls some way short of achieving this aim.

Along with the contractual problems that homeworkers face, the constraints on trade union representation and the former two-year qualifying period for statutory employment rights, the National Insurance threshold poses one of the major barriers to establishing equal rights for flexible workers. The impact of the agreement on part-time work is yet to be seen. The problems are plentiful, since any legislation on flexible employment rights is likely to face the same obstacles as faced the incorporation of the Equal Opportunities Directives into UK law. In general then, this analysis paints a bleak picture of the current direction of flexible employment rights. However, as suggested, outcomes depend on the mobilisation of social agency to redress the current imbalance of benefits from flexible employment structures and move the situation in favour of flexible workers. In this sense the work undertaken by lobby groups, trade unions, grassroots organisations and individual workers to bring about change, offers possibilities for different and more positive outcomes. Eventual solutions lie in improving structures of implementation, representation and participation to enable full inclusion into social rights. Clearly, this is presently still a long way off; the incoming employment relations legislation and the EU Directives will hopefully aid this process, but radical change will still be required.

**Notes**

[1] I would like to thank the respondents who were kind enough to give up their time to help me with this research. An earlier version of this chapter appeared in *New Political Economy* 1998, 3 (2), pp.261-277.

[2] Social agency is defined here as the power of groups and individuals to have their interests included in the development of policy and legislation.

[3] The Equal Opportunities Directives 76/207/EEC and 75/117/EEC were incorporated into English Law by the 1995 Statutory (UK) Amendment to the Employment Protection (Consolidation) Act 1978, which accorded part-time employees equal rights with full-time employees, that is, the right to a contract of employment, unfair dismissal, redundancy, and the right to return to work after maternity leave. (Terms and Conditions of Employment - the employment protection of part-time workers regulations, no. 31 *Statutory Instruments*, [1995] pp.1-3).

[4] 610,000 men worked part-time in 1984 compared with 1,328 in 1997 (Social Trends, 1998:80).

[5] 4,356,000 women worked part-time in 1984, compared with 5,367,000 in 1997 (Social Trends, 1998:80).

[6] Some writers argue that flexible employment is positive for women and has been chosen by women specifically in the form of part-time work. See debates between Hakim (1995), and Ginn et al. (1996), Phizacklea and Wolkowitz (1995).

[7] 'Secretary of State for Employment ex parte EOC', (*2-WLR409*, 1994), resulted in

the Amendment to the Employment Protection (Consolidation) Act 1978, 'Terms and Conditions of Employment - the employment protection of part-time workers regulations'.

[8] Reference to flexible work as 'atypical' poses severe problems, resulting in typical work being associated with men, and atypical as the realm of women's employment. See Christine Cousins (1994) for discussion of the problems of viewing flexible work as 'atypical'. See also Walby (1997) for discussion of the inaccuracies of viewing women's employment as peripheral and men's employment as core.

[9] Although the eight and sixteen hours thresholds were abolished in 1995 ('Secretary of State for employment ex parte EOC'), one of the most fundamental legal barriers to flexible workers accessing employment rights, the two-year qualifying period still remains. This is currently under judicial review and continues to be an obstacle to employment rights access for many workers. See Court of Appeal in 'R v Secretary State for Employment, ex parte Seymour-Smith', (*IRLR465*, 1995).

[10] For example, the limits placed on trade union rights in the Trade Union Reform and Employment Rights Act 1993, and the cuts made to the welfare state.

[11] Meaning is generally clarified over time by the ECJ, for example, the changes in interpretation of Chapter 189 in the Treaty of Rome. The original interpretation of this is that Directives are a contractual agreement between the member state and the EU. The interpretation of Chapter 189 has now been given additional scope by the ECJ; the Francovich decision extends it to a contract between the individual and the member state, see case 6/90, *ECJ Reports* (1991); Steiner (1992).

[12] EU Directives 76/207/EEC and 75/117/EEC *Official Journal of the European Community*, L45 (19.2.75) p.19 and L39 (14.2.76) p.40.

[13] To some extent, successful tribunal decisions are built upon, due to the pro-active work of organisations such as NGH and the trade unions.

[14] See Steiner and Woods' (1996) discussion of 'Posthuma-Van Damme v Bestuur van de Bedrijfsvereniging voor Detailhandel, Ambachten en Huisvrouwen' *(Case C 280/94)*.

[15] The term 'gender regime' is used in feminist research as a broad description of embedded structures of gender inequality which permeate the public and private spheres. For further discussion of gender regimes see Ostner and Lewis (1995), Hoskyns (1996), and Walby (1997).

[16] For expansion on the importance of social agency see Giddens' (1984) theory of structuration. Also Williams (1994).

[17] Hoskyns' (1996) research found that EU women's policy promoted networks and contact between women only at an elite level. See also Mazey and Richardson (1993) and Bretherton and Sperling (1996).

[18] These difficulties are demonstrated by the problems encountered by unionised part-time workers. USDAW stated that they are reluctant to pressure their members into taking cases against their employer because workers are terrified of losing their jobs,

and facing the recriminations afterwards. This also acts to discourage membership (Interview, USDAW, 1996).

[19] Neathey and Hurstfield (1995) identify conflict between trade unions' priority of protecting their full-time members and negotiating conditions on behalf of fixed term workers. This was a particular problem in the banking and finance industries they studied.

# 3 Equal Opportunities at Work in France and Spain: Theory and Reality

HILARY ROLLIN AND JEAN BURRELL

## Introduction

There are a number of obvious parallels between the context of women's employment in France and Spain. Both are Romance-language-speaking countries with judicial systems based on Roman law, members of the European Union (EU) and subject to EU legislation, and post-industrial nations, although there are dramatic differences in the stage of development in each country. They have both experienced accelerated economic and industrial restructuring in the latter part of the twentieth century, characterised by a rapid increase in women's employment, particularly married women's employment. Both are essentially liberal democracies with a constitution which contains a commitment to equal opportunities. Moreover, both have highly segmented industrial and occupational workforces characterised by gendered occupational segregation and persistent gendered pay differentials. On the other hand, there are marked differences between the two countries, particularly in terms of recent political and social history. Chief among these is the fact that, whereas France is highly centralised, Spain is divided into autonomous regions.

This chapter will start by looking at key features of women's employment in France and Spain in comparison with the United Kingdom, and move on to outline the main issues covered by EU legislation and other measures relating to equality of opportunity for women in the workplace. It will then discuss their application in France and Spain and conclude by attempting to evaluate their impact on women's employment.

**Women in the Labour Market**

Economic activity rates vary between and within countries, and constitute one of the most significant differences in the employment patterns of France and Spain. The 1997 Eurostat Labour Force Surveys show that the UK has overtaken France in both male and female activity rates, ranking third and fourth respectively in the EU.

**Table 3.1  EU activity rates**

| 1997 | Men % | Women % |
|------|-------|---------|
| EU15 | 66.0 | 45.3 |
| B | 60.7 | 41.0 |
| DK | 72.1 | 59.0 |
| D | 67.9 | 48.2 |
| EL | 62.9 | 36.2 |
| E | 62.3 | 36.7 |
| FR | 63.3 | 48.2 |
| IRL | 68.5 | 42.7 |
| I | 61.8 | 34.8 |
| L | 64.7 | 38.1 |
| NL | 71.5 | 50.6 |
| A | 69.1 | 48.7 |
| P | 67.1 | 49.4 |
| FIN | 65.9 | 54.9 |
| S | 65.3 | 56.5 |
| UK | 70.8 | 53.2 |

*Source:* Eurostat http://europa.eu.int/en/comm/eurostat/indic/indic13.htm

Although in France, as in the UK, women currently form approximately 50 per cent of the labour force, employment patterns have evolved differently in the two countries over the past few decades. Since the 1970s there has been a remarkable increase in the proportion of French women in the labour market in the 25-54 age group, from 45 per cent in 1968 to 79 per cent in 1994 (Brondel et al., 1996), an increase which is largely attributable to married women's employment (Letablier, 1995). The M-shaped curve, still typical of women's work history in Britain and most of the rest of Europe, where child-rearing breaks are the norm, had been transformed in France by the 1980s into an inverted U curve which is similar to men's working profile. French women now tend towards the two extremes of high continuity in employment or low participation, depending largely on numbers of children and occupational status.

Almost three-quarters of French women with two children and over, and 40 per cent with three or more, remain in the labour force (ILO, quoted by Lebaube, 1998). In spite of rising job losses in recent years, French women have not withdrawn from the labour market. Indeed, contrary to the situation in the UK, the unemployment rate for women is higher than for men, at 13.3 per cent as opposed to 9.4 per cent in 1994 (Letablier and Daune-Richard, quoted in Letablier, 1995). In December 1997 they made up nearly half those seeking work and just over half the long-term unemployed (Van Eeckhout, 1998).

Spain has a marginally lower male, and considerably lower female, activity rate than France, broadly comparable to Italy, and much lower than the UK. This is in spite of a 38.7 per cent rise in Spain's female activity rate between 1984 and 1993. Clearly a result of increased participation in all levels of education, this was felt in all age groups except the over 55s and 16-19 year-olds. Expressed in other terms, one and a half million women joined the active population (employed and unemployed), compared to little over 200,000 men. This constitutes one of the most significant recent sociological changes in Spain. The female employed population, however, had grown by only 27.6 per cent, which shows that much of the increased activity rate is attributable to those seeking work, and highlights the seriousness of Spain's female unemployment (Rollin, 1995), to which we shall return.

Part-time work has always been much more common in Britain where, in 1987, 45 per cent of working women were employed part-time, compared with 23 per cent in France and 14 per cent in Spain (Secrétariat d'Etat aux Droits des Femmes and INSEE, 1991). This may be due to the appeal to employers of part-time contracts, with their previously more limited employment rights under UK law, or to the greater flexibility offered by part-time work when childcare is in short supply. In Spain domestic responsibilities were cited by 9 per cent as a reason for their working part-time in 1993, whereas 43 per cent attributed working part-time to the requirements of the job. Far from being seen as a desirable compromise, reconciling paid employment and family commitments, part-time work is viewed by the Spanish workforce with suspicion, and little wonder, since the working day for full-time employees is often structured to end at 2.30 p.m. The chief factor limiting part-time work in both France and Spain in the past was employment law that made part-time jobs uneconomic for employers. However, legislation was introduced in France in the 1980s and 1990s, and in Spain in 1994, aimed at bringing greater flexibility into the labour market. Together with the inexorable rise in service sector employment, where women predominate, this has increased the proportion of women employed in part-time and other forms of 'atypical' work.   By 1995, stimulated by the 1992 introduction of partial exemption from social overheads for employers creating part-time posts, it had risen to 29 per cent (Bisault et al., 1996) in France, where almost half of all part-time workers, and more than half of those under 25, had been forced to accept, rather than had chosen, this form of work.

Job-sharing (a form of part-time employment whereby two people voluntarily share the responsibility for one full-time position), which has enabled mothers of young children to remain in the labour force, is virtually unknown in France and Spain.   It is favoured by UK employers due to its potential for reducing staff turnover, thus retaining expertise and minimising investment in recruitment and training.   It has, however, generated a considerable volume of case law (Equal Opportunities Commission, 1997) in the area of indirect discrimination, given the uncertainty surrounding the mechanics for calculating years of service in job-share posts, and the disproportionate number of women employed on this basis.

The real female employment rate is harder to calculate than men's, given the greater frequency with which women enter and leave the labour market, being more likely than men to be on short-term contracts (Hantrais and Letablier, 1996). This is particularly the case in Spain with its high proportion of fixed-term contracts.   Disraeli's 'lies, damned lies and statistics' takes on new meaning in the interpretation of cross-national statistics.   Countries differ in their calculation of part-time workers: for example, Italy, unlike most other member states, adds together several part-time workers to count them as one unit, giving the impression of a lower female participation rate than would otherwise be the case. Such anomalies bring into question the credibility of Eurostat figures (Rollin, 1996).

The proportion of temporary employment in the total employment figures is normally smaller than the proportion of part-time employment.   Spain, together with Portugal and Greece, is an exception to this, temporary employment being more common than part-time (Delsen, 1994).   In both Spain and France protection against unfair dismissal is high.   Furthermore, there are very few restrictions on fixed-term contracts, hence their appeal to employers and widespread use.   Indeed, in the France of the 1990s, such contracts have become an instrument designed to absorb and retrain the unemployed, and women figure in large numbers as beneficiaries of *contrats emploi-solidarité* and *contrats initiative-emploi* which, however, do not lead to a guaranteed permanent contract.

In France a factor explaining the large numbers of women working full-time has been the availability of affordable public childcare and pre-school education.

Over 80 per cent of children between the ages of two and five attend *écoles maternelles*. This makes full-time work feasible for many women, although the uneven distribution and the cost of provision, as well as opening hours which do not cater for women working in some highly feminised sectors such as hotels/restaurants, are all issues which make the picture less than completely rosy. Unlike France, Spain has no tradition of nursery education. Spain's LOGSE education reform of 1990 (Ministerio de Educación y Ciencia, 1995) made pre-school education, from the age of three, part of the education system, a step welcomed by those wanting to combine a career and motherhood. However, data on provision, cost and uptake do not seem to be available, which is all the more surprising given the positive impact that the falling fertility rate should have had on the percentage of children who could be accommodated.

French public policy concerning mothers in the workforce was for many years a battleground between the demographic scaremongers, who warned of irreversible national decline unless women were given every encouragement to devote themselves to their family, and those who advocated women's right to self-determination in employment as in other areas. The uneasy compromise that has been reached between them has resulted in a framework which emphasises choice and solidarity while continuing to support the specifically French version of 'family values' (Hantrais and Letablier, 1995). France has some of the most generous family provisions in Europe: for example, even before the adoption of the Parental Leave Directive, a French parent of two children under three could stop working or work part-time and receive up to £300 a month in benefit; this is still the case. This benefit is the *allocation parentale d'éducation*, which was introduced in 1987 for families with three or more children, and extended to those with two in 1994, with the declared intention of allowing parents to reconcile work and family life. However, a recent INSEE study estimates that up to a quarter of a million women have withdrawn from the labour market since 1994 (Aulagnon, 1998a). The danger for women inherent in this situation is clear and proven: although employers are obliged to re-employ staff returning from such leave, a 1995 INSEE report found that six out of ten did not find work.

In marked contrast, Spain's one-year unpaid leave (with no length of service requirements, and with possible extension to three years) is seldom taken, conforming to the pattern of low take-up in countries offering no payment (Equal Opportunities Review, 1996a). Until the Labour government signed up to the Social Chapter of the Maastricht Treaty in 1997, the UK, in the name of non-interference in the private affairs of families and businesses, made no provision at all for parental leave. The Equal Opportunities Commission (EOC) welcomed the implementation of the Directive; not only does it accept the changing realities of the labour force, but it allows scope for adoptive parents and gives men official recognition of their parental role for the first time.   However, as the UK is working through the two-year transitional period allowed for implementation, working parents did not benefit from (probably unpaid) leave until 1999 (Equal Opportunities Review, 1997a).

Sectoral segregation is much more pronounced in women's employment than in men's, women being concentrated in relatively few sectors of activity and a limited number of occupations within these.   Moreover, since the areas in which women are employed are growth areas, this segregation is becoming more, not less, pronounced with time.   Alongside significant parallels between countries, there is one striking, but not unexpected, difference.   Despite a more marked increase in women's employment in the service sector in France and Spain than in the UK since 1991, the UK still has a higher proportion of women engaged in services and a much lower proportion in agriculture.

**Table 3.2   Harmonized unemployment rates**

|        | 1997 | May 1998 |
|--------|------|----------|
|        | %    | %        |
| EU 15  | 10.7 | 10.2     |
| B      | 9.2  | 9.9      |
| DK     | 5.5  | 4.6      |
| D      | 10.0 | 9.8      |
| EL     | 9.6  | -        |
| E      | 20.8 | 19       |
| FR     | 12.4 | 11.9     |
| IRL    | 10.1 | 9.2      |
| I      | 12.1 | -        |
| L      | 2.6  | 2.2      |
| NL     | 5.2  | 4        |
| A      | 4.4  | 4.5      |
| P      | 6.8  | 6.4      |
| FIN    | 13.1 | 12.6     |
| S      | 9.9  | 8.9      |
| UK     | 7.0  | 6.2      |

*Source*: Eurostat http://europa.eu.int/en/comm/eurostat/indic/indic14.htm.

As mentioned earlier, it is important not to be misled by Spain's rising female activity rate into thinking that equality has been achieved in terms of employment. Whereas French and British women form 45 per cent and 44 per cent of the labour force, their counterparts in Spain and Italy account for only 37 per cent. Two significant points emerge: first, the UK shows an interesting deviation in having a lower female than male unemployment rate; second, Spain's male unemployment rate is high, but the female unemployment rate is even higher. Spain has, nonetheless, more unemployed men than unemployed women. Women seeking employment account for 36 per cent of the female activity rate. The Eurostat figures for May 1998 in Table 3.2 outline the seriousness of Spain's unemployment problem. Despite marginal improvement over the 1997 figures, these show Spain still having by far the highest rate of unemployment in the Community, 19 per cent, compared with 11.9 per cent in France and 6.2 per cent in the UK. However, as has been pointed out (Irazusta, 1996), of the 6 million people engaged in unpaid work in Spain, 96 per cent are women. It is largely thanks to this unpaid work, the prevailing culture in Spain and the nature of the family structure, that the current level of well-being can be maintained despite the alarmingly high rate of unemployment.

For Spanish women in the 16-19 age bracket, the rate of unemployment in the third quarter of 1997 stood at 59.8 per cent, while that of 20-24 year-old women was better, if still extremely worrying, at 41.6 per cent, comparing with male unemployment rates of 43.6 per cent and 28.5 per cent respectively (Encuesta de Población Activa and Instituto Nacional de Empleo, 1998). The increase in female labour market participation in Spain has not been matched by an increased demand for female labour. Official statistics, particularly at cross-national level, may of course give a distorted impression, underestimating the actual activity rates, if, as in Italy, part-time workers are not counted as a unit, or if the black economy is very active. This is most evident in low-level occupations, where women have jobs rather than careers.

**European Equal Opportunity Measures**

We will now look at the EU equality legislation relating to women in the workplace. The European interest in equality of opportunity between men and women is rooted in two concerns which are fundamentally economic: first, that women constitute an under-utilised resource and should be encouraged to develop and use their skills for the benefit of the European economies; and second, that similar conditions should obtain for workers in all member states in the name of fair competition. France was a prime mover in insisting that the Treaty of Rome (1957) should include Article 119 on equal pay for equal work, but largely for fear of the competitive advantage other member states might gain by not subscribing to it.

It was not until the 1970s and the adoption of the Social Action Programme, which led to the elaboration of several Equal Opportunities Directives, that a more properly 'social' concern for European cohesion began to make its appearance. It is important to bear in mind that, where pre-existing national legislation offered terms that were more advantageous to employees, these were allowed to stand. The 1975 Equal Pay Directive, which developed the concept of equal pay for work of equal value, was followed in 1976 by the Equal Treatment Directive, laying down the principle of equality in access to employment, training, promotion, etc. More recently the 1992 Pregnant Workers Directive included provisions for maternity leave and pay, and protection from dismissal on account of pregnancy-related illness. Such dismissal, as it could only affect women, was deemed discriminatory (Equal Opportunities Review, 1998a). In the same year the Recommendation on Childcare encouraged member states to make progress in this area. The Recommendation identified governments, local authorities, employers, individuals and relevant organisations, for example unions, as responsible for promoting family-friendly policies, but without specifying their respective roles (European Commission Network on Childcare and other Measures to Reconcile Employment and Family Responsibilities, 1996). EU childcare measures are regrettably restricted to a Recommendation, hence not legally binding on member states. It is no surprise, therefore, that Eurobarometer (Directorate-General for Employment, Industrial Relations and Social Affairs, 1997) reports that 48 per cent of women and 46 per cent of men consider that financial assistance or better childcare facilities should be provided to help reconcile family life and employment.

In 1996 employers and trade union representatives agreed a framework for parental leave which was subsequently adopted by the Council of Ministers as the Parental Leave Directive. It lays down the right of parents to take up to three months leave on the birth or adoption of a child, but decisions on payment are left to member states.

Although a binding instrument on sexual harassment at work has not yet emerged, this is a topic that has been high on the EU agenda for some years because of its prominence in relation to both employment equality, and health and safety. In 1991 the Commission adopted a Recommendation and a Code of Practice intended to guide employers, unions and employees, and in January 1999 the topic was still the subject of further consultation among employees' and employers' representatives. The delay in developing acceptable legislation arises less from the difficulty of defining sexual harassment than from the task of interpreting the definition, which is necessarily subjective and culturally bound. Member states have incorporated provision into their national arrangements in differing ways: through specific legislation, through inclusion in equality laws or penal code, or through sector or company level collective agreements.

**Movement Towards Workplace Equality in France**

Many feminist commentators have remarked on the contradiction between France's theoretical commitment to *Liberté, Egalité, Fraternité* and the patriarchal bias that was the practical result of the Republic's universalising rhetoric (Cross, 1997). A series of statements of principle, running from the 1946 Constitution of the Fourth Republic, which guaranteed women 'equal rights to those of men in every field' (Duchen, 1994), through to 1970s legislation including declarations on equal pay and discrimination at work, failed to provide any working definitions or implementation machinery and often allowed for 'exceptions' or 'just cause' for discrimination.

In the early 1980s François Mitterrand made women's rights a major issue in his bid for the presidency and by 1983 the Minister at the newly created Ministry for Women's Rights, Yvette Roudy, had piloted a law on equality at work through Parliament and on to the statute-book. Although it amended the *Code du Travail* to provide a definition of equal pay for work of equal value and strengthened earlier anti-discrimination measures, the main thrust of the Roudy law was enabling. Companies with 50 or more employees were to be required to present to works councils an annual report, as part of the *bilan social* or social audit, on the relative situation of female and male workers, including comments on action taken during the previous year and costed objectives for the year to come. On the basis of this information companies were encouraged to formulate 'equality plans' which could be part financed by the State.

In addition a new Council for Workplace Equality (*Conseil supérieur de l'égalité professionnelle*) was set up as a tripartite interministerial body to promote these measures and monitor implementation. Its deliberations and intentions were to be informed and transmitted at the regional and departmental level by the newly created *Déléguées des droits des femmes* working with the local administration of the Employment and Training Ministry.

In the second half of the 1980s an attempt was made to break down horizontal segregation with the introduction, on a pilot basis in six regions only, of individualised contracts (called *contrats pour la mixité des emplois*), signed by state, employer, and employee. Their purpose was to finance training or job creation for women in small and medium-sized companies and in traditionally male occupations. After this measure was extended to all regions roughly 100 contracts were signed each year (Conseil Supérieur, 1995).

Before the introduction of the Pregnant Workers Directive, France already allowed 16 weeks leave paid at 84 per cent of salary, whereas UK provision had hitherto been hedged about with length-of-service conditions for both leave and pay. Provisions in France now allow 26 weeks if the expectant mother already has two or more children. The corresponding leave for adoption is 10 and 18 weeks.

French law relating to sexual harassment in the workplace, introduced into the penal code and employment law in the early 1990s, rightly recognised the phenomenon as an abuse of power but restricted the application of the new measure to harassment by an employer or supervisor. It therefore fails to cover colleagues of similar status, even though a survey of 1,300 French women carried out in 1991 identified the harasser as a colleague in almost a quarter of cases experienced (European Industrial Relations Review, 1997 and 1998). Somewhat surprisingly, only 21 per cent of the women questioned claimed to have experience of sexual harassment at work (compared with 73 per cent of 2,000 women responding to a German survey).

## Equality of Opportunity Developments in Spain

In Spain in 1975 civil liberties and political parties, now taken for granted, did not exist. The 1978 Constitution banned discrimination, making men and women equal in law, regardless of race, social class, sex, or religion (Constitution, Article 14). This opened the way for the long process of change: re-shaping attitudes, influencing behaviour, and bringing changes to conventions and social structures that had prevented women participating in the country's economic, cultural and political life. The 1978 Constitution also clarified the situation regarding employment:

> All Spanish people have the obligation to work and the right to paid employment... to promotion at work and to a salary that is adequate to satisfy their needs and those of their family, without there being any discrimination on grounds of sex (Article 35).

Enormous social change followed, particularly over the thirteen years of socialist rule, building on the economic expansion of the late 1950s to the 1970s. Administrative decentralisation, another key reform ushered in by the 1978 Constitution, offered employment in regional administration, at a time when women were ready to join the labour market. Joining the EC only in 1986 meant Spain has had less time in which to adapt national to EU legislation than have the founder members. One hundred and twenty measures were approved in

September 1987 by the Council of Ministers in Brussels to reform discriminatory aspects of Spanish law and raise awareness of women's rights and problems.

The *Instituto de la Mujer* (Institute for Women's Affairs, hereafter referred to as the *Instituto*), set up in 1983 under the Ministry for Social Affairs, now the Ministry of Employment and Social Affairs, has been the catalyst for the promotion of awareness of women's rights and collaborates with the National Employment Institute (INEM), organising training and vocational guidance. It co-ordinates IRIS (network of vocational training programmes) and NOW (New Opportunities for Women) initiatives, draws up and evaluates the impact of Spain's Equal Opportunities Plans, manages a database on women's matters, offers support to the dynamic women's networks, promotes research, and publishes reports and surveys. All seventeen autonomous regions set up bodies working towards equality; eleven produced their own plans and set up free Women's Advice Centres (CIDEM).

Spain's first equality plan, *Plan de Igualdad de Oportunidades de las Mujeres* (PIOM*)*, 1988-90, sought to promote change in Spanish women's social and legal status. The second PIOM, 1993-95, designed as a stimulus to enable women to participate actively in professional, cultural and political life, aimed at bringing about qualitative change in structures and attitudes of both individuals and groups. The third PIOM, 1997-2000 (Instituto de la Mujer y Ministerio de Trabajo y Asuntos Sociales, 1997a), is extraordinarily comprehensive, but short on detail or specifics. It spans ten topics ranging from education to sport, women's health, decision-making, the environment, balancing work and domestic responsibilities, sexual harassment, feminisation of poverty, with intermittent reference to partnership and mainstreaming. Lack of prior consultation with women's organisations, undue haste in launching it on the eve of International Women's Day in 1997, the conspicuous absence of attention to the outcome of Beijing, lack of new ideas, unfortunate contradictions, omission of concrete details as to means of implementation, monitoring and evaluation, all mean it was not well received (Actualidad Política, 1997).

On the legislative front, maternity/paternity leave was extended (by Law 03/03/89) to sixteen weeks, the last four to be taken by either parent. Provision was made for jobs to be held open for a year, later extended to three years (Law 24/03/95), for parents wanting to take care of small children and then return to the same or a comparable post. Reporting of discriminatory practices was made easier for women by placing the burden of proof on the accused (Art. 96 RDL 521/90) (Unión General de Trabajadores de Andalucía, 1992). Clauses in the Constitution not deemed explicit enough to cover equal pay for work of equal value were reinforced by new legislation (Law 03/03/89). Also in 1989, the Workers' Statute was amended, prohibiting sexual harassment in the workplace.

Spain was the first member state to take any such action, defining sexual harassment as 'verbal or physical offence of a sexual nature' (European Industrial Relations Review, 1997 and 1998). Employees were also given the right to request their contract to be terminated in the event of behaviour at work adversely affecting their personal dignity. Furthermore, this was ruled to constitute grounds for unfair dismissal and if the case were deemed valid, the individual would be eligible for reinstatement or compensation.

Spain has had a minimum wage (SMI, *Sueldo Mínimo Interprofesional*) since 1961. However, at 68,270 ptas. per month (c. £300) in 1999 for workers aged 16 and over, this is so low as to be unrealistic, the sectoral *convenios* instead being the instrument used in wage determination. With the labour market reform's apprentice contract legalising payment of only 70 per cent of the SMI, the proportion of workers earning less than the SMI (27 per cent in 1993) was destined to rise. Whether the drop in unemployment can be attributed to the reforms, aimed at reducing unemployment particularly among the under-25s, or whether this has happened as a result of the economic upturn, it is hard to say. Women have taken a high proportion of the new contracts. With 80 per cent of the part-time contracts being in the service sector, for only the minimum duration of six months and largely restricted to the tourist season, these contracts could be viewed as compounding the problem of precarious, 'atypical' work. Further measures are being taken (García de Sola, 1998) in an attempt to enhance women's employability, increase their participation rate, and by offering in-service training, reduce the risk of their leaving the labour force.

The recent desegregation of certain sectors, ironically, is more than offset by increased segregation in, for example, services, which, as the major growth area, has taken on increasing numbers of unskilled female workers (Directorate-General for Employment, Industrial Relations and Social Affairs, 1996) at a time when agriculture and industry were declining. With 40 per cent female workers, it is now the sector employing the highest proportion of women. Discrimination is exacerbated by segregation (Pérez del Río, 1990). The most likely result of feminisation is a drop in pay levels: the sector becomes less prestigious, less valued, the remaining men seek alternative employment, and women's bargaining power is weakened. It is significant for Spain that the Fourth Action Programme had among its objectives the desegregation of the labour market and a consultation on 'atypical' work (Equal Opportunities Review, 1996b).

**Impact of EU and National Provision**

This overview demonstrates that national legislation in response to the EU initiatives of the last 15 or so years is no more than a first step. Women have not been able to take full advantage of the legal provisions theoretically available to them. Moreover, as in Britain, women in France and Spain are deterred from pursuing cases under equal pay and equal treatment provisions by the complex and time-consuming nature of procedure and by the fact that the persistence of occupational segregation makes comparison with men difficult. Mazur (1995) has also identified the very nature of the French legal system, compared with the Anglo-Saxon recourse to case law and precedent, as an obstacle to the development of equal opportunities practice and a hindrance to feedback. It is possible to identify a number of other factors that may account for the failure to effect a perceivable change in women's position in the workforce.

In neither country is there a monitoring body independent of government, such as the Equal Opportunities Commission, to ensure continuity and take the initiative, or, as the EOC is currently doing, change the emphasis from combating discrimination to promoting the positive right to equal treatment. The appointment of Baroness Jay as head of the Women's Unit in Britain is encouraging. Moreover the Unit's move to the Cabinet Office is seen as scope for leverage and likely to facilitate mainstreaming (Equal Opportunities Review, 1998b). An autonomous body similar to the EOC had been proposed in the original bill formulated in France in 1981 but eliminated from the final draft (Mazur, 1995). Subsequently, changes of government and the shuffling of ministerial responsibilities that has accompanied them have slowed down progress. What support Aznar's PP Government[1] actually gives to the *Instituto* and to women's interests in Spain is a matter of some contention, despite the presence of four women in the cabinet. In France, on the other hand, the return of the Left under Prime Minister Lionel Jospin in June 1997 also meant the return to the Employment Ministry of the energetic Martine Aubry, who frequently includes references to the particular situation of women in her pronouncements on employment measures. However, the policy caravan appears to have moved on: the focus of activity in relation to women is now parity of political representation rather than parity of employment opportunity and treatment.

For France factors that could be interpreted negatively include the gradual downgrading of equal opportunities issues and bodies and the ineffectiveness of the traditionalist *Inspection du Travail*, which was charged with enforcing annual equality audits. Both go some way towards explaining why the enabling measures of the 1980s have had relatively little effect. Laufer's analysis (1992) of the early 'equality plans' identified a strong resistance among employers to their aims, and a working group of the Council for Workplace Equality reported that only 30 plans had been signed since 1983, bemoaning 'a certain lack of interest in discussion of equality at work... at company level' (Conseil Supérieur, 1995). The Council itself seemed to confine its activities to collecting data and issuing worthy statements of intent. In the two full years that have elapsed since 1995, only one equality plan per year has been added to the total; the movement appears to have run out of steam.

France has attracted the criticism of European institutions on at least four occasions for failing to remove discriminatory pay or treatment provisions or to implement European Directives with due speed. The rhetoric of equality has not been translated into real improvement in working conditions and opportunities for the majority of French women and this is in part due to a lack of will on the part of politicians and employers. The story of the dilution in cabinet and parliament of Yvette Roudy's proposals, which eventually became the 1983 law, bears witness to that (Mazur, 1992). Geneviève Fraisse, appointed interministerial delegate for women's rights in November 1997, asked in an interview published the previous year: 'We have a law on workplace equality, but it isn't applied. Why?' She has subsequently criticised the Jospin government's handling of social and economic issues affecting women and pointed out that the budget allocated to the *Service des Droits des Femmes* is lower for 1998 than it was for 1982.

The Commission singled out Spain for the influence and impact on women's lives of Spain's Second Equal Opportunities Plan 1993-95 (European Commission, 1995), and for information exchange with the Commission. Notwithstanding the abundant informative literature written in comprehensible language and the network of CIDEM advice centres for women, precisely the women who most need assistance are least likely to have an awareness of their rights or the confidence or skills to pursue their cause. Problems facing those wishing to seek redress when confronted with infringements include lack of experience of the procedures involved, delays in cumbersome legal procedure, and tight deadlines for submission of the claim. Claims against dismissal, for example, must be made to the *Juzgado de lo Social* within 20 days. Changes intended as enabling are having a boomerang effect; maternity leave is perceived by private sector employers as too generous, making women staff a poor investment. Moreover, it is not only men who are a barrier to women's success, but women's own lack of ambition. For all the awareness-raising campaigns, prejudice remains ingrained in the national psyche. In the face of evidence to the contrary, women in Spain are still regarded as prone to greater absenteeism (Martínez Quintana, 1992). Despite the minimum wage and commitment to equal pay, the gender pay gap persists. As in other countries with an enforceable minimum wage (West Midlands Low Pay Unit, 1992), discrimination continues to distort the operations of the labour market, the economic value of the work being assessed by the gender of the worker.

**Conclusions**

Despite their massive and continuous presence on the job market and their clear belief in and commitment to their 'right to work', and despite measures aimed at reducing inequality at work which have sometimes appeared imaginative, women in France and Spain today suffer from greater insecurity and marginalisation than two decades ago. The increase in 'atypical' work, the economic downturn, increased competition and employment crises have exposed them to unemployment, part-time work that is imposed rather than chosen (particularly among young women), and reduction in pay brought about by attempts to redistribute work in the name of solidarity. In April 1998, the French Employment Ministry announced that the recent annual narrowing of the gap separating male and female pay (29 per cent in 1991 falling to 22 per cent in 1996) had started to open up again in 1997 (*Le Monde*, 1998).

The preamble to the EU's Third Medium-term Community Action Programme for Equal Opportunities, 1991-95 (Directorate-General for Employment, Industrial Relations and Social Affairs, 1991), had recognised that legislation can rarely do more than provide a framework for remedying inequalities. Despite the marked improvement on paper, customs and attitudes have not kept up with legislative changes. It is axiomatic that, in order to benefit from equality legislation, women have to be familiar with the law: enabling them to exercise their rights was among the priorities of the Fourth Community Action Programme (Directorate-General for Employment, Industrial Relations and Social Affairs, 1995), not least because of the substantial differences between member states in terms of knowledge, information, access to seek redress, likely delay in enforcement of the law, etc. Sadly, Eurobarometer (Directorate-General for Employment, Industrial Relations and Social Affairs, 1997) found that 34 per cent of those taking part in the survey said they did not know that national equality legislation existed; 11 per cent said they believed it did not. A mere 22 per cent said such legislation existed and was implemented. Over 60 per cent of respondents did not know that the institutions of the EU were working on issues relating to equality in the workplace. Women were even less informed than men. It is predictable and inevitable that social changes, involving fundamental shifts in attitudes, expectations and values of both employers and employees, can be brought about only gradually, but given this level of ignorance, despite awareness-raising programmes and media coverage, very little concrete progress appears to have been made.

The current orientation of EU action on equal opportunities is to promote mainstreaming, that is the integration of sex equality considerations into all policy-making. Fraisse fears that this could be a backward step: 'We don't say single mothers any more, but one-parent families. We don't talk about women's part-time work but part-time work in general, even though 80 per cent of part-time workers are women.... When we used categories, we could see where women were. When we generalise they disappear' (Aulagnon, 1998b).

**Note**

[1] The Partido Popular is the Spanish centre-right party, founded in 1977 and voted in by a slender majority in 1996 under the leadership of José María Aznar.

# 4 Vive la Différence?: Equal Opportunities and Access to Training at Work for Women in France and Britain

CATHERINE FLETCHER

## Introduction

This chapter is concerned with the issue of equal opportunities in the field of ongoing training, as an important element of advancement at work. Placing particular emphasis on the insurance industry, this study investigates whether women are given a 'fair crack of the whip' in terms of access to training courses and promotion, particularly into managerial positions. A cross-national comparison between Britain and France is used because the regulation of provision, and practice, of training at work is quite different in each country.

The French system, *Formation Continue*, was instituted in 1971 following the demands for worker participation in 1968. Its aim is to provide every worker with the chance of advancement and personal development at work. As part of the *Formation Continue* training levy system, which is heavily regulated by the state, all companies employing over 50 people are obliged to spend 1.5 per cent of their wages bill on continuous vocational training for employees. In contrast, the British system is voluntarist and has been moving away from any state intervention, particularly evident since the disbanding of the Training Boards in the 1980s. This system has been heavily criticised over the years as the onus is placed on the employer without legal compulsion to provide training. As such, training is often seen only in relation to market competitiveness rather than staff development per se. Professions such as engineering and the law have training requirements which are overseen by their respective professional bodies but not controlled by the state. Equal opportunities in training is perceived quite differently within the French and British systems, as will be discussed below.

France and Britain were chosen for this study partly due to their geographical proximity which, with increased labour mobility within the European labour market, may enable mobile women workers to decide on whether to work in France or Britain based on the conditions of work offered, including that of equal opportunity of access to such things as ongoing training and the advantages this gives.  Cross national comparison is particularly useful in demonstrating best practice and policy difference.  The insurance industry is further selected for investigation because of its importance as a service sector industry employing large numbers of women.  Moreover, it is currently at an interesting stage as it is undergoing a period of rapid change as a result of new technology and consequent changes in working practices linked to the increased use of direct telephone sales.

It is difficult to compare like with like when comparing French and British figures on training expenditure.  The French system requires records to be kept for audit, whereas under the British system employers provide estimated figures.  This leads to the current situation where estimations of training expenditure figures in Britain are vastly inflated and may bear little resemblance to reality.  The figure of £2 billion per year spent on training supplied by the British government to the European Commission publication, 'Social Europe', (European Commission, 1993) is a good example of this phenomenon.  In investigating the issue of gender and training, the immediate problem is that statistics have only recently been disaggregated by gender.  The European Commission realised the importance of working towards equal opportunities, and the first report comparing continuing vocational training in the original 12 member states where gendered figures are provided was published by the FORCE (FORmation Continue en Europe) Bureau in 1997.  The survey considered all vocational training activities undertaken by employees of the enterprises included.  With the exception of initial training of apprentices or trainees with a special training contract, the survey, carried out in the calendar period 1993, considered all vocational training activities of employees in 50,000 companies with a workforce of ten or more.  The sample was designed to ensure representativeness of the national economy as well as the size and sector of each enterprise included.  The results for both Britain and France were surprising.  For Britain the figure of £10.6 billion training expenditure was given by International Facts and Forecasts (IFF), the company which provided the statistics for the FORCE report, a big increase on the £2 billion previously quoted.  Moreover, preliminary results showed that fewer French (87 per cent) than British (93 per cent) companies had provided training in 1993.  This is not what would have been expected considering the different approaches to training in the two countries.

The raw figures seem to show that women have nothing to complain about in terms of equal access to training but this can be misleading as women in certain industries, such as construction, receive more training than male workers simply because they do different jobs, for example office administration which necessitates computer training.   When the figures are examined according to profession or industry, a different picture emerges.

## Gendered Employment in the Insurance Industry

This chapter contains a brief overview of the issue of gendered employment within the insurance industry, raising some of the particular problems encountered by women in that industry, but which are not unique to it.  Questionnaires received from training managers in France and Britain and the interviews carried out with respondents are then analysed to draw conclusions.  Problems encountered in the first part of the fieldwork are also discussed.

The study, undertaken in 1995, involved sending questionnaires to training managers in the head offices of 30 major insurance companies in France and 30 in Britain.  The purpose was to discover whether equal opportunities for men and women with regard to training was perceived as an important issue.  The final sample was made up of ten British companies and eight French companies.  The study does not aim to be statistically representative but the intention is, rather, to provide a snapshot of activity in the area of training provision for women in the insurance industry.

Ongoing training at work is an essential part of any equal opportunities policy which aims to tackle gender segregation in the workplace.  Many writers (Crompton and Sanderson, 1990; Dex and Walters, 1990; Duru-Bellat, 1990; Gadrey, 1992; Maruani, 1989; Philips and Taylor, 1986; Toutain, 1992; Walby, 1988) have looked at the issue of horizontal segregation where women are not represented in certain professions and are vastly over-represented in others.  Other writers (Ashburner, 1992; Cockburn, 1991; Laufer, 1993; Rees, 1992; Wajcma, 1996; Witz and Savage, 1992) have analysed the phenomenon of vertical segregation where women are employed in large numbers in an industry but are not represented in the higher levels of management.  Vertical segregation exists within the insurance industry where most workers at the base of the pyramid are female but most managers are male.  Furthermore, horizontal segregation is evident where anti-female bias can be seen in recruitment of the salesforce.  The segmented nature of the insurance industry has been commented upon by Crompton and Lefeuvre (1992), Crompton and Sanderson (1994), and Collinson, Knights and Collinson (1990), who noted the division between primarily male salesforce staff and primarily female support staff.  For example, to be promoted above the level of team leader in British companies, workers need to demonstrate experience of management, and field management is overwhelmingly male, effectively barring most women within insurance companies from one avenue to promotion to senior level. The issue of recruitment is obviously linked to what sort of training is seen as appropriate for which workers, and there appear to be rigid divisions between the two areas of the industry.

Women's presence within the salesforce in insurance companies in Britain is as low as 3 per cent and not much higher in France at 5 per cent, while promotion opportunities are further limited by a stated need that candidates must be mobile and have continuous service. The criterion of mobility may not in reality be applied but can be used to undermine and discourage women who want to broaden their experience and get promoted (Collinson, Knights and Collinson, 1990). This can be added to the list quoted by Gadrey (1992), who states that if inferior physical strength can no longer be used to exclude women from the workplace, factors such as noise, smells, dirt and danger will be used to underline the 'fact' that the workplace is an unsuitable place for a woman. The use of the mobility criterion to exclude women takes place within an industry characterised by paternalism where managers often present the outside world as a dangerous place in which women are in more physical danger than men, for example, in going to visit clients in the evening. This issue was clearly illustrated in an interview carried out with an insurance training provider in 1995 for the current study. Here the example was cited of Suzy Lamplugh, an estate agent who was abducted and presumed murdered in the course of her job. Conversely, it could be argued that the reluctance of female clients to let a strange man into their homes should be perceived by enlightened companies as a reason to employ more female sales representatives.

In her study of the tourism industry, Adkins (1995) highlights how women are clustered in front-line service jobs where their sexuality is an integral part of the kinds of customer relations which women are expected to carry out and men are not. Gendered work relations contribute to the production of what she calls compulsory heterosexuality. This is particularly visible in the tourist industry where uniforms issued to female staff are often designed to signal sexual availability to men. It could also be argued that the dress code for women in office work is explicitly framed to meet the male gaze, to avoid overt sexual invitation but to be, nevertheless, 'attractive'. Collinson, Knights and Collinson (1990) give examples of how women who did progress into sales jobs in insurance were accused of sleeping with managers to get promoted. They also give examples of how some customers suggested sexual favours might be part of the deal in order to ensure obtaining an important contract. The position of front-line staff in the insurance sector could be seen as gendered in the same way as it is in the tourism industry, although the roles are different in each industry. Women, who make up the vast majority of insurance support staff dealing with claims, are perceived by customers as being more sympathetic and maternal than male staff in times of crisis. The insurance industry can be seen as providing an interesting example of how gendered work relations operate to hold women back.

## Statistical Information on the Insurance Industry

In France all personnel classed as employees, including those working part-time, have training rights, and are seen as part of the workforce which may benefit from training. In Britain, the salesforce is often classified as a mixture of full-time staff, staff working on commission or staff attached to the company but not classed as employees, and who are therefore not counted as part of the workforce eligible to receive training by the company. The salesforce is overwhelmingly made up of male workers in all companies studied in both countries. Rather than surveying the minority of women who work in sales, it was thought preferable for this research to survey the administrative personnel where women make up a much higher percentage of workers. Tables 4.1 and 4.2 show the percentage of the administrative workforce which is female, in order to track the percentage of women in management positions and the number of training hours received by women. Figures given are at the national level but a second questionnaire was distributed to staff at a local level to ensure easier access.

French companies prefer to express their training spending in terms of the percentage of the wages bill spent. While the law requires companies of over 50 employees to spend at least 1.5 per cent of the wages bill on training, insurance companies are known to be good training providers and figures of 4-5 per cent are usually documented by companies. The insurance industry in Britain was the largest industry training provider in terms of percentage according to the British report published for the FORCE Continuing Vocational Training Project (IFF, 1993). As British companies do not have figures available on percentage of the wages bill spent, it was decided in this study to express training in terms of numbers of training hours per person per year to facilitate comparison. However, many British companies could not provide accurate figures for this study as no central records were kept.

## Questionnaire Results

Statistical information on the following four areas was obtained: the percentage of women staff; the percentage of women employed part-time; training hours per person per year (pppy); number of training hours received by women; training strategy; whether the training strategy included measures specifically aimed at women (strategy for females); and external qualifications which employees hoped to obtain.

*French Companies*

**Table 4.1  French companies**

| Company | Hours pppy | % Female Staff | | Strategy for Females | Qualifications |
|---------|-----------|------|------|--------------|----------------|
| | | F/T | P/T | | |
| A | 46.0 | 67 | - | None | BTS, CAP, BP |
| B | 22.0 | 57 | - | None | BTS |
| C | 24.0 | 66 | 13 | None | BTS |
| D | 32.0 | 60 | - | None | Internal |
| E | 29.0 | 62 | - | None | BTS, CAP |
| F | 16.6 | 56 | 1 | None | BTS, ENAS |
| G | 25.0 | 45 | 5 | None | BTS |
| H | c.50.0 | 55 | - | None | BTS, CAP |

CAP=Certificat d'Aptitude Pratique
BTS=Brevet de Technicien Supérieur
BP=Brevet Professionnel
ENAS=Ecole nationale des assurances (diploma from a selective higher education establishment specialising in insurance).

In the French companies, women were in the majority in all but one company and even there they made up 45 per cent of the workforce. It can be seen from these figures that the part-time rate is small in France, no more than 13 per cent. One company representative said that three quarters of part-time workers worked four days a week, which is a popular option in France for women with childcare responsibilities since many children go to school on Saturday morning and have Wednesday free. None of the French companies stated that they regarded gender as being a relevant issue where training is concerned. They all stressed individual needs, thus disregarding gender. About half of the companies kept figures disaggregated by gender and in all these cases the incidence of training received was slightly below the expected level for the female percentage of the workforce with male employees benefiting disproportionately. When the figures are further examined in terms of training hours it is very clear that men benefit more. For example, in 1996, in Company H, 385 women and 351 men received training. Despite women making up 57 per cent of the workforce, they do not receive 57 per cent of training given, which would have given a figure of 420 women trained. The pyramid pattern in this company can be seen with 229 male workers, classified as *cadres* (managers) and who received training, compared to 64 female workers at this level. The remaining workforce comprised 40 male and 50 female *agents de maitrise*, and 281 female and 82 male workers classified as *employés*. The number of training hours was not proportionate to the gender divisions in the company. Of 26,385 hours training received, 10,105 were taken up by managers. This clearly indicates the greater benefits received by males, probably due to their greater presence in the management category.

Similarly, in Company F, which spends 4.3 per cent of its wages bill on training on the general insurance side, women made up 4,191 or 67 per cent of the 6,281 strong administrative workforce but benefited from only 61 per cent of 201,606 training hours received. This means that male employees again benefit disproportionately as 33 per cent of the workforce have 39 per cent of the hours devoted to them. Men therefore gain from a larger number of hours, probably linked to higher quality training courses, whereas women participated in more short courses. Women made up 68 per cent of trainees, and although this seems high, some did two courses and were therefore counted twice. Although there are twice as many women as men in the administrative workforce, there are more male managers within this section (18.7 per cent male and 13.3 per cent female). This means that if one encounters a man from the administrative side of this company he is more likely to be a *cadre* (18.7 per cent) than *non-cadre* (16.1 per cent). Women are even less well represented in management of the sales section.

In Company D, gender disaggregated figures show that men once more benefit disproportionately from training within the company. This is again linked to the structure of the workforce which favours managers who are predominantly male (65 per cent plus 5 per cent senior management), whereas only 35 per cent of the female employees are classified as *cadres*. As *non-cadres* only receive 27 per cent of the 28,263 training hours, this inevitably disadvantages the female workforce.

All companies encouraged employees to aim for a BTS (*Brevet de Technicien Supérieur*, which is roughly equivalent to two years post A-level) specialising in the insurance industry, or for in-house qualifications. Qualifications at lower levels such as the CAP *(Certificat d'Aptitude Professionnel)* or BP *(Brevet Professionnel)* were seen as less useful but could be used as stepping stones.

*British Companies*

**Table 4.2  British companies**

| Company | Hours pppy | % Female Staff | | Strategy for Females | Qualifications |
|---|---|---|---|---|---|
| | | F/T | P/T | | |
| 1 | 3 | 25 | - | Maybe | FPC, ACII |
| 2 | - | 41 | - | None | FPC |
| 3 | (estimate) 45 | 45.5 | - | None | CII |
| 4 | - | 70 | - | None | ACII, CIP |
| 5 | - | 30 | - | None | CII |
| 6 | (Field) 144 | 22 | - | None | FPC |
| | (HQ) 5 | | | | |
| 7 | - | 46 | - | None | CII |
| 8 | - | 40 | 7 | None | CII |
| 9 | - | 42 | 2 | None | CII |
| 10 | - | 60 | - | Sometimes | Relevant degree CII, NVQ |

ACII=Associateship of the Insurance Institute
FCP=Financial Planning Certificate
CII=Chartered Insurance Institute
CIP=Certificate of Insurance Practice
NVQ=National Vocational Qualification

All information was given by fairly large companies, ranging from 420 staff up to 10,000 staff, but typically having more than 1,000 employees. The training hours per person per year were unknown in the vast majority of the British companies which raises the question of how British firms monitor training and ensure effectiveness. Where figures were given they were higher than the French ones, which could indicate that the companies involved in good practice in training provision see the value in keeping records. The percentage of women employed in the British companies ranged from 20 per cent to 60 per cent with the exception of one Scottish company which stated that their workforce was 70 per cent female, and that 100 per cent of the part-time workers were women. However, women made up the majority of the workforce in only two out of the 10 companies but were 40-50 per cent of the workforce in another five companies. A small percentage of the workforce in the insurance industry appears to be employed part-time, but, unsurprisingly, women make up the vast majority of this category. The percentage of part-time workers is likely to increase as more companies find they have to compete by offering telephone services for longer hours and therefore use flexible working practices which usually means more part-time workers used at peak hours.

All the companies had employee schemes and training strategies linked to staff needs but none had any measures linked specifically to women. One company reported discussion of the possibility of a training package geared to women's needs but on further investigation it was found that the questionnaire had been filled in by a freelance consultant who had since stopped working with the company and no further information was available on such plans. One company stated that they would run single sex courses for women if there was a perceived need but regarded this as an 'eighties issue' with much less relevance in the 1990s and beyond. The vast majority of training managers that were interviewed considered women-only courses to be totally inappropriate for their company culture and stated that women themselves did not want differentiated treatment.

Most companies were fairly clear about externally sanctioned qualifications and examinations run by the Chartered Insurance Institute being important. Employees involved in giving financial advice are legally required to pass financial planning certificates at different levels.

## Company Training Strategy

The following information is given in bullet points to attempt to give the flavour of the questionnaire.

*French Companies*

*Company A*
Connect national policy with local needs.
- Link training to personal objectives.
- Increase internal mobility.
- Allow everyone to keep up successfully with changes in career directions.
- Have the right person in the right place at the right time.

*Company B*
Be the leaders in the sector.
- Apply national policy according to local needs.

- Revise policy according to needs.
- Increase skills levels across the board.
- Prioritise technical training, participative management, communication training.
- Encourage staff to obtain BS and BTS qualifications.

*Company C*
No stated strategy. The general direction of policy is decided centrally but is linked to local needs.

*Company D*
National strategy, revised every 3 years.
- Prioritise management of communication and professional mobility.
- Reinforce skills of on-the-job staff.
- Enable staff to cope with change in job content.

*Company E*
National strategy, revised annually with the *comité d'entreprise* (workers' committee).
- Encourage development of commercial spirit.
- Encourage development of professional attitude.
- Encourage the acquisition of human relations skills.

*Company F*
National strategy.
- Focus on knowledge of insurance products.
- Develop information technology skills and management training.

*Company G*
*Polyvalence* (flexibility) seen as more important than specialisation which may become outmoded.
- Prioritise customer relations, computing training, quality control and technical training.

*Company H*
The training strategy is linked to the training plan, drawn up every year with workers' representatives, using information from the yearly appraisal of employees.

*British Companies*

*Company 1*
Strategy being reviewed. National strategy but central and local delivery.
- Encourage all staff to take up training. The issue of separate training for women is being discussed.

*Company 2*
Achieve business objectives and support objectives of business.
- Provide training related to roles not gender. There is no reduction of take-up in training by women.

*Company 3*
Human Resources Development is part of the corporate plan, cascaded down to the training department. It is revised every 12 months. There is a quarterly appraisal where training needs and development are linked. No difference is made between male and female employees.
- Increase technical skills.
- Improve levels of professionalism and quality of team-working.
- Consolidate operation of performance management.

*Company 4*
New strategy, to be revised annually. Courses are mixed. Men and women have different natural skills(!) Provision of quality service for the majority of staff.
- Provide training for varied needs according to job.

*Company 5*
National policy on training, identical for men and for women.

*Company 6*
- Continue to provide training to new recruits (new recruits are given 20 per cent of all training).
- Prioritise Information Technology skills to cope with change.
- Give training on product knowledge, leadership and management skills.
- Provide a personal development programme.
- Encourage acquisition of professional qualifications. 'This is a traditional firm but we want to tap everyone's potential. Women should be encouraged to go into sales.'

- 'Change is needed now - the glass ceiling is imposed by the traditional approach but women-only courses are inappropriate.'

*Company 7*
Annual group training plan gives a clear framework for training policy.

*Company 8*
Strategy is company policy. No details given. Telephone comment made that equal opportunities is 'an explosive subject'.

*Company 9*
Focus strategy to meet individual's needs.

*Company 10*
Company policy sits within the wider group. The company is committed to Opportunity 2000 and getting women into management. They run women's development courses. Occasionally both men and women take part in single-gender training. Many others refuse to attend as they regard it as discriminatory. The training manager sees training for women as 'an eighties issue with far less relevance now'.
- Support the business in a cost-effective way.


**Any Explanations? Training Managers Comment**

Because of the inconsistencies in the record keeping of the British companies it is difficult to see how they can monitor the training which is being delivered. Equal opportunities and differentiated training for women are viewed as difficult issues, 'contentious' and 'explosive' being two descriptions given by British managers. Another British training manager said the latter was an issue which was no longer relevant. Although the British training managers in this sample do not consider gender to be important, they at least recognise that it may be on the agenda at some point. This contrasts with French training managers who refused, in most cases, to consider gender as an issue, preferring to claim that they were gender-blind. One manager (male, Company A) claimed that gender was as unimportant to him as eye-colour. Another manager (female, Company D) stated that women were not discriminated against in terms of training hours allocated, then had to revise her opinion in the interview while discussing the gender breakdown of figures which proved otherwise. Another (male) manager of the regional delegation (Company G) had very firm beliefs that women could make either very good workers or very bad workers, depending on whether they were really committed to the job. This echoes research by Gadrey (1992) which notes the opposition between male and female characteristics perceived by employers such as male strength and female dexterity, greater female than male absenteeism but also greater female *conscience professionnelle* (being reliable in doing one's job thoroughly). Only one French training manager (female, Company B) was encountered who was familiar with the concept of the *plan d'égalité* (an optional equal opportunities statement to run alongside workers' agreements with management). She stated that she had been complaining about the lack of equality in training given to women for many years, and had threatened her employers with instituting such a scheme to highlight their poor record on equal opportunities.

Qualifications were seen by most training managers to be important but many stressed the preference for internal qualifications so that the firm could provide the specific training which was most useful for its needs. National qualifications were seen as important as a benchmark of achievement, and to identify motivated individuals who were willing to put in extra hours to get on within the company. However, physical accessibility of training courses for some women was seen as a potential difficulty. For example, the problem for women of travelling to external training courses was mentioned by several training managers, and also by the women's rights representative for the Breton region. Female employees were often limited in their ability to attend courses which necessitated staying away from home due to childcare responsibilities and more prosaic problems such as lack of good transport. The women's rights representative commented that women often had the second, less reliable, family car in which they were wary of travelling long distances and that this problem could be overcome by provision of a hired car if the company were serious about providing equal access to training for women.

The few British firms in the survey with Equal Opportunities Officers did not seem to be concerned with equal opportunities in training but rather with issues related to dismissal or maternity leave. In Britain training managers were part of human resources teams and another member of that team would normally have responsibility for equal opportunities issues. The nearest equivalent found in a French company was a female Personnel Officer in Company D who was responsible for issues of promotion and mobility in the company. Otherwise there was a belief in French companies that equality was already dealt with in the statutes governing training provision and was therefore not an issue. A small number of companies had been affected by training champions who had left their mark by implementing new procedures. Company C had, up until a few years ago, a female Managing Director who had instituted a modular scheme which allowed women to build up their portfolio of skills based on previous experience at work and obtain an internal qualification. This is analogous to the provision of National Vocational Qualifications in Britain, which are considered to be a useful route which women can use to obtain accreditation of prior learning. This type of 'portfolio' qualification accumulation is easier to fit into a career pattern which may be marked by periods outside the workforce because of childcare responsibilities. During one particular year the same female Managing Director had allowed promotion only to female employees, in order to redress a gender imbalance in the management. Interestingly, the regional office of the company became so female-dominated that males were actively recruited in order to redress the gender imbalance which had swung in favour of female management. In Britain, Company 6 had a new training manager who found the under-representation of women to be a great change from the previous company he had worked for and was resolved to encourage women to take up training. The importance of these training and equal opportunities champions cannot be overestimated.

Overall, the American concept of management of diversity is now being used in the insurance industry, particularly in British companies. This suggests that needs should be considered on an individual basis rather than treating employees as having any identity as part of a grouping such as gender or race. This is obviously useful to avoid any male backlash since if we are all a minority of one, white middle-class heterosexual males can also be treated as having special needs.

**Where Do We Go From Here ?**

Access to training and development is only one area where equal opportunities for women in the labour market influences their chances of mobility, promotion, salary increase and power within the organisation. The issue of training and development cannot be divorced from its cultural context and it is not really feasible to isolate it as a variable to make cross-national comparisons. However, it is possible to draw a picture of the situation in Britain and France and compare defining features, even if the picture may sometimes be hazy. This study does not claim to be comparing two representative sample populations. Difficulty of access to private companies which have to be persuaded to allow researchers to use employee time means that such a study is inevitably based on co-operative research with access controlled by gatekeepers within the company.

An internal report on women and management carried out at British Company 2 on 541 employees found that female employees in that study were more aware of inequality than male employees, with 75 per cent of male employees believing that there were equal career opportunities compared to 51 per cent of females. Similarly, 72 per cent of male employees believed that women were promoted just as quickly as male employees, whereas only 37 per cent of female employees believed this. This indicates that the perception amongst female employees is that the system does not give women an equal chance. Thus it is possible that training and official validation of skills used in the workplace is an objective way of struggling against this unfairness. In other words, there is a high level of awareness among British female employees that the system is not gender-blind and that they suffer from discrimination. This mirrors national studies carried out by Wacjma (1996) and Crompton and Sanderson (1990) which indicate awareness that all-male networks, including those in sports clubs, can be advantageous to those involved. For example, golf seems to play a peculiar role in promoting male bonding and excluding female employees within British companies, although no sporting equivalent in French companies was found.

*Training Officers' Perceptions*

In French companies, there was a general refusal to believe that gender was an issue. Training officers repeatedly stated that female employees were treated the same as male employees, despite company statistics which did not support this. When giving figures that clearly showed that male employees were getting a bigger share of the training cake than the percentage of the male workforce warranted, the female training officers seemed particularly puzzled that they had not noticed this disparity before, even though gendered statistics are held by French companies as a matter of course. The theory advanced by many French training officers interviewed was that it was a question of generation. Things had changed so much for women now in their twenties and thirties that they had the same aspirations as men, whereas the current, admittedly hierarchical, structure was a product of previous generations where women's work was always seen as subordinate to their role as wife and mother. With time, these younger women would take their place in the management structure and gendered vertical discrimination would diminish. Besides being a hopelessly optimistic case of 'jam tomorrow', this also places the onus on women fitting into the system and assumes that women's aspirations are the prime element in changing management structure, which is patently not gender neutral.

At the same time, many training officers interviewed were of the opinion that women were less available for employment between the ages of 25 and 40, the crucial time for establishing a career pattern, as this was when they were starting families. One male training officer also divided his female employees into those who were not serious and were just passing time and those who were motivated career-minded women who were more useful than their male counterparts.

In the French insurance industry, as there is no perception that discrimination against women at work is an issue, the companies do not monitor and evaluate the progress of women in the organisation, and all employees are seen as individuals. If a problem with discrimination is perceived then this should be dealt with by the training manager, with the employee having the right to call on the services of the *comité d'entreprise*. Indeed, training managers interviewed in France were most emphatic that female employees would not like to be given special treatment and that any application of, what would be seen as, positive discrimination would lead to a backlash in which women would be accused of benefiting from favouritism. The notion of the *plan dégalité* has obviously had little impact outside of the literature on equal opportunities. On the other hand, it is possible for a champion of equal opportunities to effect change fairly rapidly if she or he has the management position to do so, as the example of Company C demonstrates (p.65). Such a champion is arguably the most important prerequisite for action to establish equal opportunities within a company, appearing to be more significant than systems set up on a national level.

In Britain, monitoring and evaluation are impossible even where personnel staff are employed with responsibility for equal opportunities. In some cases, when the question of equal opportunities in training was broached, quite negative responses were evoked. One training manager refused to answer the questionnaire for managers, and it was not until his (female) manager was contacted that it was possible to speak to a personnel representative with responsibility for equal opportunities issues. However, as mentioned, the issues that training managers tended to be most concerned with were linked to maternity benefit, and there is little evidence concerning the allocation of training resources to male and female employees. A positive outcome of the interviews was that officers spoke with enthusiasm about getting the issue of equal opportunities in training on to the agenda.

Mainstreaming has become a much discussed subject both on a European level and in French and British research groups, with notable platforms such as the MAGE (*Marché du Travail et Genre* or Gender and the Labour Market) conferences on women and the labour market in Europe which took place at the Centre National de Recherche Scientifique (CNRS) in Paris in the late 1990s. This is obviously the first stage in raising awareness amongst managers that discrimination is a problem but, inevitably, it is all too easy to incorporate an equal opportunities statement into company policy and simply pay lip-service to it without there being any tangible results. Programmes such as 'Investors in People', in the UK, do not have a strong policy on equal opportunities and make recommendations of good practice rather than making the issue a cornerstone of compliance with the programme. The European Commission has adopted an approach to mainstreaming whereby inclusion of an equal opportunities element is compulsory to obtain funding for social projects and this may well have the desired effect on the companies which receive funding from the Commission. Similarly, public sector organisations can show themselves to be equal opportunity employers on paper but in practice it is the educated white female who benefits rather than those from ethnic minorities or from educationally disadvantaged backgrounds.

*Recent Developments Regarding Women in Management*

The importance of equal opportunities and training has been highlighted by a number of recent developments in major companies. A landmark case, in which the Zurich Insurance Company made a significant out-of-court settlement may now force employers to offer job-share opportunities to women in senior management positions after maternity leave. Janet Schofield, a marketing manager at the company, stated that while lip-service was paid to the idea of equal opportunities, she had been told that if she wanted to work for the company she would have to be prepared to work a seven-day week. Countering criticism following the case, Linda Taylor, Zurich's Employee Relations Manager underlined the company's strong commitment to equal opportunities, noting that the workforce was almost exactly 50 per cent male and 50 per cent female. However with only 42 out of 315 managers being female (and 2 out of 11 senior directors) this does not even match the average national figure. Thus, in the same article, Elizabeth Hodder, deputy chairwoman of the Equal Opportunities Commission, pointed out that nationally women made up 55 per cent of workers in non-manual jobs but still accounted for only 15 per cent of senior and middle managers. She stated:

> Intelligent employers already know that practices which encourage mothers to return to work maximise the return on their financial investment; keeping the skills and experience of senior staff and reducing re-training and turnover costs is good business sense (*Independent*, 28th August 1997).

The initiative by Asda, the supermarket chain, in October 1998 to encourage job sharing at all levels of the company by both men and women was hailed as a major move in shattering the glass ceiling. The decision was taken to improve equal opportunities within the company where only 10 of the 220 store managers are women, and none of the seven divisional directors are female. Jayne

Monkhouse, Employment Policy Manager at the Equal Opportunities Commission, said:

> While many retailers create part-time jobs which exclude people from employee rights and training and where women tend to be ghettoised, what we want is for people to realize that any job can be done part-time, including senior managerial roles. (*Guardian*, 1st October 1998).

## Conclusion

Whether they are working in companies which operate a voluntarist training system, as in Britain, or a state-run levy system, as in France, women do not have equal access with men to training and development opportunities within private companies in the insurance sector. This is easier to prove under the French system, as clear statistics are kept, but the evidence points to the same conclusions in Britain. It is, of course, quite possible that even with equal access to training, promotion and progress up the hierarchy would not automatically take place as so many other variables, such as selection procedures and company culture, may cause bias towards males in management recruiting staff in their own image. The level of awareness of existing discrimination seems to be lower amongst employees and training managers in France than in Britain, and the belief stronger that no structural measures to combat this are necessary since the situation will change with stronger work affiliation from the younger generation of women at work.

Recent studies by Eurostat have highlighted the disparity of training received by men and women throughout Europe. The issue of training and equal opportunities has so far not received the attention it deserves and the gap between reality and rhetoric is still very wide. Work done by the European Commission highlights best practice in the area of equal opportunities, and national organisations such as the Equal Opportunities Commission in Britain and the MAGE research group in France have produced studies which may in the future inform national policy. However, prospects for equal opportunities in the workplace are fairly bleak, although the move to encourage cases brought as class actions on the American model, to combat unequal treatment will take the onus of contesting areas of discrimination away from the individual and does give cause for cautious optimism. Until national governments in France and Britain start to treat equal access to training in the workplace as a priority by bringing in strong legislation to sanction miscreant employers, both countries will continue to waste the talents of a large proportion of the workforce which could otherwise be harnessed for increased efficiency and competitiveness.

# 5 'It's No Place for a Lady': An Empirical Study of the Implementation of an Equal Opportunity Policy within Northshire Fire Service

ANDREA LEE

It's difficult to know about her as a female, she did everything that they did. You did not know there was a female on the yard...she had no illness or ill-effects of periods. I asked her to give me the nod when she came on so I could monitor any dip in performance.

These earnest words of an instructor on the Recruits' Training course at the Northshire Fire Service discussing the progress of the first female recruit, suggest that despite equal performance 'on the yard', the underlying assumption remained that women were different and quite definitely problematic. Clearly within the Fire Service it made a great deal of difference if you were a man or a woman! The Fire Service more than most organisations remains 'dominated by gender-related values which bias organisational life in favour of one sex over another' (Morgan, 1986:178). This chapter aims to show how the gender-related bias frustrated any opportunities for change presented by the Service's Equal Opportunity Policy. It identifies those processes which ensured that dominant, white male interests remained protected and existing patterns of power were unchanged. So that, despite the title 'Equal Opportunity Employer', Northshire Fire Service remained 'no place for a lady'.

This study is based on qualitative research and is part of a large project exploring the 'implementation gap' (Dunsire, 1978) between the intention and achievement of a local authority equal opportunity policy. The study used implementation context analysis to focus on individuals and groups seeking to put policy into effect, combined with an understanding of the processes which structure their action. Such actions reflect the subjective attributes, values, perceptions and beliefs which constitute the 'assumptive world'[1] of the actor (Young and Mills, 1980). The material for this chapter was drawn from a range of exploratory techniques including participant observation, documentary evidence, attendance at meetings and training sessions, but most particularly from 25 in-depth interviews with fire officers from all levels in the Service. The results presented here show how gender-related values shaped the assumptive world of fire officers to ensure the limitation of equal opportunity and a restricted scope for change. This was done in three ways: firstly, gender-related values shaped the understandings of equal opportunity held by fire officers; secondly, gender bias was mobilised to define women as *the* problem whilst denying issues of 'race'; and thirdly, gender bias was maintained by a range of processes which effectively excluded women from the Service and maintained existing patterns of power and access. Each of these will be explored in depth in the following three sections of this chapter. The web produced by the superimposition of these values, processes and mechanisms constitutes the fabric of institutionalised racism and sexism, which will always frustrate the implementation of equal opportunity framed in terms of merit and access in any organisation.

## Women as a Threat: Gender-related Values and Understandings of Equal Opportunity

A key assumption underpinning most local authority equal opportunity policies is the belief that 'equal opportunity' is a unitary term commonly shared and understood by all the actors in any policy system. However, within the Northshire Fire Service quite distinctive understandings were evident, shaped by the assumptive world of the occupational community. Basing their concerns on their understanding of what happened in the London Fire Brigade, equal opportunity seemed to threaten the continuing professionalisation of the service by the intention to introduce women into the all-male environment. The Fire Officers therefore sought to maintain the status quo and protect the position of the Fire Service as a highly-paid elite amongst manual workers.

The Fire Service is a close-knit community replete with stories, myths, and legends. Northshire Fire Officers have more in common with their counterparts in other brigades than with departments within the County Council, which has responsibility for strategic services including Fire and Civil

Defence. Many views of equal opportunities came from this national brigade network, often based on reported experiences of the London Fire Brigade:

> The London Fire Brigade set people's teeth on edge. They didn't want women in the Fire Brigade for the sake of the Service but because they wanted to change society. The GLC report stated that the Fire Brigade was the toughest nut to crack...everything was done since then pointing to the idea that they should have women in the Fire Service (Chief Fire Officer).

The Chief Fire Officer was thus resistant towards the equal opportunity policy in Northshire, and he felt that 'there is a certain wrestling with us as a male-dominated service'. He was adamant that rules should not be changed, and whatever the policy entailed it 'must be without affecting the Brigade'. The prevailing interests which underpinned this view were very clearly articulated; he believed that, 'there are some jobs that are different, some jobs that women cannot do, and the pay difference is important too'. Women were thus perceived to be a threat in terms of status and pay. Officers felt that they were well-paid with scales linked to the top section of skilled manual workers, with a progressive scale for more senior officers which far exceeded these levels. Women threatened vested male interests and forces were mobilised to ensure that dominant interests were protected.

Within the Fire Service equal opportunities was constantly described in terms of a 'fair crack of the whip':

> Equal opportunities is about a fair crack of the whip to everybody and it is needed. I don't agree with advertising in Asian languages, but I think probably Afro-Caribbeans would ideally fit into the Fire Brigade - they would work better as a team as the Asian Community often have self-imposed isolation. I don't agree with pre-entry training either, that certainly smacks of discrimination the other way (Divisional Commander).

Equal opportunities was shaped by the interplay of prevailing interests, values and beliefs, themselves the plausible interpretations of everyday experiences of the Service. The senior officers assume they are being fair, that there are 'no problems here', but to an outsider their words betray that fairness and illustrate institutionalised racism and sexism. Note in particular the opposition to Asian languages, the stereotypical views of Afro-Caribbean groups, and the opposition to pre-entry training as 'unfair'. In reality, to the Senior Brigade Officers a 'fair crack of the whip' actually meant the maintenance of the status quo, doing nothing to disturb the existing patterns of power and access. Cynthia Cockburn described such 'cultural resistance' by men to form a common pattern wherever areas of male control were challenged.  In such situations she noted that

> men are observed to generate a masculine culture in and around their work, whether this is technical or managerial, that can make women feel, without being told in so many words, 'you are out of place here' (Cockburn, 1991:65).

The remaining sections of this chapter seek to explain these processes of the mobilisation of gender bias within the Fire Service, which effectively made women 'out of place'.

## Defining Women as a Problem: the Processes of Problem Ascription

In the words of a Divisional Commander, 'Women in the Fire Service are looked at in the same way as with a problem person, in other words they are treated as different and that is the problem'.  According to Guillaumin, 'to speak of difference is to articulate a rule, a norm... it is the statement of the effects of a power relationship' (1995:250).  The notion of difference thus represents a relationship of a particular type, where there is a fixed point, a referent.  In Northshire women were seen as the problem demanding special attention because of their difference or deviation from the implicit, normative, white male model.

Defining any problem is a social and political process which involves the values, attitudes, perceptions and interests of the actors concerned.  It is a process which selects some issues for attention and ignores or screens out others.  It is essentially a subjective process whereby issues are perceived as problems by interested parties, who in turn will be influenced by the structures within the organisation (Hogwood and Gunn, 1984).  The particular ways in which women were constructed as *the* problem, thus becomes a significant aspect in the understanding of cultural resistance.

### *The Nature of the Problem*

> the issue we really want to look at is sexual discrimination.  Race is not a basic problem, and the operational fire-fighters do not have to deal with disability.  But sex discrimination is important - women fire-fighters are the main issue, let's lay this on the line.

The words of the Assistant Chief Fire Officer, quoted at a seminar given to each division, closely reflected the views held by the Fire Service. In the discussion which followed the seminar on sexual harassment[2] the issue of women in the Fire Service was openly aired. It emerged just how clearly women were perceived to be a problem, in particular the extent to which they were different or deviated from accepted male norms. These differences were expressed as problems in four ways: biological unsuitability; emotional unsuitability; sexuality; and the differences that would cause managerial problems.

In the case of biological unsuitability, women's 'menstrual cycle' was noted as a potential cause of difficulty affecting their performance on the job. Pregnant women were a problem because of health and safety issues. Women were also discussed in terms of their emotional unsuitability ('would they be able to cope with road traffic accidents') and their sexuality ('beds on stations is always an emotive issue'). Managerial problems were also raised, in terms of women potentially down-grading the standards and status of the Fire Service, of women being given 'preferential treatment', and finally of women's presence forming a barrier between managers and the men, disrupting the all-male world.

What cannot be emphasised sufficiently from this selection of statements is the consistency with which the same sentiments were expressed by numerous officers across the entire Service. The resonance of a shared language embedded in the organisational culture was striking. Many of the comments echoed the views expressed by the Chief Fire Officer (as outlined on p.3) and the arguments were seen as accepted 'truths' and remained over time as persistent myths. To explain such views merely in terms of sexist attitudes would be to miss significant processes of problem ascription in operation.

*Processes of Ascription*

The processes of ascription refer to those factors which mould the attitudes, perceptions and interests of fire officers, which in turn shape the way some issues are defined as problems and others are not. Within Northshire, women were defined as *the* problem whereas 'race' did not emerge as an issue. Women were treated as a problem because they threatened the self-image of firemen; the prevailing discourse emphasised the difference between their male world and outsiders; the equipment was perceived to be unsuitable; women disturbed the private world of the fire station; women posed a dilemma in terms of equal treatment; and in comparison 'race' was alleged to be a non-issue. Each of these will be examined in turn.

Women threatened the self-image of firemen, which was defined in masculine terms to encapsulate 'manly work virtues' such as pride in the occupation, and membership and control of an all-male world (Salaman, 1986:53). In Northshire that self-image was perfectly captured in a familiar lithograph found at the Training Centre, Brigade Headquarters and most fire stations. It shows an heroic fireman bravely carrying the body of a young lady, in a virginal white night-dress, out of a burning building. The title is 'Saved'. The picture emphatically defines gender difference in occupational terms.

Language and the prevailing discourse reflects the culture of an organisation and conveys not just words but meanings which are both implicit and explicit. For example, the term 'ladies' a term of politeness excessively used at all levels in the Fire Service evokes a striking resonance to the outsider. Such superficially courteous behaviour is both 'protective and paternalistic' and is underpinned by the belief that women are subordinate (Benokraitis and Feagin, 1985:65). The term implies gentility: ladies are affronted by bad language; ladies are protected by gentlemen; ladies do not fight fires, they are rescued from them. Perhaps this *is* 'no place for a lady?' In Northshire, work defined masculinity which was perceived to be embedded in the fire-fighter's job, and so there was absolute conviction that women were incapable of the work. Evidence to the contrary, from the presence of women in other brigades, was dismissed and rationalised in terms of lower standards which operated elsewhere compared to the very high standards in Northshire.

Many of the masculine work-virtues related to bodily strength and the nature of the equipment used, for example, the ladders and the hose-lengths used. Running whilst carrying a hose formed a major exclusionary factor in recruitment, discussed in the next section of this chapter. The Building and Supplies Officer, giving details of the equipment used, explained that 'the stores are unsuitable for a lady'. Cynthia Cockburn dispels such arguments very clearly as the very material of male power,

> Men having been reared to a bodily advantage are able to make political and economic use of it by defining into their occupation certain tasks that require the muscle they alone possess; thereby barricading it against women (Cockburn, 1981:106).

She goes on to say how work equipment is political in design, overwhelmingly produced by males and assembled in ways that make it just too big or too heavy for the average woman to use. That all equipment was seen as standard and accepted as the normative state of affairs is to demonstrate the results of pre-existing patterns of power. It is this unquestioning acceptance of the status quo which demonstrates the pervasive power which reinforces the interests of those exercising power and operates against the real interests of those excluded (Lukes, 1974).

Women were also a problem because of their threatened invasion of the private world of the fire station, where the 'atmosphere is not receptive or conducive to females'. As the Assistant Chief Fire Officer explained,

> The organisation is designed to promote cohesive teams through training and developing a common spirit through physical recreation. On every working shift there are teams of volleyball, handball, touch-and-pass, a sort of indoor rugby. The problem would be to integrate female fire-fighters into this setting, or would they just not fit in? However, I don't see a lot of problems with race.

Firemen lived in a closed world where the same colleagues formed work groups on the watch system and social grouping related to the Benevolent Fund and other activities, all of which 'stressed the mutual obligations in both life and death'. In this way strong bonds of loyalty developed along with a common language, values and beliefs. Such homosocial grouping constitutes the fabric of male monopolies designed to exclude outsiders.[3] Life on the fire station had its own particular ambience, for, despite close bonding, acts of intimacy were not included but disguised as 'horseplay', 'pranks' or 'messing about'. When such strong bonds of loyalty develop, individuals acquire an 'organisational personality' rather distinct from their individual personality, 'developing as a group archetype' (Simons, cited in Bowles, 1990). Further, excessive group solidarity can become dysfunctional and lead to 'group think' (Janis, 1972) whereby there is resistance to different ideas. Organisational structure deliberately fostered a stereotypically masculine culture as an exclusionary circle which influenced thought and action and prevented learning on equality issues. Discussions on fire stations continually went over the same ground, defining and redefining the problem of women, whilst denying any problem with 'race':

> The subject about women on stations regularly comes up here. They talk about living and working with women and the effect it may have on their lives. Most believe it is not a job for a woman. I wouldn't want my wife to do it. On the other hand they see a need for a coloured input into the Service (Divisional Commander).

Women remained 'the problem' and as such the dilemma of treatment proved difficult in a uniformed service when normal practice aimed to achieve uniformity. The Fire Service faced such problems in the recruitment of the first women when differences were exaggerated in a process of 'boundary heightening' (Moss Kanter, 1977). In the 1991-2 recruitment campaign, seven females reached the practical assessment stage. The ways in which women reported their experiences clearly demonstrated how they were made to feel different and excluded:

> I walked into the room and everyone looked at you and I thought, oh dear am I doing the right thing here? I felt uncomfortable.

> That was embarrassing. I felt alone and I really stuck out. They all looked at you thinking what's she doing here? The instructions were broadcast as if there were no women present at all.

All the feelings expressed were of isolation, the visibility of difference, and the outsider being excluded. If an attempt was made to treat all applicants equally, it appeared that only men were being addressed, the women rendered invisible. If efforts were made to include them, 'Any ladies here today?' for example, then attention was focused on them and the difference between them and other male candidates made all too apparent. These factors added to the disadvantage felt by female applicants as outsiders to such an extent that one applicant submitted an equal opportunity complaint. Similar issues continued to emerge as the first female recruit joined the Brigade. She was expected to be both invisible performing alongside males, and yet, highly visible as the focus of considerable interest and curiosity. By emphasising difference and framing the key issue in those terms, women were the problem, not the exclusionary nature of the Fire Service. The latter perspective would demand a more complex and detailed analysis of the issues, including 'race'. Indeed, it was interesting to compare how 'race' was perceived.

'Race' remained a 'non-problem' and any racial questions were perceived as essentially male issues and so never pursued in the same way. To recall the comments of the Assistant Chief Officer, 'I don't see a lot of problems with race', and the Divisional Commander who saw 'need for a coloured input into the Service'. The only problem identified was the lack of Black applicants. The Chief Fire Officer expressed the same sentiments:

> Ethnic minorities are a source of puzzlement. There are 50,000 Asians living in Northshire, yet we have very few applicants. They would have a very useful role

to play within the service - it is very difficult to get the fire prevention message across to minority groups, particularly the women.

However, despite the belief that 'race was no problem', the language of the statements reveals a different picture. It is interesting to note how the Chief Fire Officer sees a contribution in terms of outreach or fire prevention rather than 'real' operational work. The facts are also stark: in 1992, out of a total of 967 whole-time fire-fighters in the county, only three were Black. There was further evidence that serious problems had been brought to the attention of both the unions and the senior officers. The Equality Officer registered an official complaint regarding racist comments made at her lectures on stations,

> At every lecture there were particularly racist comments from those areas where there is a large Asian population. For example, 'Oh, you've come to talk to us about coons have you?' 'My son has been unemployed for x years and these people are taking our jobs', 'Prayer times - they want to pray all the time, they don't want to integrate with us, why should we integrate with them', 'I object to my children learning Urdu at school', these are just some of the comments made.

The Community Liaison Officer had also expressed concern to the Chief Fire Officer in writing, noting that the Asian community thought that, 'the Fire Brigade only employed white people as fire-fighters', and that the Service was no place for Asian people expressing their fears that, 'fire station canteens would not serve suitable food' and that 'firemen were required to live at the station during their tour of duty'. The Asian community clearly perceived the Fire Service to be an overtly racist organisation, and yet the Chief Fire Officer still maintained that ethnic minorities were 'a source of puzzlement' and he failed to understand the reasons for the lack of applications from the Black population.

The problems were evident, yet the issues failed to emerge and racism remained unacknowledged. A process of inaction filtered out the issues and a lack of interest ensured little had changed. Clearly, to do nothing is a political act. The status quo was maintained by a process of non-decisions (Bachrach and Baratz, 1963) and problems were ascribed in favour of the normative white male model. In this way the dominant interests determine outcomes and repressed interests remained neither expressed or represented. The bias was maintained by a range of exclusionary processes, and it is to these the discussion will now turn.

**Keeping Women Out: Exclusionary Processes to Maintain Gender Bias**

The gender bias was maintained throughout the recruitment and selection process which, despite the equal opportunity policy, ensured that the Fire Service remained white and male.  The recruitment and selection process is a long and detailed one, which adheres to procedures established by the Home Office, supplemented by additional requirements within Northshire.  Whilst the process was professionally administered, it remained inherently biased towards those individuals with family or friends already employed within the Service.  Four exclusionary barriers were identified which result in the replication of the existing labour profile, and the frustration of change.  These were: pre-entry barriers; advertising; fire station visits; and the hose-running element in the practical assessment.  Each will be discussed in turn.

*Pre-entry Barriers*

Pre-entry barriers refer to those factors which influence the supply side of the labour market.  With job segregation as marked as that of the Fire Service, factors which deter potential female applicants become significant.  In the 1990-91 recruitment campaign seven female applicants reached the practical assessment stage in the selection process.  They all reported scepticism and hostility towards their application from family and/or friends:

> Dad said, 'Don't be stupid, you'll not get in'.

> They laughed. 'It's really difficult to get in. Do they take women?'

> I'm aware it's male dominated and a lot of firemen don't think a woman can be a fire-fighter.

Such comments may be described as 'supportive discouragement', a form of 'subtle sex discrimination when women receive mixed messages about their abilities and potential performance' (Benokraitis and Feagin, 1986:68).  Not all females pursued their applications through each stage of the selection process.  Some gave up, but clearly all perceived the Fire Service to be a male service, from which women were effectively excluded.  There was further evidence to suggest that officers sought to maintain such perceptions rather than utilise opportunities for change.  For example, station officers often attend careers conventions or activities organised by schools. They respond by sending personnel available at the time from the nearest fire station.

At careers conventions many girls are interested in the Brigade. We tell them what it's like on the station, we'll say there will be pranks played on them and fooling about, that they'd better be able to look after themselves (Station Officer).

These comments perpetuate the existing view of the Fire Service that it is no place for a lady. They provide an example of the 'cooling-out process' identified by Benokraitis and Feagin (1986) whereby women are led to doubt their abilities and purpose and recognise potential limitations. It is impossible to say how many applicants might be deterred in this way, but it is clear that opportunities for change are ignored.

A second example comes from the work of the School Liaison Officer who visits schools to put across the fire prevention message. At the time of the research he had visited over 60 schools in Northshire. However, he stated: 'the equal opps. policy has no effect on my job at all', and he saw no connection between equal opportunities and his work: 'It has not affected what I do in any way'. Later during the interview, when describing the teaching materials used, he did comment that on one occasion a teacher protested that the scenarios used portrayed stereotypical male and female roles. He implied that the teacher had the problem, and he did not see it, and he 'just carried on doing things the same'. In both of these examples, the lack of understanding of the appreciative context[4] of equal opportunity frustrated any opportunities provided within the organisational context to implement and promote change. These processes show the gender bias inherent in practices which maintain the status quo and the 'perceived vested interests in the reproduction of job-segregation' (Collinson, Knights, and Collinson, 1990:132).

*Advertising*

Advertising represents a second exclusionary process. Within the Fire Service there is a long-standing tradition of informal recruitment using familial networks and unsolicited letters of application. However, in the 1991-2 recruitment campaign a strategy was employed of advertising vacancies as widely as possible placing advertisements in the local evening newspaper, in Job Centres, and the Careers Service, along with an Open Day and a poster campaign. These methods produced 56 per cent of all female applications. The newspaper advertisement was the most effective single strategy yielding 22 per cent of the applications from women. Significantly, in the 1992-3 recruitment campaign when the Brigade reverted to their traditional approach and used no external advertising, the total number of female applicants was reduced by a third, and the limited number of applications from ethnic minorities was noted as a 'source of puzzlement' by the Chief Fire Officer. The exclusionary results of this strategy were rationalised by Officers in terms of the need to 'consider the prudent use of resources', reflecting that, 'there is no pressure to use scarce resources to increase the number of applicants'.

Informal and internal methods of recruitment clearly produced a sufficient number of the 'right type' of applicants, white males, who would 'fit in' to the organisation. Whilst external advertising might generate more applications from women and ethnic minorities it was also problematic and produced increased administrative costs. Closer examination of the familiar local authority discourse reveals a hidden layer of bias or gender rules (Mills, 1989). The seemingly rational, logical, detached and unemotional reasoning given for the unequal opportunities in operation provides evidence of the masculinity embedded in bureaucratic organisations which tends to benefit one sex over another. From the apparent neutrality or 'desexualisation of the organisation' (Burrell, 1984), a pattern emerges which confirms male dominance and produces a system for attaining defined ends (Ferguson, 1984). As Jenkins notes, 'The politics which frame administrative allocation means that these judgements often derive from or reflect ideology and policy agendas' (1996:159). Therefore, it is only a matter of perspective which justifies the systematic exclusion of women and ethnic minorities in terms of comparatively minimal administrative costs. It is a measure of hegemonic power that the discourse which relates equality of opportunity to the acceptable level of administrative costs is seen as legitimate, and was unquestioned.

*Fire Station Visits*

A further exclusionary barrier may be identified from fire station visits. Within the Northshire recruitment process the Fire Service encouraged applicants to visit fire stations as a measure of their initiative and commitment. However, in practice this operates as an exclusionary process with a bias towards those with inside knowledge of the service. The female applicants reported quite different experiences of such visits:

> They gave us some tips on the running out of the hose and said you must give it 100 per cent but that was all really.

> They were very helpful, got us running carrying a hose. The officers encouraged us with a lot of shouting, 'Get those backsides moving!'

At x they were really helpful. They will spend as long as it takes with you. It started off with one bloke and then another, and most people offered information. If you go somewhere where there's a special appliance then the driver only goes out to particular calls, so the guy took me round as he had more time.

None of the candidates made adverse comments about the treatment received, but clearly they were treated differently. Some received much more help than others and, as one applicant herself noted, the time available for discussion will vary from station to station. Her father was a Station Officer and clearly this aspect in the recruitment process favours those with existing knowledge of the Fire Service. In effect this pattern replicates the existing labour profile and reinforces the status quo.

*'Hose-running'*

A further exclusionary element was the 'hose-running'. Part of the full day practical assessment test, the hose-running exercise is a gruelling two hours of running with the hose, rolling it out and back up. It involves not just a general level of fitness, but stamina and sustained upper-body strength. The strength required is far in excess of the standards set by the Home Office in the hand-grip and leg-back pull tests[5]. To overcome the difficulties of running for considerable periods carrying the hose, women require particular training such as that devised by the Fire Service for use on the Recruits' Training Course. In the absence of a standard programme, the successful candidate borrowed a hose and trained as follows:

I went to an old folks' area of sheltered accommodation, running round there every day, running it out and rolling it back up. I worked up to four then six times round this circuit, say about 200 metres in a circuit. My arms used to go dead, nearly numb. Although I was fit I didn't have adequate strength. If I hadn't done the training I wouldn't have got through the day.

Without prior knowledge and rigorous training to develop upper-body strength the majority of women would fail the hose-running exercise and so be excluded. The Fire Service are therefore implicitly demanding from women, an extremely high level of training and preparation at the recruitment stage. Although only a small part of the whole selection process, the hose-running is highly significant to selection outcomes: over half of all candidates, and five out of six females, were rejected at this point. The stringent demands of the hose-running represents an effective exclusionary barrier for women:

...getting through the practical assessment day, that was all my Dad wanted to see. He was sceptical to be honest, like 99 per cent or 100 per cent of blokes. He doubted a woman would be physically strong enough to get through.

The ability to run carrying a hose is a blunt instrument of selection for a modern, highly technical Fire Service.    It over-emphasised strength requirements which could be acquired by technique and training.   The hose-running however, was staunchly defended by officers of the Fire Service.   To them it represented a rite of passage measured by a test of masculine virtue, to secure access to a privileged group.   It was rationalised as a test of the strength and stamina required in the job.   Although it should be noted that fire-fighters are not regularly re-tested to ensure that the requisite levels of fitness were maintained, and the Fire Brigade Union protested vociferously at the very suggestion.

Details of selection instruments change over time, but the significance lies in the processes of exclusion whereby a range of mechanisms produces a web of practices which leads to the reproduction of the existing labour profile and the restriction of change.   All of these processes are underpinned by the way masculinity is built into the job and the fear that, 'somehow if a woman can do it, it ain't that masculine, not that tough' (Schroedel, cited in Mills, 1991:89).   The study has also attempted to demonstrate the operation of male power, or the 'capacity to control social interaction' (Bradley, 1999:33).   In this context, male power has been exposed in several dimensions and it has been seen how men have tried to protect their economic power, and retain the higher pay and status of an all-male occupation.   Technical power was evident in the nature of the equipment used, which had been designed to require male strength.   Physical power was permanently maintained by the enduring image of the fire-fighter captured on the ever-present lithograph, 'Saved'.   The image remains of the fireman carrying a woman out of a burning building, although the everyday reality of the work is often quite different.   Most pervasive, however, are the symbolic power and collective power of the strong work groups established and entrenched by male bonding on stations.   Taken together, all of these processes create an exclusionary web which make women out of place and sustain the belief that 'it's no place for a lady!'

## Conclusion

To dispel any remaining myths that change is only a matter of time, a review of the figures proves illuminating.   After considerably more than a decade of equal opportunity in Northshire there were, in 1999, six female whole-time fire-fighters out of a total of 1,013. This constitutes 0.6 per cent of the total number of whole-time fire-fighters. Such numbers might be described as 'tokenism', a false power which masculine society offers to a few women who 'think like men' (Rich, cited in Benokraitis and Feagin, 1986). However, it is perhaps even more significant that the numbers of Black and Asian fire-fighters is lower still at 0.4 per cent.

For those women who have entered the male domain the environment remains unchanged as the essentially all-male group continues to act collectively, noting, identifying and exaggerating gender difference:

> As far as the environment itself, in the back of the personnel carrier they leer out of windows jeering, banging and whistling...that does not bother me.... A nurse came round one day for a medical - imagine all those yellow helmets gawping through the window because it was a nurse... the language, the first few days they watched their language but by the end of twelve weeks I knew words I didn't know were in the English language. As long as you don't bother with that, they make suggestive comments and all sorts. But that is the environment you are going to get on stations, it never bothered me.

In the name of equal opportunity, a few women have moved into an all-male environment, but access remains on male terms. The only accommodation to the status quo is made by the women who, in effect, become 'honorary men'. The overtly engineered male grouping of the Fire Service continues to structure the actions and collectively shape the perceptions, values, and beliefs, or the 'assumptive world' of the fire-fighters. The Equal Opportunity Policy did little to alter that 'assumptive world' and, consequently, the implementation gap between the intention and the achievement of the Equal Opportunity Policy remains firmly entrenched. This chapter has thus attempted to illustrate those processes by which the rhetoric of equal opportunity becomes the reality of limited change, persistent job segregation, and the Fire Service ultimately remains 'no place for a lady!'

**Notes**

[1] The term 'assumptive world' was coined by Ken Young (1977) and refers to the set of assumptions by which actors interpret and understand the complexity of their everyday world, drawing upon their values, attitudes and beliefs.

[2] The seminars reviewed the case of fire-fighter Lynne Gunning, who took a case of sexual harassment against the London Fire Service, and was awarded an out of court settlement of £27,000. Following the recruitment of the first females into the Fire Service, the possibility of sexual harassment was evidently a major concern for senior officers.

[3] For further discussion and thought refer to the work of Michael Roper (1996).

[4] The use of the term 'appreciative context' (Young and Mills, 1980) refers to those particular aspects of the organisational culture involving the beliefs, values and assumptive worlds of the participants which captures the subjective experience of the actor.

[5] The hand-grip and leg-pull tests are standard tests set by the Home Office to assess the basic strength requirements for the job of fire-fighter. Arm strength and upper leg/back strength are assessed to nationally established minimum levels.

# 6 Women Choose Low Pay?

LINDA WALSH AND LIZ JAMES[1]

## Introduction

In 1997, 70 per cent of low paid workers in Britain were women (Low Pay Commission, 1998). The experience of low pay has important implications for women's lives. Dex, Lissenburgh and Taylor (1994:vii) have outlined a number of these. Firstly, low pay contributes to gender inequality. Secondly, it makes it harder for women to escape from the benefits system, and therefore is a disincentive to taking paid employment. Thirdly, it reduces the ability of women to become economically independent. Fourthly, low pay throughout a working life reduces the levels of women's pensions and increases the likelihood of poverty in old age.[2] Finally, there are overall implications for women's access to justice. In June 1998, the Low Pay Commission (LPC) published its first report, which contained recommendations for the level of the UK's national minimum wage. The Commission's terms of reference stated that the minimum wage should address issues of low pay, the exploitation of homeworkers, and the unemployed (Low Pay Commission, 1998), with another key issue being the inequality of pay between male and female workers.

This chapter will examine the position of women in the British labour market, with its distinctive national context of high rates of part-time work, weak collective bargaining and a governmental strategy of deregulation as a response to globalisation. It will focus particularly on the dimensions of activity rates, wage differentials, occupational segregation and part-time work. It will then consider the prospects for the national minimum wage as a means to reducing the incidence of low pay for women and increasing gender equity.

## Women and 'Rational Choice' in the Labour Market

Turn to any first year undergraduate economics textbook and an elaborate yet simple explanation of the labour market will be found, extolling the virtues of the supply and demand model. In this model the greater the demand for workers, the higher the wages offered or demanded, contrasting with the situation of over-supply which brings wages down. However, when applied to women in the labour market the rules of the model appear not to work. Thus, despite being highly sought after workers since the Industrial Revolution, mainly for their cheapness, docility and disposability (Miles, 1989:186), women's wages have always been considerably lower than men's. The model claims to be gender-blind, perceiving all individuals as utility-maximising, rational, or selfish beings. In the context of the neo-classical model of labour supply, utility is not the usefulness of any commodity or action but the benefit or satisfaction an individual derives from particular activities, in the main, consumption enabled by the receipt of wages. Work, the source of income, and thus consumption, for most of us has a disutility; we have to turn up and do it. However, for women, historically, the : has been little choice about work and consumption and the disutility is greater than just the location outside the home: their domestic labour is continuous, unpaid, unrecognised by economic models, and inside the home; and their paid labour, often done in conjunction with domestic duties, is usually a vital part of, if not all, the family income whatever the work or wage. It appears that, in practice, the rational choice concept applies almost exclusively to men, who are in a better position to make choices that appear rational in this model than are women.

Within economic theory there are two types of explanation of labour market patterns: those which stress individual agency and those which concentrate on the structure of the labour market. In terms of women's employment patterns, the first explanation draws on the model of rational economic man to argue that women make a rational choice: they choose to work part-time, preferring to make a fuller contribution to raising their families and maintaining their households. In this model, women are less concerned about promotion, are less career-orientated and hence choose low pay. Catherine Hakim has now argued in a number of places (1996a, 1996b, 1998) that part-time and low paid work represents the preferred choice of a large number of women workers who, she claims, have a primary orientation towards home and family. She even goes so far as to argue that women's 'genuine choices' and 'preferences' have become social factors of such significance that they will potentially outweigh 'the demographic, social, economic and institutional factors that have historically been so important' (1996a:215). Any analysis which does not centre on 'choice' in this positive manner, Hakim brands as 'victim feminism' (1998:137). Other commentators, however, prefer to maintain a notion of choice as taking place within a context of structural constraints on women's lives, particularly in terms of domestic labour, childcare and other caring work.

In the light of this debate, then, the next section of the chapter engages with women's position in the labour market, to see how far it can be described as the result of 'rational choice'.

## Women in the Labour Market

*Economic Activity*

According to neo-classical economics, individuals have a choice between market and non-market activity. A woman's 'choice', as opposed to the choice made by a man, however, is not simply a choice between the wage rate and leisure time, but is affected by additional factors. These include marital and parental status and household income. Training and educational qualifications have also, historically, been limited for women.

Since the Second World War, the role that women have played in the labour market has changed dramatically. Typically, women worked prior to marriage, and then fulfilled a predominantly household function including the bearing and rearing of children. Now, increasing numbers of women work full-time and/or combine the roles of mother, carer and employee. Unlike their male counterparts, women tend to alter the pattern of their employment throughout their lives, often taking breaks from paid work for several years to raise their children to school age.

The concept of economic activity is an important one when discussing the constraints on women's participation in the labour market. It usefully removes those who do not wish to work, categorising them as students, people with disabilities or those looking after the family or home. In addition it removes the thorny issue of unemployment. In 1988 69.9 per cent of women aged 16-59 years were economically active. By 1998, the rate had increased to 72 per cent, lessening the gap between the rates of working men which fell from 88.2 per cent to 84 per cent over the same period (Thair and Risdon, 1999). For women with dependent children, marital status has a key influence on their rate of economic activity. Whilst 71 per cent of married women with dependent children were economically active in 1998, only 53 per cent of non-married women with dependent children were.[3] The age of dependent children affected women's economic activity rates, the highest being for women whose youngest child is over 11 years old (Sly, 1996; Thair and Risdon, 1999). Women without dependent children were the most active group of women. In the age group 16-24 years, 70.5 per cent of women without dependent children were in employment or looking for work, and in the 25-39 age group 91.2 per cent were active.

Women with higher qualifications, that is, above A level, were more economically active (86 per cent) than women without qualifications (50 per cent) (Thair and Risdon, 1999). The impact of educational achievement was most marked for women with pre-school children, where 76 per cent of women with higher qualifications were active compared to just 27 per cent of unqualified women. This is partly explained by their being able to earn more and thus be able to pay for child-care. In addition, women with higher qualifications were likely to have less difficulty in securing and maintaining a full-time position and, for these women, taking time away from work would have a more serious impact on household income (Brannen et al., 1997; Thair and Risdon, 1999).

*Wage Differentials*

Women's labour market activity is generally not rewarded at the same rate as men's. Despite the fact that between 1970 and 1998, the earnings differential between men and women has fallen, women still earn on average over 20 per cent less than men (Sloman, 1998; Thair and Risdon, 1999; Sly, 1996). Much of the reduction in the wage gap occurred between 1975 and 1978, and reflects the impact of the legislative changes. The 1970 Equal Pay Act is well-documented as having had the effect of a one-off increase in women's relative earnings (Sly, 1996), although slippage in this advance and progress towards the definition of equal work of equal value has resulted in two more updates of the Act. Consequently, women's relative earnings have risen steadily. A comparison of New Earnings Survey data for 1977 and 1997 shows that women's hourly earnings compared to those of men have risen from 74 per cent to 80 per cent during that time, and their total weekly earnings from 65 per cent to 73 per cent (EOC, 1998).

Moreover, as Table 6.1 demonstrates, by the late 1990s, relative to men, women were earning proportionately more in manual work, with a 72 per cent wage gap, although manual work is less well paid than non-manual work in absolute terms. The smaller earnings gap even accounts for the greater overtime potential of male manual workers whose average weekly overtime payments and other additions contribute 22 per cent of their average weekly pay compared to 13 per cent for women. Manual workers of both sexes tend to earn more from overtime as a proportion of their weekly pay than non-manual workers (White, 1999). Despite the continuing wage differentials

between women and men, skills differentials may also be a part
for the level of inequality. The concept of skill, how
problematic and contested. Feminists have argued that the assessm
of any particular job depended on the gender of the worker, rath
anything intrinsic to the work itself (Phillips and Taylor, 1986; Cockbu
1981, 1983). Skills, or the lack of them, tend to emphasise gender segregation
in the labour market, although, as seen below, fewer women are employed in
manual occupations thus raising their comparative earning potential, as can be
seen from Table 6.1.

**Table 6.1  Percentage of women's hourly wage compared to men's, 1998**

|  | Manual £ per hour | Non-manual £ per hour |
|---|---|---|
| Women | 5.14 | 8.89 |
| Men | 7.10 | 12.94 |
| Women's wages as a % of men's | 72.0 | 68.0 |

*Source*: New Earnings Survey, April 1998.

An explanation of the wage differential related to skills development is
given by Becker (1975). His concept of human capital explains how
individuals rationally choose to spend different amounts of time and effort
developing the skills for labour market success. As women know that they
will be taking breaks from employment, they choose to invest less in building
up a portfolio of skills and qualifications. This is then reflected in the position
of women in the occupational structure as well as the level of pay they
receive. It also explains why employers will be less keen to train and promote
female employees of child-bearing age, if indeed they employ them in the first
place. Empirical studies have demonstrated that human capital differences do
explain part of the gender difference in pay, but nevertheless leave a
substantial proportion unaccounted for (Dex, Lissenburgh and Taylor, 1994).
As stated above, however, the skills and qualifications which comprise human
capital are deeply gendered, and these notions need to be seen as social
constructions, rather than absolute standards of measurement.

Attempts to account for the pay gap have led economists to admit that
labour markets are not shining examples of perfect competition, but may
allow discrimination. Discrimination in the labour market on the basis of
gender can take two forms: first, workers undertaking identical work can be

paid different wage rates; and second, workers can be treated differently in terms of promotion or employment. Becker gave neo-classical economics a model for discrimination in the labour market, based on the idea of employer taste being incorporated into a utility function. According to this view, while the monetary cost of employing women and men is given by their respective wage rates, there is a perceived disutility associated with hiring women. However, if women's wages are lower as a result of this, the competitive firm will take advantage of such differentials and over time these will be eliminated. The firm employing female labour at a lower wage rate will have lower costs and a competitive advantage over firms who discriminate and do not employ women. If, however, market imperfections, in product markets or labour markets, exist then wage differentials can persist. If this is the case then it could be argued that there is a role for anti-discrimination legislation on both the recruitment and wage fronts. In this model, discrimination is either a temporary 'blip' or can be cured by making labour markets work better.

Other approaches to this issue draw on a wider disciplinary base than the economic model presented here. They recognise that the labour market is a product of history, institutional practices and attitudes. An early version of this approach is found in Edgeworth (1922), where he argued that it was the trade union movement which tended to crowd women into certain occupations and that this resulted in the depression of their wages. Such an approach was elaborated in the dual labour market hypothesis, first propounded by Doeringer and Piore (1971). Although originally designed to consider the impact of education and training, this model has been adapted by Barron and Norris (1976) to analyse the impact of sex discrimination in the labour market. Summarising the model, the market is split into two segments, the primary and the secondary, with barriers to movement between the two segments. The primary segment is characterized by high pay, secure career-oriented employment, whereas the secondary market suffers low pay, insecure occupational structure and a high labour turnover. Sly (1996) considers the importance of these issues and accepts that women's shorter average length of time with an employer is an explanatory variable in why they receive less pay than men. However, the model of a dual labour market has been criticised for being dated (Hakim, 1996a:148), based on 'masculinist conceptions of work and of workers' (Adkins, 1995:21), and not taking into account the polarisation process occuring between different groups of women workers (Walby, 1997:78-79). There is, therefore, no simple and direct equivalence between women and secondary work.

*Occupational Segregation*

While women do not wholly constitute a secondary sector, employed women are not evenly distributed among occupational classifications. By breaking down employment into just nine major groupings, it begins to be evident that women and men are employed in different types of occupations.

**Table 6.2  Employment by occupation, 1998**

|  | Men | Women |
|---|---|---|
|  | % | % |
| 1. Managers and Administrators | 19.4 | 11.8 |
| 2. Professional occupations | 11.3 | 9.5 |
| 3. Associate professional and technical occupations | 9.0 | 11.2 |
| 4. Clerical and Secretarial occupations | 6.9 | 25.2 |
| 5. Craft and related occupations | 20.2 | 2.4 |
| 6. Personal and protective service occupations | 6.5 | 16.4 |
| 7. Sales occupations | 5.1 | 11.2 |
| 8. Plant and machine operatives | 13.9 | 4.0 |
| 9. Other occupations | 7.4 | 8.2 |

*Source*: Labour Force Survey, Spring 1998.

As demonstrated by Table 6.2, women are mostly employed in clerical and secretarial occupations and personal and protective service occupations, such as security work, cleaning and hairdressing. These types of occupations clearly relate to the concept of women as support workers. Women are much more likely to work in non-manual jobs (70.6 per cent) than in manual. Taking a finer definition of occupation, the segregation of men and women into different occupations becomes even more clear. Table 6.3 presents three of the nine major occupational groups which illustrate the greatest extent of segregation.

**Table 6.3  Employment: breakdown of occupational groups, 1998**

|  | Women as a percentage of all in employment |
|---|---|
| Associate professional and technical occupations | 49.6 |
| a. Science and engineering associate professionals | 19.0 |
| b. Health associate professionals | 86.7 |
| c. Teaching associate professionals | 43.3 |
| Clerical and secretarial occupations | 74.3 |
| a. Clerical occupations | 67.2 |
| b. Secretarial occupations | 96.4 |
| Personal and protective service occupations | 66.6 |
| a. Protective service occupations | 12.8 |
| b. Personal service occupations | 78.1 |

*Source*: Labour Force Survey, Spring 1998.

Women's waged labour is predominantly found in a narrow range of occupations. Moreover, these occupations generally contain a high proportion of female workers (Hartmann, 1976; Rubery and Fagan, 1993). Segregation has been found to exist both in terms of type of work and grade or seniority (Hakim, 1979; Walby, 1990). While recent years have seen a notable increase in the numbers of women at the higher levels of occupational structures, significant levels of both horizontal and vertical segregation by sex still exist (Walby, 1997:37). Part-time workers in particular are crowded into occupations with high rates of segregation (Walby, 1997:75-76), and both part-time work and high rates of segregation are characteristics associated with low pay (Dex, Lissenburgh and Taylor, 1994).

The areas in which women are most highly represented are those traditionally deemed as 'feminine' activities, extensions of women's domestic and caring roles. The link between paid and unpaid activity enables the argument that this work comes 'naturally' to women, is unskilled and therefore perceived as not deserving of high rates of pay. To admit that these activities when performed in the workplace are highly skilled and worthy of remuneration throws traditional ideas concerning the 'housewife' into question. Heidi Hartmann has argued (1976, 1981) that occupational segregation has arisen because male labour organisations historically operated to exclude women workers from particular occupations, specifically those with higher rates of pay. By confining women to lower paying occupations without a living wage, men force women into economic dependence. They can then benefit from women's unpaid domestic labour. Responsibilities for childcare and domestic labour in turn reinforce women's disadvantage in the labour market. These exclusions are further reinforced by the effects of the twin ideologies of domesticity for women and a family wage for men, which argue that a woman's place is in the home, and that a man has the right to earn enough to keep his wife and children.

*Part-time Work*

The phenomenon of part-time work is an interesting case to consider as it brings together the issues of rationality, choice, segregation and levels of earnings. A considerable proportion of women in paid employment work on a part-time rather than a full-time basis.[4] In 1988, 37 per cent of employed women worked part-time, increasing by 1998 to 43.5 per cent, of which 47.5 per cent were married and 35 per cent unmarried (Thair and Risdon, 1998). This raises the question of 'choice' and whether part-time employment is freely taken, or results from constraints on women's ability to take on full-time work. While the responsibilities associated with marriage and the bearing and rearing of children now have less of a negative impact on women's economic activity than in past decades (Walby, 1997:50-55; Brannen et al., 1997), they still retain a significant impact in terms of earnings and leisure time (Chambers, 1986; Seymour, 1992). The major constraints on women's labour market participation are domestic labour, childcare and other informal caring work. On a positive note, there is evidence to indicate that greater participation in paid employment is matched by a higher likelihood of a male partner taking on a share of domestic labour (Kiernan and Wicks, 1991, cited in Crompton, 1994). Speakman and Marchington (1999), however, argue that while there is an assumption that paid work and housework are competing activities, and an increase in one would lead to a decrease in the other, the reality of the situation is different. Gendered constructions of identity, which mark jobs as 'belonging' to women or men, and power relations within the household have a significant constraint on women's employment. Indeed, British Social Attitudes Surveys frequently find more people believing in the sharing of domestic work and childcare than actually practising it (Hewitt, 1993). Speakman and Marchington review a wealth of evidence which suggests on the whole that 'the imbalance between the amount of child care and domestic work men and women undertake has not been redressed' (1999:85) and that this is the case regardless of women's paid work or men's lack of it. Morris (1993) notes that in couples where the man is unemployed, 'flexibility' is at its greatest where the woman works full-time, but lowest where the woman is in part-time employment.

In addition to the physical caring and domestic responsibilities of women impinging on their employment choices, the need for external childcare remains a constraint on employment for many women, in terms of cost. Costs of childcare often have to be borne out of women's own wages (Harman, 1993:96), making it an option largely taken up by those on higher incomes (Ginn et al., 1996). In particular these costs add to the difficulties lone parents experience with regard to the job market (Ginn et al., 1996; Walby, 1997). Childcare costs are, therefore, a significant factor in the process of polarisation that is occurring between groups of women (Ginn et al., 1996; Walby, 1997). Responsibility for sick children also resides with women (Dex, Lissenburgh and Taylor, 1994). The problems of childcare have been demonstrated above with the large difference in economic activity between women with and without dependent children (Thair and Risdon, 1999). Similarly, mothers with pre-school children tended to work part-time (66.7 per cent) with only 33.3 per cent employed full-time, and women with children in secondary school, who are possibly more able to fend for themselves for short periods of time, were divided fairly equally between full- and part-time work. Approximately half of part-time women workers do not have children under 16 years of age (Breugel, 1996). However, most of these are mothers of older children and adults, and are mainly over the age of 30. This suggests that 'non-dependent' children still represent a source of caring and domestic work for 'midlife' women (Ginn and Arber, 1994).

It is important to recognise that childcare and the domestic labour involved with the presence of older children form only a part of women's caring responsibilities. The context of Care in the Community, where care for chronically ill, disabled and elderly people has been passed out of long-term care institutions and placed in 'the community', especially the family, has shifted a variety of caring roles on to women (Finch and Groves, 1983). Arber and Ginn argue that while there is an assumption in the literature on the increase in women's employment that this will make them less available for the provision of informal care, there is no evidence to suggest that this is the case. Indeed, for the majority of female carers total work hours per week are 'extraordinarily long'. Individual women are left to devise strategies of 'work accommodation', fitting in work and their caring duties (1995:468). Part-time work is thus both a cause and an effect of caring for, for example, resident and non-resident parents and parents-in-law, and is often used as a strategy 'to avoid the emotional and psychological exhaustion which would otherwise result' (Ginn and Sandell, 1997:417). This correlation between caring responsibilities and part-time work has been found by several extensive national surveys (Ginn et al., 1998:169).

To shed light on the choice versus constraint debate, research has been conducted on the motivation, satisfaction and commitment levels of part-time workers. While Hakim (1996b:178) argues that part-time work does not shift women's 'primary self-identity' as housewives, Ginn et al. cite a range of evidence to suggest positive changes in terms of identity, family roles and poverty resulting from women's engagement in waged work (1996:168). The United Nations Development Project holds the view that paid employment is essential to enable women to fulfil their potential for human development (cited in Walby, 1997:23).[5] Hakim draws on survey data which she interprets as demonstrating high levels of satisfaction and low levels of commitment in this group of workers. She argues that differences between full-time and part-time female workers are qualitative rather than simply quantitative, resulting from 'fundamental differences' in self-identity (1996a:107). Nevertheless, she fails to consider where these attitudes come from and how they are formed (Bruegel, 1996:175; Crompton and Harris, 1998:120). There are also methodological issues to consider when analysing this type of survey data, such as the superficiality of the questions asked (Dex, Lissenburgh and Taylor, 1994:28). Measures of satisfaction depend on both the wording of the survey questions and the perception of alternatives, and comparison with other Western countries suggests that shorter hours in the same job would be preferred to part-time work with its attendant poor conditions, were this option to be available (Ginn et al., 1996). Both Ginn et al. (1996) and Crompton and Harris (1998) point to the usefulness of biographical data in contributing to an understanding of how women construct their working lives in the context of 'historically available opportunities and constraints' (Crompton and Harris, 1998:119).

While she stresses the heterogeneity and polarisation within the female workforce as a whole, Hakim has also been criticised for failing to recognise differences within the category of part-time workers (Walsh, 1999). A crucial distinction, for example, is between voluntary and involuntary part-time workers (Barling and Gallagher, 1996). The latter group are constrained by '[e]mployers' inability or unwillingness to create suitable full-time positions...' (Walsh, 1999:192). The deliberate creation of part-time jobs as an alternative to investment in new machinery is significant here (Dex, Lissenburgh and Taylor, 1994:37). There is evidence that women's employment orientations vary throughout their lives, which conflicts with Hakim's view that part-time workers are a qualitatively different type of worker (Crompton and Harris, 1998; Rubery, Horrell and Burchell, 1994; Burchell, Dale and Joshi, 1997).  As such, the fact that only 10 per cent of women in part-time employment, compared to 29 per cent of men, stated that they would prefer a full-time job, may well be a condition of their work/domestic circumstances at the time rather than a psychological aberration.[6]  Walsh argues that women's part-time work needs to be viewed in the context of their previous employment history and their expectations for the future.  She concludes that the 'presence and age of dependent children and past employment experiences' are the key influences on women's 'choice' between part-time and full-time work (1999:194).

A major problem regarding the debate concerning women's part-time work is that further specification is required regarding precisely which women are being discussed.  If the general category of 'women' is disaggregated along other lines of 'difference' a new picture emerges.  While a focus on gender brings certain issues to light, it is not the only, or even the most salient, feature determining every woman's position in the labour market.  Gillian Dunne's work, for example, has illuminated the ways in which sexuality has an effect on women's labour market 'choices'.  Dunne (1997) demonstrates that lesbians have a higher rate of full-time work than 'women' generally, and argues that being a lesbian both necessitates and facilitates that 'choice'.  Dunne's later work with the Lesbian Household Project found that one way in which this facilitation takes place is through a more egalitarian division of household labour (ch.7).

With regard to 'race' and ethnicity, other variables in determining choice, Bruegel (1989; 1994) points out that Black women are far less likely than white[7] women to work part-time, but are more likely to be either unemployed or working full-time despite domestic responsibilities.  They are also likely to earn up to 25 per cent less than white women and are more likely to have earnings below the low pay threshold (Dex, Lissenburgh and Taylor, 1994).  This is partly due to discrimination, and partly due to the results of historical processes of settlement, in geographical and occupational terms, which have left Black communities vulnerable to unemployment resulting from industrial restructuring (Phizacklea, 1994).  Holdsworth and Dale contend that 'historically, part-time jobs were constructed for white women' (1997:453) and cite evidence from the Commission for Racial Equality that those jobs are 'preferentially available' to white women.  They conclude that, in this context, full-time employment for Black women may be the result of discrimination, rather than a positive choice.  This echoes the findings of Breugel (1989, 1994) who concluded that the option to work part-time, rather than a constraint, was a luxury that few Black women could afford.  It is also important to attend to differences between and within minority ethnic communities (Breugel, 1994; Brah, 1994). Avtar Brah, for example, discusses the 'choices' facing young Muslim women in Britain today. While Brah's work is specific to the patterns of employment of young Muslim women, she points out that, 'Patriarchal ideologies have a bearing on all women in Britain today but may take specific forms' (1994:163), and that all women are engaged in a process of negotiation with norms, practices and discourses.

**The National Minimum Wage**

The argument for a national minimum wage has been made for many years. In particular, those concerned with eliminating poverty and the low pay historically associated with particular sectors of industry and particular groups of workers, have championed its introduction. Although defining low pay is fraught with difficulties, this chapter uses as its benchmark the level of £3.50 per hour determined by the LPC (1998).

The LPC report states:

Low pay is more prevalent within certain groups of workers: women, young people, people with disabilities and ethnic minorities. Its incidence is influenced by working patterns, because part-time and some casual workers are disproportionately low paid. Low pay is also more concentrated in certain regions and business sectors and in smaller firms (1998:31).

Table 6.4 indicates the incidence of low pay amongst groups of male and female workers.

**Table 6.4  Percentage of women and men earning below the £3.50 benchmark, 1998**

|        | Manual | Non-manual | Part-time | Full-time |
|--------|--------|------------|-----------|-----------|
| Female | 38     | 29         | 23        | 43        |
| Male   | 24     | 9          | 25        | 9         |

*Source*: LPC (1998).

The report provides further evidence of the occupational pattern of low pay. More than half of all low-paid work is concentrated in a few industries:

retail, contract cleaning and security, social care, hairdressing, hospitality, agriculture and clothing and footwear, the very industries, as indicated in Table 6.3 (p.96), in which most women are employed (Low Pay Commission, 1998).

Obviously, trade unions have as one of their aims raising the wages of their members. However, besides the occupational segregation which would typically exclude women from certain unions, such as the Associated Engineering and Electrical Union (AEEU) whose membership is only six per cent female, the industries most susceptible to low pay are typically not represented by trade unions (Sly, 1996). Thus, a proportion of women's low pay has been largely ignored, or passed unnoticed, in pay negotiations. Lack of union representation for women in low-paid employment was recognised as a factor which increased the likelihood of low pay (Low Pay Commission, 1998).

The introduction of the minimum wage was achieved under the Labour Government in 1999. Trade unions and other champions of the minimum wage wanted the wage floor to be around £4.00 an hour, but it was originally set at £3.60 per hour for adult workers and raised to £3.70 from June 2000, following LPC recommendations. At this level 55 per cent of those benefiting from the minimum wage will be women working part-time, and 17 per cent full-time women workers (Low Pay Commission, 1998).[8] This amounts to approximately 1.6 million women. Overall, the LPC forecast that approximately two million workers will directly benefit from the national minimum wage in the form of higher pay. In particular workers in the following sectors will benefit most: retail (500,000 workers); hospitality (340,000 workers); cleaning and security (90,000); social care (80,000); horticulture (40,000) and clothing and footwear (40,000) (Low Pay Commission, 1999). These estimates are based on the proportion of workers employed in these sectors who are paid below the £3.60 per hour threshold.

The LPC claim that the national minimum wage 'will have a significant effect in reducing inequality of income among working families' (Low Pay Commission, 1998:145). Whilst this may well be the case, it is questionable whether the national minimum wage will reduce the 20 per cent pay differential between male and female workers. However, the Labour Government is introducing the national minimum wage as part of a package of measures, including the New Deal for Lone Parents, Working Families' Tax Credit, and parental leave, which it claims will improve women's lives and reduce gender inequalities (Women's Unit, 1998). Together, these are intended to improve the prospects for women to work and escape the poverty trap. Prior to the minimum wage, and these initiatives, many low paid women were financially worse off by working since they not only lost their entitlement to state benefits and other welfare provisions, they also had to pay tax and national insurance contributions (Low Pay Commission, 1998).

Traditional economic theory presents a case against minimum wages, arguing that they increase unemployment (Lipsey and Crystal, 1999). In the UK, the only evidence of the likely impact of the minimum wage is derived from the experience of Wages Councils whose introduction in the 1960s had fixed minimum rates for workers in low paying industries (Riddell, 1991:61). These were thought to herald a significant rise in unemployment but the applicability of evidence is reduced as low paid workers in the sectors covered by the Councils were shifted to sectors not covered. Again, their abolition in the 1980s resulted in only a minimal impact on employment (Low Pay Commission, 1998). In his foreword to the LPC report, Bain emphasises that: '... there needs to be a real incentive to make work pay, without unnecessarily jeopardizing job opportunities' (Low Pay Commission, 1998:x). Empirical evidence from other countries offer competing consequences of instituting a minimum wage. Bazen and Martin (1991) and Card and Krueger (1995) present cases supporting the traditional economic model, while van Soest (1994) and Chapple (1997) cite other instances where a minimum wage has actually increased the number of workers employed (cited in OECD, 1998). The LPC also claims that the national minimum wage, rather than causing substantial job losses, will create opportunities for the unemployed to work and develop skills, and for businesses to improve productivity and competitiveness.

Strong evidence does suggest that minimum wages result in a compression of the pay distribution. There are a number of lessons from international use of minimum wage systems. Countries with relatively high minimum wages have fewer low paid workers and inequalities in wages are less. However, unskilled workers are priced out of jobs if the wage is set too high, especially in the case of young people and, presumably, women. At least the UK government is now accepting that women do *not* choose low pay. Indeed, the National Minimum Wage Act (1998) is included as part of the Fourth Report of the United Kingdom of Great Britain and Northern Ireland to the United Nations Convention on the Elimination of all forms of Discrimination Against Women (CEDAW, 1999). Minimum wage legislation sets a 'moral level' or 'decency standard' (Dex, Lissenburgh and Taylor, 1994) below which wage levels are deemed unacceptable. Reviewing wage regulation across Europe, Almond and Rubery conclude that:

wage determination systems involving the minimisation of wage dispersion, including protection for low-paid workers, offer better prospects for gender pay equity than the decentralised systems which most European countries seem to have as an aim (1998:691).

Thornley and Coffey argue that despite the LPC report's rhetoric of social partnership and a 'balancing' of interests, implying that a 'common purpose' between different parties is possible, the Minimum Wage Act does represent a shift in ideology and policy from those of previous Conservative governments, and as such provides leverage for further changes (1999:528, 535).

There are, however, a number of factors that militate against the success of the national minimum wage in terms of both alleviating poverty and increasing gender equity. National minimum wage measures are perhaps likely to be used as a 'means of reducing the rate of wage increases' (Almond and Rubery, 1998:680) rather than as a means to furthering social justice. The British government has chosen to implement a rate which is calculated not to have a negative impact on the Treasury (Metcalf, 1999) and has not yet considered other measures which may have an impact on low pay, such as the changing conditions of, and pay for, work that is contracted out from public sector organisations. For example, in 1995 the Equal Opportunities Commission reported that Compulsory Competitive Tendering (CCT) in local government had resulted in a 22 per cent fall in employment for women, compared to 12 per cent for men, and that their pay levels had fallen, often below the National Insurance threshold (EOC, 1995). Although CCT has now been abolished, the trends in contracting-out are still strong and the disadvantages to workers in terms of pay and conditions may still apply. Obviously, close monitoring will be necessary to see if the national minimum wage fulfils its promise, the experiences of the Wages Councils and CCT suggesting that strict measures of enforcement are necessary (Dex, Lissenburgh and Taylor, 1994:88). In addition, it must be acknowledged that other measures besides a minimum wage can help low-skilled workers and the earnings of the low paid (OECD, 1998; Cash, 1998).

Even if the minimum wage is successful in its own terms, its impact in terms of women's economic independence is likely to be constrained by a number of factors. Part-time work, even at slightly higher rates of pay, is unlikely to enable women to command a full, rather than a component, wage (Siltanen, 1994). Thornley and Coffey (1999:534-535) also point out that the LPC report 'fudged' the issue of the lack of recognition and remuneration for women's skills by emphasising training as a route out of low pay. Therefore, it does not address the issue of how jobs come to be low paid by being classified as 'women's work'. Neither will the national minimum wage help the poorest women, for example, those living on social security benefits, or whose wages are supplemented by benefits with an increase in pay being deducted from benefit by the agency concerned. As many women earn below the threshold for National Insurance contributions, it is possible that employers will re-write contracts to keep hours worked down in order to keep wages below this level. Overall, income levels may therefore not improve, and women's position with regard to pensions will remain precarious. In other words, the national minimum wage will make little impact on the consequences of low pay outlined by Dex, Lissenburgh and Taylor in the introduction to this chapter. Moreover, if workers on the minimum wage still need to claim benefits to sustain themselves and their families, ought the initiative be called the national *minimal* wage instead?

**Conclusion**

This chapter has examined the idea that low pay is the result of choices by women who prefer part-time jobs requiring little human capital because of their commitment to their domestic role. Hakim (1998) argues that women's choices are key determinants of labour market patterns. The evidence, however, strongly suggests that these 'choices' take place within a system of 'structures of constraint' (Folbre, 1994). Walby, while not seeing rational choice theory and a social structural analysis as necessarily opposed, believes a sense of each to be necessary for a complete analysis. Paraphrasing Marx, she argues that, '[w]omen make choices, but not under conditions of their own choosing' (1997:25).

The ideal of rational economic man, on which neo-classical models are based, is tied into the modernist liberal concept of the self which has been extensively criticised from psychoanalytical, feminist, postmodern and poststructuralist positions. Folbre (1994) argues that the concept of rationality within neo-classical theory is highly gendered. The use of such a narrow definition of rationality has implications for what can then be considered a 'rational choice'. By defining rationality as inherently selfish, many decisions women make appear irrational. Caring for others, whether by choice or due to the operation of 'compulsory altruism' (Land and Rose, 1985), has no place in this model. Folbre puts forward the alternative concept of 'purposeful choice' (1994:28) which, she contends, avoids extreme individualist interpretations of rationality while maintaining a sense of agency, linked to the notion of culturally constructed identities. It also 'avoids any implicit dichotomy between rational and irrational (1994:28). For Folbre, these 'purposeful choices' take place within the context of 'structures of constraint' (1994:51) which set the boundaries of choice.

Feminist analyses have tended to focus more on constraint than on choice in determining labour market behaviour. As has been pointed out, however, not all women experience these constraints in the same way, and differences exist between groups of women. While some versions of this argument stress the significance of caring work, it is not possible to present a single aspect of women's lives, such as childcare responsibilities, and argue that this is the main cause of constraint. Similarly, in the case of those arguments stressing the operation of the labour market, it would be wrong to argue that a single factor, such as the creation of part-time jobs, has the same impact for all groups of women. Different issues present themselves to women in different life circumstances and at different times in their life cycle. They may then 'choose' part-time work, and therefore low pay, as a solution to having to balance work with other responsibilities, but this is neither a solution open to all women or even an 'ideal' solution to those who do take it up. An adequate model must also take into account differences between women including, but not confined to, 'race' and sexuality. 'Choices' are therefore structured for different groups of women in different ways.

The issue of women's low pay is a complex and multi-faceted problem. As Brah argues, 'structure, culture, and agency; the social and the psychic are all implicated' (1994:169). Walby (1997) emphasises the significance of geographical and historical dimensions. Recent analyses of women's work, including those influenced by poststructuralism, demand that we pay attention to the ways in which gendered and sexual(ised) identities are constructed in the workplace (Pringle, 1988; Adkins, 1995). An adequate framework for analysis would need to address each of these. Similarly, in policy terms, a single measure, such as a national minimum wage, will not provide a complete answer. An approach is required with as many facets as there are to women's lives.

**Notes**

[1] The origin of this chapter is a conference paper written by Derek Routledge and Linda Walsh.

[2] Whilst more than 70 per cent of male workers in non-manual jobs contribute to a pension, only two-fifths of manual women workers do (Nichol, 1998).

[3] Interestingly, only one per cent of men were economically inactive and looking after their family or home (Thair and Risdon, 1999).

[4] The Labour Force Survey allows the respondents to class themselves as either full-time or part-time workers (Sly, 1996).

[5] Some feminists, however, question the notion that work leads to empowerment for women, either because they believe sexuality to be a more significant factor in women's oppression (Dworkin, 1981; MacKinnon, 1989), or because the types of employment available to working-class and ethnic minority women are not seen as life enhancing (hooks, 1984).

[6] Survey data reveals that most women who work part-time state that this is because they do not want a full-time job (79 per cent of part-time workers) compared to only 27 per cent of part-time male workers (Thair and Risdon, 1999; Sly, 1996).

[7] The language used to denote racialised categories is always contentious. Here, the term 'Black' has been capitalised to denote its politicisation as a category. As 'white' is frequently used in a descriptive sense, it is left lower case. This also follows the usage of contributors to this debate, at their time of writing.

[8] Twelve per cent of the gainers are part-time male employees and 16 per cent are full-time male employees (Low Pay Commission, 1998).

# 7 Balancing Acts: On the Salience of Sexuality and Sexual Identity for Understanding the Gendering of Work and Family-Life Opportunities

GILLIAN A. DUNNE

## Introduction

For a number of good and not so good reasons there has been a tendency towards an unfortunate division of labour within the academy between those interested in sexuality and those interested in gender and gender inequalities. Insights gained from both areas of inquiry often pass like ships in the night. With few exceptions (Blumstein and Schwartz, 1985; Duncan, 1991; Van Every, 1995), mainstream research on the organisation of gender, work and family life has had an entirely heterosexual focus and framework of analysis. We know very little about the working lives of ordinary lesbian (Dunne, 1997a) and gay people, and it is rare to find any reference in mainstream work to the small but growing literature on divisions of labour in non-heterosexual households (Blumstein and Schwartz, 1985; Peace, 1993; Tasker and Golombok, 1998). The need for integration is not simply a matter of 'political correctness'. The absence of alternative voices indicates a lack of awareness that the experience of lesbian and gay people may be different from the norm, and that these differences could be of intellectual interest and have theoretical relevance for understanding the organisation of work, family life and gender inequalities more generally. It is through the charting and exploration of commonality and difference, whether they be experienced by lesbian women, African Caribbean women or whoever, that we are offered crucial insights into the complex processes which impede or support equality.

My thinking on the salience of lesbian and gay experience for wider feminist concerns is based on two separate pieces of research: firstly, a life-history study of lesbian experience of work and relationships (Dunne, 1997a);

and secondly, a recently completed ESRC-funded[1] project on divisions of labour in lesbian partnerships with dependent children, entitled The Lesbian Household Project. Together these studies suggest that much of what has been described in the abstract as 'women's situation' in relation to work and family life simply does not apply to women who form primary relationships with women.

In this chapter I will consider briefly why lesbian experience is relevant for broader questions about gender, work and family life and then summarise some of the more interesting themes which emerged in the Lesbian Household Project.


## Relevance

> I feel that most lesbian couples have had to make it up as they go along really, because even within the lesbian community there may well not be anybody who is doing quite what they're doing  (Juliet, co-parent of three-year old Jonathan).

My approach to thinking about the relevance of non-heterosexual experience is informed by four overlapping features of lesbian lifestyles, although these are not necessarily unique to lesbian experience nor are they always present:

• The first relates to institutional heterosexuality.  Feminists have mounted a strong critique of the naturalness of heterosexuality pointing to its socially constructed origins and its centrality in maintaining and exacerbating gender inequalities (Rubin, 1975; Rich, 1980), by, for example, facilitating the appropriation of women's unwaged labour by male partners (Pateman, 1988a; Delphy and Leonard, 1992; Dunne, 1998a).  This thinking would suggest that a comparative framework incorporating non-heterosexual experience of, for instance, divisions of labour would help illuminate the significance of heterosexuality itself for reproducing the status quo.

• The second relates to the material dimension of the construction of sexuality and sexual identity. Given that most women do not earn a living wage, the capacity for women to live independently of men and to prioritise primary relationships with other women can be seen as an economic achievement.  In the earlier study (Dunne, 1997a) I explore the relationship between lesbianism and empowerment: firstly, the ways that, for example, the extension of choice beyond heterosexuality tends to necessitate financial self-reliance (manifest in their struggles and choices in relation to education and occupation); and secondly the way that women's approaches to their relationships with women (attitudes towards employment and the allocation of domestic work) tend to facilitate the mutual development of employment opportunities. As we will see later, the more long-term self-reliant approach to income generation often experienced by lesbian women can provide greater scope for reconciling the demands of work and family life in partnerships.

- The third feature of lesbian lifestyles relates to the gender context in which lesbians experience and negotiate their relationships. For example, women in relationships with women occupy the same position in the gender hierarchy and share broadly similar gendered experience, skills and so on. *A focus on lesbian partnerships offers the possibility of exploring what can be achieved when gender difference as a fundamental structuring principle in interpersonal relationships is minimal.*

- Finally, their differences place them outside conventionality. Most of the parents in the Lesbian Household Project had children via donor insemination and all were relatively positive and open about their sexuality.

Together, these features mean that when approaching the allocation of paid work, domestic and parenting responsibilities, lesbian partners cannot easily draw upon the dominant frameworks for guiding practice available to heterosexual couples. In making sense of their lives, and in negotiating everyday routines and practices, lesbians engage in an inordinate amount of reflexivity; in their approach to the allocation of work and family responsibilities, to borrow Juliet's words, lesbians 'have to make it up as they go along'. While these circumstances do not guarantee the construction of more egalitarian approaches to financing and caring for children, it does provide a head start over most heterosexual couples, and this makes their arrangements worthy of more general interest.

**The Lesbian Household Project**

This project focuses specifically on the detailed examination of divisions of labour between lesbian couples, with and without dependent children. A primary objective was to provide empirically grounded theoretical insights to extend contemporary debates on gender and the organisation of work and family life. A key concern in these debates is the intransigent nature of gender-differentiated outcomes. Women in partnerships with men continue to take responsibility for care and the bulk of time-consuming routine domestic work (Berk, 1985; Hochschild, 1989; Brannen and Moss, 1991). Thus a vicious circle is perpetuated whereby women balance their lives around the competing worlds of income generation and the management of home life, while men can be more single-minded in the pursuit of employment opportunities.

The persistence of gender differences in the organisation of work and family life has led researchers to focus on developing better understandings of what constitutes a constraint on people's ability to organise their intimate relationships differently. Most commonly cited factors include: men's greater earnings; the organisation of waged employment on a traditional masculine model (Bradley, 1989; Brannen and Moss, 1991); gender ideologies, including ideologies of motherhood, fatherhood and traditional family life (Berk, 1985; Lewis and O'Brien, 1987; Hochschild, 1989; Morris, 1990); and minimal childcare provision (Morris, 1990; Melhuish and Moss, 1991). As these are often interdependent and mutually reinforcing, difficulties in untangling them are exacerbated by the almost exclusively heterosexual focus framing analysis. Dunne's earlier study (1997a) suggested that lesbian partnerships provided greater opportunities for egalitarian arrangements. A key question shaping this research is whether these opportunities extend to lesbian couples with dependent children.

*Sample*

Much effort was devoted to publicising the study and recruiting the sample through as wide a range of different sources as possible. The study was advertised in relevant media, publicity leaflets were sent for distribution to Women's Centres and Lesbian Parenting Groups across England, and signs were put up in a number of alternative bookshops. Leaflets were also distributed at a non-academic lesbian and gay parenting conference in London, and through two law firms who specialised in lesbian family law. The most successful method of recruitment turned out to be a snowball technique: participants in the study were encouraged to publicise the study within their own friendship networks. The only selection criteria for the parent sample was that the household comprise a co-habiting lesbian couple with dependent children. All who contacted me in this situation agreed to participate in the research and were interviewed. The sample tended to live in the inner-city neighbourhoods (usually with a high ethnic minority population) of three major northern cities and three major southern cities; few lived in suburban or rural areas. The sensitivity of the topic together with the general invisibility of lesbians in the population means that no study of this nature can make claims of representativeness. However, there is no reason to assume that the sample is particularly unrepresentative, especially in relation to couples who have experienced donor insemination.

When designing the project I had anticipated difficulties in locating lesbian couples with children via donor insemination, hence the original intention for half the parents to have had their children in a previous heterosexual relationship. However, during the recruitment stage it soon became apparent that the majority of couples who contacted us had children via donor insemination (DI). I decided to depart from our original 50/50 specification as the focus on DI couples was more relevant to my aims. Consequently, DI couples represent 75 per cent of the parent sample. As recruitment continued I decided to include all the couples with children who had made contact (n=37) and reduce the sample of non-parents (from 15 to six). Any loss with respect to the reduced sample of non-parents was greatly exceeded by the advantages of charting the arrangements and experiences of DI parents who were usually sharing parenting responsibilities. This re-emphasis illuminated interesting themes around experience and conceptions of parenting in a same-sex context, the negotiation of donor/father involvement and the construction of kinship relations (Dunne, 1999b). Additionally, the majority had pre-school-aged children. As this stage in family formation represents a time when pressure towards polarisation is most extreme I had an excellent opportunity to fulfil my main objectives and increase confidence in my findings and theoretical conclusions.

**Methods**

A wide range of methods, both qualitative and quantitative, innovative and conventional, were employed to illuminate the work and caring strategies of 43 lesbian households, including 37 with dependent children. After the completion of detailed background questionnaires, a series of in-depth taped interviews (two-three hours) were carried out, time-task allocation data was collected and participants were re-contacted two to three years later. A key concern was that participation in the research should be as pleasurable and informative as possible.

*Joint Interview*

The first interview involved both partners. I began by focusing on their journey to parenting. Respondents then mapped out their social/kin networks of support on paper; an advantage of this technique was the less directive prompting of memory. The interview moved on to the main focus which was the production of a 'household portrait'. This is a new 'participatory' method, first developed by Doucet (1995) for her research on divisions of labour between heterosexual parents, and modified for this study. This technique involves partners placing colour-coded task/responsibility tokens relating to a wide range of household, financial, and parenting activities on to a continuum presented on a large board. This allows the participation of respondents in analysis; by visually representing their perceptions of 'who does what', respondents are encouraged to discuss, negotiate and reflect upon their arrangements. This proved to be a powerful tool, illuminating for both participants and researcher. While respondents generally expressed feelings of enjoyment and validation on doing this activity, its potential for exposing contradiction and conflict at the heart of a relationship means that its employment requires high levels of care and sensitivity.

*Time-Task Allocation Diaries*

These offered an alternative perspective on divisions of labour and were completed by each respondent over a seven-day period. One advantage of this method is that by providing a sense of how an individual's time is distributed across a range of activities, I move beyond an account of household dynamics based on perceptions and the possible desire to present an ideal. The diaries and coding frame were designed to facilitate comparison with other time-use studies, most specifically data collected by Jonathan Gershuny (with whom we were collaborating) derived from the *Social Change and Economic Life Initiative* (SCELI) collected in 1987. Respondents' commitment to the project was reflected in the comparatively rich data supplied in doing what was an onerous task for people with young children.

*Individual Interview*

A second interview was conducted several months later with each partner on her own. The first part of this interview returned to domestic arrangements, providing the opportunity for clarification and for offering a more personal view. Respondents were then presented with some preliminary analysis of the dynamics of their household. The task allocation outcomes from their Household Portrait and the data from the diaries were visually summarised with the aid of a graphics programme, Excel. Early comparative findings, within the project and with a sub-sample from the SCELI study, were also presented. This feedback stage was beneficial all round. Respondents welcomed the opportunity to receive information and to comment on different methods employed and, more usually, on the difficulties and stresses related to doing the diary. Drawing on their expertise, respondents were again encouraged to participate in analysis.

The interview moved on to collect life-history data. A Lifeline Technique facilitated the charting of continuity and change: on one side of the line respondents recorded transitions in relation to education and employment, and, on the other, the focus was personal events, relationships and children. They were then asked to discuss hopes for the future. The last stage of the interview explored respondents' attitudes to employment. This was fairly structured, using a combination of open and closed questions as well as statements for evaluation. By asking respondents to think out loud, the statements usually provoked extended discussion which aided clarification.

*Longitudinal Dimension*

Contact was maintained with participants through periodic telephone conversations. Time-depth was provided by the completion of an individual questionnaire which was administered two to three years after initial contact. At this time respondents also received a short progress report and copies of publications. Most of the questions were open-ended and focused on change and continuity in relation to employment, domestic life and children. It also invited comments on the papers and on the impact, if any, of being involved in the project. When necessary, supplementary clarification and elaboration was gained by telephone contact. Analysis of this longitudinal data continues. However, worth mentioning is the extent to which participants commented on the impact of being in the research, the sense of re-assurance and validation which came from discussing their own practice and learning about that of others. Some suggested that they had adjusted or become happier with the weighting of domestic contributions in their partnership after looking at their completed Household Portrait or diary analysis, while some mentioned being shocked at time spent on domestic work and had made efforts to reduce this.

**Data Analysis**

My aims required analysis in two directions: firstly, extensive comparative analysis within the sample on the basis of, for example, presence of children, age of children, origins of children, parenting situation, biological motherhood, employment hours; secondly, primary and secondary comparative analysis of trends for cohabiting heterosexual parents. I am aware that the small size and particularities of our sample makes comparison far from perfect, and where possible I have made comparisons with households which are similar to the ones in the project in relation to education, occupation, and age of children.

*Quantitative Analysis*

Patterns of employment were compared with an appropriate sub-sample of households in *The British Household Panel Survey* (1993) (BHPS), as was information about task allocation. Comparisons were also made with relevant recent published research, for example, *The National Childhood Development Study* (Ferri and Smith, 1996); a study on divisions of labour for married couples who had recently become parents (Cappucine, 1996); and a study on the domestic arrangements of professional dual earner couples (Gregson and Lowe, 1994). The time-use data was coded and compared with a data-set supplied by Jonathan Gershuny of all couples with dependent children in the SCELI time-use survey. I also looked at the more recent *Omnibus Time Survey* (1995) which did not contradict the SCELI trends.

*Qualitative Analysis*

Interviews were transcribed in full and mounted on to Atlas-ti (a qualitative data analysis soft-ware package) for coding and analysis. Themes of particular interest included: journey to parenthood, locating donors, social and kinship networks of support, negotiation and logic of allocation of parenting, domestic and employment responsibilities, accounts of gender scripting, perceptions/ideals of equality, justifications of change and continuity in employment/domestic life. Because of my methodological commonalities and similarities in sample characteristics (regarding education and occupation), Andrea Doucet's qualitative research on egalitarian heterosexual couples was a particularly useful comparative reference point (Doucet and Dunne, 1999).

**Parenting Circumstances**

My sample of parents included eight households where children were from a previous marriage/heterosexual relationship, one household where the children were adopted, and 28 where they had been conceived by donor insemination. In the majority of households (60 per cent) there was at least one pre-school-age child. Worth noting is that in 40 per cent of households co-parents were also biological mothers of older dependent or non-dependent children. As both partners in parenting partnerships tended to refer to themselves as mothers, I use the term 'birth-mother' to describe the biological mother of the (youngest) child and 'co-parent' to describe her partner.

It was interesting that such a large proportion of couples with children (75 per cent) had at least one child conceived by donor insemination. This suggests that the 'gay-by' boom identified in the USA is in evidence in this country (e.g. Weston, 1991; Lewin, 1993). Worth noting also was that contrary to media representation, almost all organised conception informally; they rarely used National Health or even private fertility services. Commonly, respondents located donors through friendship networks or by advertising. They generally experienced support and encouragement in their quest to become parents from heterosexual friends and siblings. Thus the contemporary 'moral panic' about lesbian parenting which calls for greater control over access to new reproductive technologies would appear somewhat futile, and, as the findings of this research would suggest, unwarranted.

Men featured in the lives of most of the children (Dunne, 1999b). It was not unusual for donors to have regular contact with their offspring (30 per cent of households). This involvement usually took the form of 'kindly uncle', but in three households fathers were actively co-parenting. Overall and everyday responsibility for the care and well-being of children lay with the mothers except in two cases where fathers were jointly parenting. Donors were usually, but not exclusively, gay men and all male co-parents were gay. There were two main reasons for this preference. Respondents believed that the gay men in their lives represented a more acceptable, positive form of masculinity. As such, their desire to involve men in the lives of their children was usually justified on the basis of counteracting dominant stereotypes of masculinity, and certainly not by feelings about children needing fathers. They also felt that if a dispute should arise, a heterosexual donor, particularly if he were married, could mobilise formal power to change arrangements in relation to access/custody. I suggest that, unhampered by the emotional, sexual and financial constraints of heterosexuality, respondents could choose to include men on the basis of the qualities they can bring into children's lives, though this involvement was a matter of choice for the men.

In situations where children had been conceived in a previous marriage/heterosexual relationship there was more diversity and conflict regarding fathers' involvement in children's lives. In several cases fathers had unsuccessfully contested custody on the grounds of the mother's lesbianism. Indeed, two fathers had appeared on day-time television arguing that their ex-partner's sexuality conflicted with their capacity to be good mothers. There were also examples of excellent relations between the mothers and ex-husbands. While there were several examples of fathers having lost contact with their children, in most cases respondents suggested that the child/ren had more 'quality' time with their fathers post-divorce than before. Despite tensions and possible conflict between mothers and ex-husbands, these respondents suggested that they worked hard to maintain their children's relationship with the father. Thus, ironically, in this group as well as the DI group of parents there were examples of highly productive models of co-operation between women and men in parenting.

Overall, parenting was depicted as jointly shared between partners in 30 households (80 per cent) and generally their children were described as having two mothers.  I argue that rather than mirroring the dichotomy within heterosexual parenting, these women are actively engaged in a process of extending and re-defining the meaning and content of mothering (Dunne, 1999b).


**Social and Kinship Networks of Support**

The role of donors/fathers and other male friends in children's lives reminds us that lesbian parenting does not occur in a social vacuum (Dunne, 1999b). While generally hostile to the idea of the privatised nuclear family, respondents were keen to establish more extended family networks of friends and kin. Typically, they described a wide circle of friends (lesbian 'aunties', gay 'uncles' as well as heterosexual friends) supporting their parenting. The arrival of children usually had an impact on their social networks; respondents often spoke of feeling greater commonalities with other parents. Thus, their social worlds tended to become more mixed, both heterosexual and non-heterosexual than before. Those who had socialised mainly with women often suggested having made a point of befriending 'good' men to act as positive role models for boy children.

In western societies kinship is organised on the basis of sexual difference. Gayle Rubin's classic paper (1975) talks about the same-sex taboo that supports the exchange of women which establishes kinship relationships.  When the 'goods' get together, a radical and subversive act in itself, there are possibilities for fascinating and subversive kinship arrangements (Dunne, 1999b). This research revealed interesting issues about kinship which lived up to this possibility. It was not unusual for respondents to describe the arrival of children as bringing them closer to, or helping repair difficult relationships with, their families of origin. My focus on DI parents, especially those who were bringing up children as a joint project, illuminated some fascinating issues regarding the complexity and flexibility around the construction of kinship ties. In households where both partners were biological mothers (sometimes with the same donor), the children were usually described as viewing each other as siblings.  These children often had relationships with three, four and even five sets of grandparents. Those with actively involved donors/fathers often had interested and involved paternal grandparents; if there were two children with two different donors this could rise to two sets.  Alongside maternal grandparents were often the parents of the co-parent.  Respondents in co-parenting situations spoke of the importance they attached to, and the work involved in, gaining non-biological kinship recognition from extended family. One reason for their usual success in this respect, I believe, is that the presence of children helps make intelligible a lifestyle that can appear strange and 'other' to wider heterosexual observers. At one level, motherhood bridges the gap between the known and the unknown. It represents a common currency where we can predict the routines, pleasures and concerns of parents, and sexuality can be sidelined. At another level, however, as we will see, their more egalitarian experience of motherhood seems quite different to that of most heterosexual mothers (Dunne, 1998a). Importantly, by building bridges in this way friends, colleagues and extended family bear witness to these differences, and their experience reflects back into the lives of others.

## Household Employment Strategies

> Neither Helen nor I wanted to be either the one that was at work or the one that was at home all the time... I think the original reason for working part-time was to share Paul. But actually I'm not sure now even if I'd want to go back to full-time - probably not back to being a totally work person, which would be stressful and horrible.... The motivation behind it was to do with Paul, and to make sure that he was equally cared for (Maggie, co-parent of three-year-old Paul).

> I think we go about things in our own way, we don't have the role definition. We get the best of both worlds really. We get to continue along the road with our careers and also to spend time as a family and to enjoy the time with the children. Disadvantages? We could earn more money I suppose if we worked full-time, but then it takes away the point of having children I would say (Patsy, co-parent of two pre-school-age girls).

As divisions of paid labour have a major bearing on the structuring of work in the home I was interested in the organisation of employment responsibilities in partnerships, as well as the partners' strategies towards the allocation of household tasks.

The relationship between the lesbian lifestyle and the capacity to be financially independent illuminated in the earlier study (Dunne, 1997a) is reflected in the educational/occupational circumstances of this sample. Respondents tended to be well educated, with 70 per cent holding degrees or professional qualifications. It was not uncommon for respondents to have gained these qualifications as mature students, with some co-parents having timed their entry into higher education to correspond with the arrival of children to give them more time at home. They were also occupationally advantaged. The majority of employed respondents work for public sector employers or are self-employed. They are usually professionals, managers, technicians or administrators in more female occupations such as teaching, social work, local government, health and counselling (Table 7.1). Interestingly, like the women in the previous study (Dunne, 1997a), compared with the occupations of their fathers they had experienced a fair amount of social mobility: while 75 per cent of the total sample occupy professional/managerial positions in the occupational structure, this had been the case for only half of their fathers.

**Table 7.1  Respondents' normal occupations (by Standard Occupational Classification)**

| Occupational group | Birth Mothers | | Co-Parents | | All Parents | | Non-Parents | | All Sample | |
|---|---|---|---|---|---|---|---|---|---|---|
| | No | % | No | % | No | % | No | % | No | % |
| 1 Managers and Administrators | 0 | 0 | 2 | 6 | 2 | 3 | 0 | 0 | 2 | 2 |
| 2 Professional | 17 | 49 | 15 | 43 | 32 | 46 | 6 | 50 | 38 | 46 |
| 3 Assoc. Prof. and Technical | 9 | 26 | 10 | 29 | 19 | 27 | 3 | 25 | 22 | 27 |
| 4 Clerical and Secretarial | 2 | 6 | 3 | 9 | 5 | 7 | 1 | 8 | 6 | 7 |
| 5 Craft and Related | 1 | 3 | 1 | 3 | 2 | 3 | 1 | 8 | 3 | 4 |
| 6 Personal and Protective Servs. | 4 | 11 | 2 | 6 | 6 | 9 | 1 | 8 | 7 | 9 |
| 7 Sales | 0 | 0 | 1 | 3 | 1 | 1 | - | - | 1 | 1 |
| 8 Operatives | 0 | 0 | 1 | 3 | 1 | 1 | - | - | 1 | 1 |
| 9 Other | 2 | 6 | 0 | 0 | 2 | 3 | - | - | 2 | 2 |
| Totals | 35 | 100 | 35 | 100 | 70 | 100 | 12 | 100 | 82 | 100 |

NB: Includes usual occupation of three full-time mature students.  Excludes two non-employed with no specific occupation.

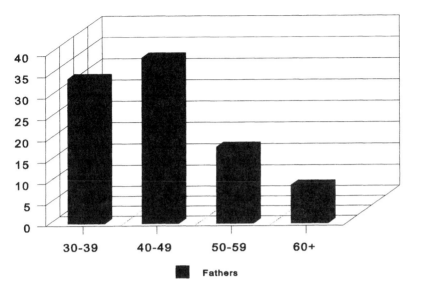

**Figure 7.1 Total hours worked by employed cohort fathers**
*Source*: Ferri and Smith (1996) from the National Child Development Study (1991).

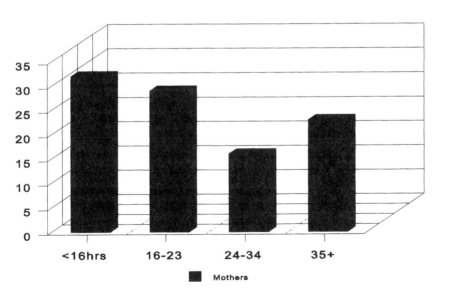

**Figure 7.2 Total hours worked by employed cohort mothers**
*Source*: Ferri and Smith (1996) from the National Child Development Study (1991).

Employment trends in Britain indicate the persistence of polarisation in the employment hours of married partners, particularly when they have dependent children. Figures 7.1 and 7.2 illustrate these disparities. For example, in 1991 77 per cent of employed mothers in the National Childhood Development Survey had employment hours of less than 35 hours per week, while 27 per cent of employed fathers had paid working weeks of 50 hours plus. Yet approximately half of that sample described parenting responsibilities as equally shared (Ferri and Smith, 1996).

Analysis of differences between the lesbian partners, on the basis of employment hours, status and income revealed little of the specialisation characterising heterosexual partnerships with children; biological motherhood was a poor predictor of partner differences in this respect.

To ensure that these differences did not simply flow from occupational/educational advantage I compared trends for the sample with highly qualified couples more generally. Comparison of the 22 couples with pre-school-aged children with parents with similarly aged children and higher qualifications in the BHPS (1993) reveals how unusual the employment circumstances of our sample are. Figure 7.3 shows that while co-parents are more likely to be employed full-time than their partners, in comparison with highly qualified fathers they are much more likely to have adjusted their employment lives around children: 41 per cent of co-parents were employed part-time or home-based, compared with 9 per cent of highly qualified fathers. Rather than using their occupational/educational advantage to maximise labour market participation and household income the parents in this study tended to use this power to develop strategies aimed at enabling both partners to combine childcare with paid employment.

Routinely birth-mothers *and* co-parents alike spoke of seeking balanced lives, valuing time for children, an identity from the formal workplace and the ability to financially contribute. Their practices and plans usually challenged the idea that the 'career' of the higher earner should be prioritised. They often operationalised joint parenting by either taking it in turns to be home-based, or by both working part-time.

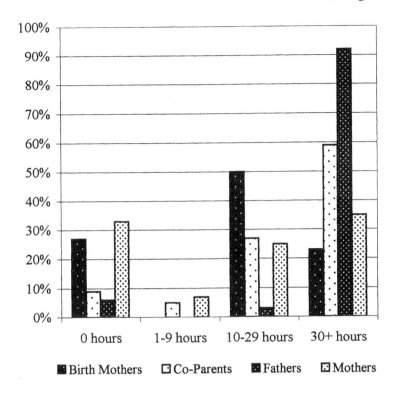

**Figure 7.3 Employment hours**
*Source*: Comparing sub-sample (n=22) with national sample of mothers (n=134) and fathers (n=160) with higher qualifications and children under five (BHPS, 1993).

As flexibility often characterised the employment strategies of both partners there was a wide range of partner employment combinations. Table 7.2, for example, shows that in seven (19 per cent) of parenting households both partners were employed part-time, and in five (14 per cent) one was home-based while the other was employed part-time. The non-parents favoured full-time employment, although two were returners to full-time training/education.

**Table 7.2  Household employment strategies for all sample**

| Partner Employment Combination | Parents | | Non-Parents |
|---|---|---|---|
| | No | % | No |
| Full-time/full-time | 8 | 22 | 4 |
| Part-time/part-time** | 7 | 19 | - |
| Full-time/part-time | 10 | 27 | - |
| Part-time/home | 5 | 14 | 1* |
| Full-time/home | 6 | 16 | 1* |
| Neither in paid employment | 1 | 3 | - |
| Total | 37 | 100 | 6 |

\* Home-based partner is in full-time higher education.
\*\* Part time is defined as less that 30 hours employment per week.

Figure 7.4 compares the parents with pre-school children with heterosexual couples where both partners have higher qualifications and children under five. Here it can be seen that the wider range of household employment combinations holds for this subsample.  In contrast, strategies of highly qualified parents more generally fall within three predictable main groupings: both full-time, full-time/part-time and full-time/at home.  Closer examination reveals that it was mothers rather than fathers who had reduced their employment hours.

Unlike the situation for heterosexual parents, where ideologies of motherhood and fatherhood exist to differentiate responsibilities for children and income generation, both birth-mothers and co-parents tended to conceptualise parenthood as the *integration* of mothering and bread-winning.  Rather than specialisation as an ideal, each usually described her approach to paid employment as being balanced around the demands and pleasures of children. Thus, the arrival of children often had an impact on the employment strategies of both parents, for example, 36 per cent of co-parents had shorter employment hours than their partners.

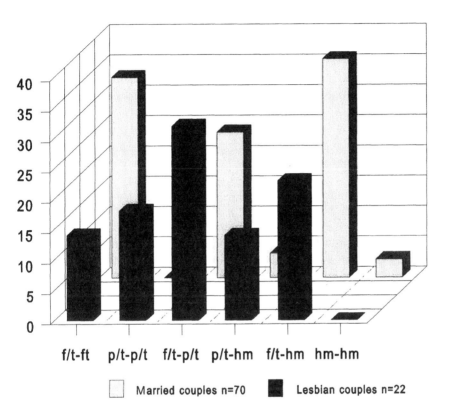

**Figure 7.4  Household employment strategies**
*Source*: Comparing sub-sample (n=22) with married couples (n=70) with children under
five where *both* partners hold higher qualifications (BHPS, 1993).

*Income Distribution*

Respondents usually described their relationships as operating on the basis of
financial co-independence.  Their structural position as women workers, and the
lack of the anticipation and experience of a sexual division of labour, meant that
income differentials in partnerships were much less than we would expect to find
in heterosexual households.   Except in the two households with full-time
students, partner income differentials were tiny for non-parents.  Ideas of fairness
and the privileging of childcare influenced the choices of higher earners who
confounded rational economic models by becoming main carers.  Despite their

being less likely to be in paid employment and more likely to have shorter paid working hours than their partners, only 30 per cent of birth mothers contributed less than 40 per cent of total household income. Analysis of income distribution in households with dependent children in the National Childhood Development Study (Joshi et al., 1995) showed that only 17 per cent of married mothers contributed half or more to total household income, compared with 50 per cent of our birth mothers.

## The Allocation of Work at Home

> I think it is impossible [to get balance in a heterosexual relationship]. I've had to do so much rebellion against the status I was expected to have in a heterosexual relationship.... It's just too complicated. I mean it's difficult for feminists anyway.... If there's a problem then it's between June and me, it's not a problem between men and women like the world over, or history conspiring against us (June, birth-mother of two pre-school-age children, employed full-time as a technician).

### Non-routine Task Allocation

> I think it's much more acceptable to take on whatever role you want, or whatever you're happy with. I mean it doesn't matter if I want to go and chop down a tree in the garden, that's fine, there's not some man being put out because I am doing heavy work, or if Liz wants to go and fiddle with the car, that's fine. I think it's the whole society man/woman thing. I think there are an awful lot of new men, new relationships.... But, I think it's a lot easier for us because we don't have any sort of roles to live up to (Judith, birth-mother of a two-year-old boy).

Using the Household Portrait, I examined the detailed information on perceptions of who did what to see if similar patterns of task allocation to those identified in research on gender segregated heterosexual partnerships emerge for different reasons in same-sex partnerships. Exploration of the allocation of gender stereotyped tasks such as car maintenance, baking or sewing, revealed no such specialisation. If performed, these tasks were either undertaken jointly (especially DIY), or one partner might take responsibility for a task like car maintenance and the other minor household repairs. Interestingly, there were several examples of someone taking responsibility for sewing/knitting *and* carpentry, indicating, perhaps, transferable skills. Another interesting point relates to kin-keeping. This is usually a female responsibility, but my respondents tended to retain responsibility for remembering birthdays etc. for their own kin/friends.

*Routine Domestic Task Allocation*

I suppose because our relationship doesn't fit into a social norm, there are no pre-set indications about how our relationship should work. We have to work it out for ourselves. We've no role models in terms of how we divide our duties, so we've got to work it out afresh as to what suits us.... We try very hard to be just to each other and... not exploit the other person (Dolly, who has been living with her partner, Jo, for the past 19 years, and has grown-up children).

**Table 7.3  Core routine domestic tasks in parenting households**

| | | | Birth mother | | Co-Parent | |
| Task | Exclusively | Mainly | Shared Equally | Mainly | Exclusively | |
| | % | % | % | % | % | N |
| Washing-up | 5 | 16 | 62 | 16 | 0 | 37 |
| Cleaning & Dusting | 6 | 24 | 58 | 9 | 3 | 33 |
| Grocery Shopping | 5 | 24 | 57 | 5 | 8 | 37 |
| Ironing | 13 | 3 | 53 | 7 | 23 | *30 |
| Bathroom Cleaning | 14 | 11 | 49 | 17 | 9 | 35 |
| Vacuuming | 15 | 27 | 45 | 6 | 6 | 33 |
| Cooking | 8 | 24 | 41 | 19 | 8 | 37 |
| Laundry | 14 | 27 | 38 | 11 | 11 | 37 |
| Mean | 10 | 20 | 50 | 11 | 8 | |

* It was not unusual for households to dispense with ironing. Eight households employed a cleaner for a few hours a week (a man in two instances and a daughter in another).

I then examined participants' strategies in relation to routine labour-intensive domestic tasks such as laundry, ironing, grocery shopping and cooking on weekdays and at weekends. Table 7.3 summarises the outcomes for the parents. To aid comparison within the sample, a simple 'domestic contribution' score was calculated by taking an average of each partner's percentage contribution to eight *core* tasks. In addition, a fairly crude 'domestic responsibility' score was calculated by averaging each partner's percentage involvement in taking/having responsibility for: compiling the shopping list, remembering to buy groceries, planning meals, deciding what needs doing for housework, and remembering to pay bills (Dunne, 1997b).

The domestic contribution scores of all but one of the non-parenting households fell within a 40–60 per cent threshold, indicating fairly even partner contributions. For the parents, the contribution scores of 21 households (57 per cent) and responsibility scores of 17 households (46 per cent) fell within this shared threshold. Being the biological mother of the youngest child was, however, a poor predictor of contribution imbalances. Taking the domestic scores of all 37 parenting households, birth mothers have an average domestic contribution score of 52 per cent to co-parents 48 per cent, and their average share of responsibility was 55 per cent. Domestic contribution imbalances were more likely to be, although not necessarily, influenced by differential time availability.

Respondents spoke of the importance of sharing domestic tasks and responsibilities and in individual interviews frequently described both themselves and their partners as being involved in the rhythm of domestic life. Commonly respondents described an absence of gender scripts to inform practice and that this enabled flexibility in the allocation and performance of tasks. I argue that their similarities as women make disparities in contributions much more visible and less easy to justify than in heterosexual relationships where gender difference shapes both the allocation of tasks and evaluations of fairness (Dunne, 1998b, 1999a).

## Time-Use Patterns

> I think that because you have been through the situation yourself you have a real understanding. If you are at home all day with a baby you cannot think of anything that is more demanding than that or more tiring. But if you have been out at work all day you cannot think of anything more tiring than that. But because we have done both, we can really understand. There wouldn't be an argument about who has had the hardest day because we both had a very clear understanding of the experience of being at home all day and the experience of being at work all day. They are both very demanding in different ways (May, birth-mother and co-parent of two pre-school-age daughters).

[When I was married] my husband came home from work and his day was finished, in terms of work, whereas when I come home from work I don't have that sense... I take my coat off and assess what's going on and act - get on with it. If they're in the bath I go and get their pyjamas or whatever. You don't have that kind of demarcation line (Ella, sole-earner, birth mother of a grown-up son and co-parent of two primary school-age boys).

This is the first published study to collect time-use data on lesbian couples with children. Analysis of this data confirmed many of the employment and domestic trends noted above. I describe these more fully in Dunne (1998a). As anticipated, being the birth mother was a poor predictor of partner differences in time devoted to paid employment and domestic work, and birth-mothers average proportion of total household time devoted to childcare was 61 per cent, with 40 per cent of households coming within a 40–60 per cent sharing threshold.

Analysis of the SCELI (1987) time-use data for married couples with dependent children (supported in a separate analysis of the Omnibus time-use survey (1995)) showed that men's average working day is monopolised by work that is paid, and women's by work that is unwaged, including domestic labour, childcare and shopping. The diaries of the parents showed much less specialisation. While *total* household time devoted to paid employment for lesbian parents was fairly similar to households more generally, the difference lay in the tendency for this work to be more equally distributed between partners. For example, only 5 per cent of mothers and fathers in the SCELI sample had similar paid working hours (less than 10 hours difference) compared with 34 per cent of the lesbian parent sample, and the proportion of lesbian parents with extreme differences (30 hours plus) was 32 per cent compared with just under 70 per cent of SCELI parents. Time devoted to domestic work was fairly evenly balanced between lesbian partners, with 86 per cent of the dual earner households falling within a 40–60 per cent sharing threshold. In contrast, fathers' average time contribution to domestic labour in dual earner households was relatively small even when their paid working hours were similar to their partners, 28 per cent of average total household time. Importantly, the more equitable division of paid and domestic labour between lesbian parents enabled *both* partners to devote a greater amount of single-minded time to childcare than is usual for married mothers (Dunne, 1998a).

The size of this sample (six sets of diaries) limits conclusions for the non-parents. However, worth noting is that compared with our parents, there were more discrepancies between partners in time devoted to domestic tasks. The average contribution of the partner with the longest paid working hours in each partnership was just 34 per cent, and only one fell within our 40-60 per cent sharing threshold. The average total time spent on domestic work in these households, 2.7 hours per day, is marginally lower than the average for dual earner parents.

Comparison between the two samples suggests that rather than encouraging domestic polarisation, the additional demands of children appear to foster the more careful and conscious management of time. In this context, time-pressures appear to generate a reassessment of domestic routines, on the basis of evaluating both the necessity of specific tasks and the fairness of allocation strategies.

**Conclusions**

This research offers insights into, and highlights the importance of, the relationship between the organisation of waged and unwaged work in partnerships. While the focus of the research generally has been on the circumstances of mothers, there is a need to direct greater attention to the choices, constraints and opportunities available to fathers for enjoying more balanced lives. The more integrated approach to the organisation of work and family life desired, and often achieved, by two women parenting together suggests that there is greater scope for exercising control over the distribution of employment responsibilities in partnerships than is usually recognised, particularly for more occupationally and educationally privileged groups. This highlights the on-going salience of ideologies of motherhood and fatherhood for limiting creativity and for allowing men to see themselves, and be seen, as caring and involved fathers while absent from the home for 40, 50 or more hours a week. I suggest we need to focus less on why women care and more on civilising the paid working week and a corresponding critique of the long hours associated with masculine models of employment. This model of employment is in contradiction to the negotiation of egalitarian home-life arrangements as it is dependent on the exploitation of the labour of others, either female partners or working class women (Gregson and Lowe, 1994; Dunne, 1997a).

This study also illustrates the relationship between sexuality and the everyday accomplishment of gender. Influential household theorists such as Berk (1985) argue that the key to understanding task allocation in partnerships is its symbolic significance in affirming gender identity. This research would both support and extend this theoretical insight by highlighting the heterosexual context of observation and by thus arguing that the 'doing of gender' is mediated by sexuality: that women might find it easier to share with women because, in the absence of men, they are less likely to be engaged in a process that affirms gender difference. Thus it is important to recognise the gender dimension to sexuality.

Finally, the creativity which lesbian women can bring to 'solving' the contradiction between the demands of income generation, nurturing and maintaining a home highlights the need to be more explicit about the impact of institutional heterosexuality for reproducing inequalities between women and men. Sexuality is not simply about sexual practice. Sexual identity can shape the kind of gendered identities, experiences and opportunities available to women and men. In sociology it is recognised that sexuality, like gender, is socially constructed. Thus, it is important to critique the 'naturalness' of heterosexuality and devote greater attention to the social mechanisms that exist to limit how and with whom we may express ourselves emotionally and sexually, and our opportunities to live differently.

## Note

[1] I am grateful to the Economic and Social Research Council for funding the project (reference number R000234649). I would also like to thank my co-applicants, Bob Blackburn and Henrietta Moore for their support, encouragement and guidance. My particular thanks to my overworked and underpaid, yet always enthusiastic colleagues, Kim Perren, Esther Dermott and Jackie Beer who assisted the project over the three years.

# 8  Working Life for Spanish Women of the 1980s and its Reflection in the Novel *Amado Amo* by Rosa Montero

LESLEY TWOMEY

## Introduction

This chapter explores the interface between women at work and the novel *Amado Amo* by the Spanish novelist, Rosa Montero (1995b).[1] The first part of the study will examine the legal and social changes, which occurred during the 1970s and 1980s, affecting women and their working lives. The second part will look at issues raised by the novel.

## Democracy

After the death, in November 1975, of General Francisco Franco Bahamonde, the dictator who had held the reins of Government in Spain for over 40 years, a series of radical changes took place in Spanish life: democracy was restored step by step to Spain between 1975 and the late 1970s (Tusell, 1997). Moreover, this was achieved at breakneck speed (Montero, 1995b:315). Amendments to the law brought new focus to Spanish political life and labour relations, bringing democratic rights where none had existed: political parties, including the Communist party, were legalised; legitimate trade unions once again had the right to recruit and organise, meaning that workers' rights were no longer subsumed within the state-run vertical trade unions, which had shifted power away from the workers during the dictatorship. The first elections since 1936 were held in 1977, giving all Spaniards, including Spain's female population, the opportunity to voice their opinion via the ballot box. In all the events which go to make up Spain's transition to democracy, women participated and reaped rewards equivalent to those given to men (Escario,

1996:265). For example, in December 1978, the new constitution was ratified by referendum and, through this, equal rights were declared for all citizens. The Constitution was welcomed by women's groups, since 'it represented the promise of a new beginning, a political life offering more freedom and more responsibilities' (Escario, 1996:264).[2]   Moreover, when the Spanish state instituted its move towards devolution of power away from the centre to the *autonomías* (regions) this created new opportunities for political representation at regional level for all Spaniards.   As Rosa Montero indicates, in a chapter dealing with what she terms 'the silent revolution', 'women provide a particularly good example of the speed of change in recent Spanish society and of the unique vitality that has resulted' (Montero, 1995c:383).

Changes and opportunities for Spain's women were, thus, part of the wider vision of new legally declared democratic rights.   Article 14 of the Spanish Constitution, one of the most advanced in Europe, states that

> Spaniards are equal before the law and no discrimination is permissible on the grounds of birth, race, sex, religion, opinion or any other condition or circumstance, whether personal or social (Pujol Algans, 1992:30).

Equality for all was to be the hallmark of the new democratic Spain.   For 40 years, citizens had been categorized according to their gender.   As Garrido notes, the key policy for women in the Franco years had been to ensure their return to the private sphere (1997:527).   Following the accession of Franco in 1939, the progressive laws passed by the Second Republic were repealed, meaning that women were once again subject to the nineteenth-century Penal Code and to the 1889 Civil Code, were deprived of the rights to abortion and to divorce, both instituted under the progressive Second Republic, and were once again placed under the control of the head of the family (Brooksbank Jones, 1997:76; Telo, 1986:82).

The period saw a series of protectionist laws brought into force, many of which perceived women very clearly as second-class citizens.   For example, in education girls and boys were segregated by the Law of 17th July 1945, 'for reasons of moral order' (Garrido, 1997:535).   This dual standard can, also, be clearly seen in the Penal Code in its references to adultery and acceptance of *venganza de sangre* (revenge by blood) in force until 1958, under which a father or husband had the right to kill his wife or daughter if he found her committing an act of adultery (Telo, 1986).   The maximum penalty for men was six months exile.   Until 1975, women did not have the right either to work or travel without asking their husband or father for permission and, in the case of women granted the right to go out to work, the husband had the right to claim her salary.[3]  Telo indicates that the reform of the Civil Code which took place on 2nd May 1975 was a 'giant step forward' and one which feminsts saw as striking at the very heart of patriarchy (Telo, 1986:89).

Following the passing of the Constitution, laws were needed to give life to the statements about equality contained in it, and amongst these was the trio of laws passed in 1981.  It can be argued that it is only when Spanish women attained the right to 'administer and dispose of their property and exercise parental rights over their own children' that they attained full equality (Telo, 1986:92).  The second reform of the Civil Code once again permitted divorce (7th July 1981) and the third (13th July 1982) allowed children to take their mother's nationality rather than automatically taking the father's.  Legally speaking, it was only from the date that the Civil Code was revised in the Bill of 13th May 1981 to allow these rights that Spanish women could be considered to have obtained equality with their husbands in the eyes of the law.

Once the Socialist Party took power in 1982, they continued the legal reforms.  The so-called Abortion Law, which was put on the statute books, after a prolonged struggle, on 28th May 1985 (Pujol Algans, 1992:1017), carried forward the work of reform in the area relating to women's health.  This reform contributed to a lowering of the birth-rate in Spain which had fallen to 1.33 children per female by 1990, continuing to fall to 1.21 and by 1994 still falling (Instituto de la Mujer, 1997b:16).  This, in its turn, was a factor facilitating female entry into the workforce (Pérez, 1992).

One of the key areas of life where radical changes took place was in the field of education.  The General Education Bill, passed during Franco's dictatorship, had already given an important boost to education for women.  The Bill recognised that there had been a low level of female participation.  One important aspect of the General Education Bill is that it gave women, for the first time, unrestricted access to secondary level education.[4]  This Bill, which came into force in the twilight years of the Franco regime in 1970, was to prove a key stimulus to the increase in the number of women succeeding in education and achieving qualifications to allow them to compete in the workplace.  The number of women students quadrupled between 1940, when women represented only 13 per cent of the student population and 1984 when they were more than 50 per cent of students at University level and, since 1989-1990, they have represented a majority of the students finishing their studies at University level (Blanco Corrujo, 1995:55).  The same level of progress in the number of female students at GCSE equivalent (BUP or Baccalaureate level) and vocational diploma level is noted by María Dolores Ayllón.

**Table 8.1 Female participation at GCSE equivalent and in vocational education**

|                              | 1960-61 | 1985-86 | 1994-95 |
|------------------------------|---------|---------|---------|
|                              | %       | %       | %       |
| Baccalaureate ('O' level/GCSE) | 38.8    | 53.4    | 54.7    |
|                              | 1970-71 | 1987-88 | 1994-95 |
|                              | %       | %       | %       |
| Vocational courses           | 5.1     | 44.9    | 47.3    |

*Source*: Adapted from Salustiano del Campo (1994), cited in Ayllón (1995:37) and from Instituto de la Mujer (1997b:41).

The figures clearly show the increased number of women students in non-obligatory education after the death of Franco (Ayllón, 1995). Ayllón goes on to underline the fact that the number of women enrolled for GCSE-equivalent courses in 1985 was higher than the percentage of men enrolled. This notwithstanding, it must be remembered that the number of female students enrolled in non-traditional vocational courses in technical colleges remained low in the 1980s (Ayllón, 1995:45). To combat this situation, women called for co-education as a key way of eradicating differential education for boys and girls from their early years (Escario, 1996:199). Even by the mid-1990s, the numbers enrolled on programmes of study such as metalwork, electronics or mechanics were between 1 per cent and 3 per cent (Instituto de la Mujer, 1997b: 45).

In Ayllón's view, the advances made by women in the field of education are one of the key factors which have contributed to a higher number of women entering the workforce in the 1980s, although Ferreira (1996) considers that demography has played a significant part in the changes. Franco's policy had been to bar married women from the workforce. Telo points out how the wording of the *Fuero de Trabajo* (Labour Charter) had excluded married women whilst appearing to favour them. The statute states at Point 2 that: 'Women would be liberated from the factory and the workshop' (Telo, 1986:84). Before the end of the Franco regime, however, the situation of women in the workforce had improved. Laws were accordingly amended and the Women's Political, Professional and Employment Rights Law, passed in 1958, acknowledged women's right to equality, including equal pay, whilst continuing to exclude them from the judiciary and armed forces (Brooksbank Jones, 1997:77). Spanish economic growth, during the mid-1960s, 'made possible [...] the entry of Spanish women into the workforce' in ever greater numbers (Conde and Carballal, 1986:103). According to Conde and Carballal, the correlation between economic growth in the country and socio-demographic changes meant that more women, particularly younger women, began to consider entering the workforce.

By the 1970s, the numbers of working women was increasing annually. A rise of 2.2 per cent per annum in the percentage of working women in Spain, between 1970 and 1990, has been recorded (Sánchez-Rivera Peiró, 1995), although, as many commentators point out, Spain's official female workforce is still one of the lowest in Europe (*El Mundo,* 9th March 1999).

Labour law also sought to prevent inequities and discriminatory practices. The Workers' Statute of 10th March 1980 (Pujol Algans, 1992:526), at Article 17, outlaws discriminatory rates of pay or working conditions on grounds of sex, race, religious belief, trade union affiliation, or social status. Article 28 specifically relates to equal pay for equal work in both base salary and bonus payments (Pujol Algans, 1992:528). Nevertheless, rates of pay in Spain, as elsewhere in the western world, are far from being equitable, with women workers being paid on average some 30 per cent less than male colleagues. Female staff have been active in bringing cases against firms for wage discrimination, such as the Nestlé workers' case brought in June 1997 (*La Vanguardia* 13th June 1977). Further legislation was required to strengthen women's working conditions and to bring them into line with European Directives; these included Law 3/1989, preventing termination of contract in the case of pregnancy (Pujol Algans, 1992:532). Additional legislation indicates that the Workers' Statute was too generalist in its wording, meaning that, in individual circumstances, particularly those surrounding maternity rights, women continued to be subject to discriminatory practices.

The increased number of working women in Spain brought new questions to the fore. For example, what is expected of a woman worker in terms of commitment and how dedicated to the firm is she expected to be? What changes took place in the workplace when it began to receive an influx of women workers? One woman's answer to some of these questions is given in a novel written at the end of the 1980s, and its treatment of the labour market and women's place in it will be the focus of the second part of the chapter.

**The Novelist's Perspective**

The world of work is to be considered from the point of view of a woman who was at work throughout the 1970s and 1980s in the new democratic Spain. Rosa Montero, a journalist, had already used the world of work as the basis for one of her early novels, *Chronicle of Unlove* (Montero, 1979). In her early novel, Montero chooses to portray the working life of a female journalist, Ana. Through Ana, she recounts the story of a single parent, and her struggle to hold down a job. The scornful response of male colleagues is apparent, when Ana has to take her son to work with her when working late or at weekends:

> Despite the fact that it is Saturday, Ana had to go to work. As there is no nursery for little Curro, she has to take him with her. It will be the same rumpus as ever. The little boy running from desk to desk, annoying her colleagues and slobbering on the keyboards (*Chronicle*, p.72).

In fact, the approach of *Chronicle* is more openly polemical than the later novel, *Amado Amo* (Marcone, 1998:64). The fact that *Chronicle* relates to a working environment well known to Montero provides the opportunity for self-conscious dialogue about discriminatory practice at work.

*Amado Amo* is also an expression of women's experience of working life, a topic which is clearly of interest to Montero in that she chose to contribute a chapter dealing with the working woman to Helen Graham and Jo Labanyi's *Spanish Cultural Studies* (Montero, 1995c:381). *Amado Amo* recasts the theme of the earlier novel. However, there are marked differences in the approach taken in the two novels. As opposed to Montero's earlier novel, *Amado Amo* does not have a female main character. In this respect, it is quite different from *Chronicle*, which takes a more focused approach to the experiences of Ana, using a female narrative voice to do so (Marcone, 1998:66). Most of the events of *Amado Amo* are seen through the eyes of César, a male executive in the company, Golden Line, a multi-national with US ownership. His rambling reflections and stream of consciousness commentary on events constitute the principal narrative voice. Through César, we are made aware of the insecurity plaguing the workforce of Golden Line. Each character's personal success or failure within the company is mediated by César, whilst the intrigue which appears to permeate every aspect of life at the firm, is revealed and interpreted for the reader by César, a narrator who proves, in the end, unreliable. Unlike *Chronicle*, the majority of the characters are male. Given Montero's interest in working life and, given the fact that she can be classified as a feminist novelist in the very broadest sense of the word, it is curious that she includes so few women characters in the novel.

At one point, a brief outline of the principal female character, Paula, is given, so that she can be situated within the confines of the workforce at Golden Line. Paula works in an undetermined capacity for the company. She is the most rounded of the female characters to be presented but, having said this, there are relatively few details to be gleaned about her. Once it is realised that Paula is a former lover of the narrator, this detail becomes even more significant, as there is very little attempt to give a full picture of her psychological makeup. This woman is observed through the eyes of a male character who is little inclined to describe her positively or even impartially, despite his relationship with her. Of her life at work, we know relatively little.

Significantly, the opportunity that is given for dialogue with the character is scant. From time to time, the occasional cry of rage and impotence is heard, as Arribas' (1991) examination of phallogocentricity shows. It can be inferred that Montero deliberately uses this method of filtering out of the female voice as a concrete way of demonstrating women's lack of voice and representation in the workplace as well as in public life.

Linked to the lack of power for women to make their voices heard, there is another theme which Montero wishes to underline here and that is the fact that women are workers who are passed over by the executives. For this reason, the author does not include any powerful female character in the novel. Apart from Paula, amongst women workers, there is mention made only of Conchita. Neither of these two characters has but the slightest presence in Golden Line. Indeed, both are denied any access to power. Both are considered failures by the Board of Directors. Morton, the Managing Director, considers Paula to be 'a very nice girl but not very bright' (*Amado Amo*, p.37). Conchita has warranted being labelled as a failure for two reasons. Firstly, as a secretary, she has little hope of recognition for her own merits. Secondly, it is quite clear that the secretary at Golden Line is irrevocably allied to her boss, Matías, who provides her with her *raison d'être* to the extent that she shares his fate. Having been associated with a no-hoper, demoted from executive status, Conchita is, therefore, doomed to sink also. César categorises her as 'Matías' loyal secretary, so when he fell out of favour, she went down with him' (*Amado Amo*, p.72); hence, César's fear of association with her, when she is then passed on to him as his secretary. Although, as always, César's views must be taken with a pinch of salt, through the narrative voice provided, the reader must deduce that Conchita does not even have a worth in her own right as a worker but is dependent on the performance of others.

This theme of the invisibility of the female employee is not just used by Montero in the novel but is, in fact, a powerful tool which is deployed at its very heart. This narrative technique has been set in place by Montero to provide a narrative demonstration of how, even in the late 1980s, invisibility prevents women from having not only a voice but also from having a sense of worth in the workplace. This invisibility arises on two counts in the novel: first, from the few women characters present and also from their lack of narrative voice and, second, from the little impact any woman worker in Golden Line is perceived to make on the company. Montero does not use the novel as a vehicle for overt feminist discourse, as she did in *Chronicle of Unlove*, but the novel's discourse is at a more subtle level. Montero shows the main difficulty female workers face in operation. In *Gendered Space*, Daphne Spain outlines how the division of the workplace operates to keep women together in 'open space enclosures', whilst affording male executives the majority of the open plan space and maximum privacy, due to 'closed doors' or screening of the workplace in other ways (1992:206). These features contribute to maintaining the power base of male workers, whilst ensuring that female workers are of little significance. Space, and its division, is a key feature of the novel *Amado Amo*, although its development relates rather to the diminishing of César's own value and consonant work space in the company. Paula's space at work is never considered, and this is symbolic of the fact that, as a woman, she is not considered of value to the company at all. Montero roots women's lack of opportunity to be heard or to be considered worthy of recognition, and of space in the workplace, in the very construction of the novel as narrative, in the deliberate subjugation of the feminine voice to the masculine narrative voice.

Linked to this subjugation of the female narrative voice is the theme of the lack of opportunities for promotion, which can be seen as subjugation of the female worker on another level. The promotion issue is dealt with through its effects on Paula in *Amado Amo*. The topic of failing to be considered for the next step in the promotion stakes had already received some treatment in *Chronicle of Unlove*. There, Montero includes a scene in which Ana, a temporary worker in the firm, goes to her boss to ask to be taken on permanent contract. As a single parent, she was anxious to obtain a permanent post, pleading, 'I need security. I've got a child to look after', but her request is refused. In Paula's case, Montero makes it clear that Paula is the 'only person from the old agency who had never been promoted, they... promoted people who had much less ability, they... never gave her a chance, they... pinched her ideas' (*Amado Amo*, p.63).

Despite this obvious discriminatory practice, César voices the opinion that he does not consider Paula's situation to be at all unjust: 'The fact that Paula was not promoted was not after all such an injustice. Women are not the slightest bit ambitious' (*Amado Amo*, p.64). The insensitive assumption made by César has two main objectives. The first belongs to the narrative technique, since Montero wishes to undermine the opinions presented. This technique gradually allows confidence in the narrator to be undermined. The second is an ostensibly objective demonstration of the situation which faces working women. For these reasons, Montero allows the narrator to give his point of view without passing comment but her intention is to provide an example of the type of executive reasoning which continues to lead to a lack of women in top management posts (*Instituto Nacional de Estadisticas*, 1996; Alvira Martín, 1994).

National figures reflect Montero's concerns, pointing to the fact that they had an element of truth in them. Even though Encarnación Valenzuela states (1994a) that Spanish women are 'the strong sex', the figures quoted in her article serve to show how far down the road equality is for Spanish women.

**Table 8.2  Percentages of high-ranking women in the socialist governments of the 1980s and early 1990s and in the People's Party Government of 1996**

|                                   | 1982 % | 1993 % | 1996 % |
|-----------------------------------|--------|--------|--------|
| MPs in Government                 | 5.6    | 16.7   | 9.9    |
| Secretaries of State              | 0      | 14.3   | 0      |
| Under-secretaries of State        | 0      | 5.4    | 7.0    |
| Members of Government Committees  | 6.5    | 9.1    | -      |

*Source*: Adapted from Valenzuela (1994b:22) and Instituto de la Mujer (1997b:107).

Progress has been made in that numbers of women MPs trebled in the ten years from 1982. There were also 14 times as many female Secretaries of State by 1993. The present Spanish Cabinet, elected in March 1996, initially showed another step forward for women at ministerial level, since there were four Government ministries headed by women. However, following recent Cabinet reshuffles in January 1999, there are now only three female Ministers, with Esperanza Aguirre moving aside from her role at Education, following much publicised errors of judgement. Several articles, published by supporters of Aguirre, presented the perspective of her removal in a positive light. She was to stand as Spokeswoman of the upper chamber, the Senate, the first woman to have done so, but although her appointment to the Senate has *cachet*, in such a figurehead position, she loses the hands-on power of a ministerial post (Tocino, 1999:8). There has similarly been a great deal of capital made from the number of women heading the Parliamentary lists in recent local and European elections (June 1999). Such a leading position in the electoral lists would have been unthinkable in the 1980s, when women were regularly accorded positions on the lists such that relatively few of them were successful in obtaining seats (Eyre, 1996). Moreover, many political parties on the left of the political spectrum have implemented a quota system. This system, though much maligned by the right-wing People's Party, currently the party of government in Spain, has, nevethess, had an important impact on increasing the number of women MPs elected. In 1996, the percentage of women elected to Parliament to represent the Socialist Party was 23.5 per cent, whilst the number of women MPs elected for the anti-quota People's Party was 9.9 per cent (Instituto de la Mujer, 1997b:99). Although an advance in the number of women in political life has been undeniable throughout the 1990s and despite the fact that women in Spain do currently occupy positions of power, they have still not reached a percentage representation commensurate with their percentage of the electorate. Cristina Alberdi, an ex-Minister from the Socialist party, commented in an interview granted to *Cambio 16,* that 'the rules of the political game... are masculine', adding that, although this is changing slowly, it will not change fully 'until the day when... democracy demands that no sex makes up more than 60 per cent of MPs' (Valenzuela, 1994a:24).

However, whilst these advances are to be commended, in reality women should have made more progress. As Catherine Davies comments, 'the undeniable improvement of women's situation had defused the whole feminist issue', but she also focuses on the disillusionment Spaniards felt when the 'policies of the socialist Government which had been so promising, had fallen short of many women's expectations' (Davies, 1994:135). Montero was fully aware of the progress which had been made during the years since democracy had been introduced (Montero, 1995b and c). She was, nevertheless, conscious that injustice still existed and shows, through the novel, that complacency must be avoided.

Whilst the main focus of *Amado Amo* is on the internal machinations of the company, the novel touches, at the same time, on women in another secondary role, the company wife. Reflection on this role, reserved for women, and peripheral to the company's activities, also casts light on Montero's representation of women in the workplace. The company wife is depicted at various social functions which reunite the workforce outside working hours. She is shown as the loyal, supportive woman, who provides a foil to her husband's success in the company. The inference is that these company wives do not work, or, at least, there is no mention made of their professional lives, underpinning the fact that they take second place to their husbands. There are various examples of women in this supporting role in *Amado Amo.* The best defined is Tessa, wife of Nacho and faithful female reflection of her husband. She is from Andalusia, a province in the South of Spain, renowned for its landed gentry. Her aristocratic origins are underlined by her hair which is described as 'thick and of pure gold' (*Amado Amo*, p.50). This is surprising in itself as the majority of Andalusian women have the dark hair typical of the region. Nacho's wife's name, Tessa, is English-sounding and high-class. She provides the perfect foil to Nacho, also of aristocratic origin. Moreover, Tessa underlines the bright young executive's success replicated in the personal aspects of his life. It should be noted that for the novel's protagonist, César, a wife is considered to be a desirable possession and a useful accoutrement rather than being a companion in any real sense. There is only one other executive, Matías, whose wife fails to come up to scratch in Golden Line. It is significant that Matías is perceived as a failure, even by César, and ends up committing suicide.

The other executives not only have wives, but their wives display similar characteristics. There are key similarities but also crucial differences between them all:

> He realized that they were all blonde. The wives of all the executive Board. The front rows were a wheatfield. Dyed blonde and energetic, Miguel's wife; dyed blond and anaemic, Quesada's wife; natural blonde and athletic, Morton's wife; blonde and fluffy, Smith's wife; splendid burnished gold, Nacho's wife, Tessa. In the middle of the sea of corn, Matías' ex-wife, with her straight black hair and black dress. She looked like a crow in a cornfield (*Amado Amo*, p.123).

All are blonde but it is to be noted that not all the blondes are equal. The best are precisely the wives of Nacho, Smith and Morton, who are the most important men in the firm. Their wives have natural blonde hair and are perhaps of Anglo-Saxon origin. Quesada and Miguel are not fully in line with the power games which occur within the firm and their attempts to imitate the ways of the firm are mirrored in the dyed blonde hair of their wives. Matías' ex-wife stands out as being a 'crow', as César terms her. Her black hair is outside the norm for the firm, although normal for a Spanish woman. The *topos* of the blonde-haired wife also underlines a wider issue in the Spain of the 1980s which was the servile pursuit of things Anglo-Saxon to the detriment of home-grown talent. Montero picks up on the copying of the Anglo-Saxon wife of the American Managing Director in *Amado Amo*, using it as a critique of the way her countrymen and women set more store on foreign values, whether on the level of how the company is organised, or in terms of copying the hairstyle or life-style of foreign executives and their wives. The novel shows how Quesada and Miguel feel obliged to copy the squash-playing habits of Morton. This slavish imitation is condemned, by implication, as being bad for the workforce and for the country.

In respect of company wives, there is, however, a more notable departure from the norm and that is the case of César. As he is unmarried, he cannot display his 'possession' with the rest of the Directors. César, despite his patrician name, is of low-class origins and his lack of a female companion underlines his personal failure. César sees this lack of wife and child as a direct barrier to success at work, although it is, of course, to be suspected that this is another of the many excuses to shift the blame away from his personal responsibility for failure. Having no wife automatically means that he is excluded from the firm's socialising when it comes to family gatherings or dinner parties and it means that he is differentiated from the other executives by his failure to secure a wife. He recognises the fact with bitterness. César feels diminished by the fact that 'no woman had ever wanted to carry his seed' (*Amado Amo*, p.23). He not only sees a blonde wife as his passport to the social gatherings of the other Directors but he also has an idealised view of family life. Furthermore, paternity is considered to be a closed door, shut for him by women: 'this dictatorship of motherhood' (*Amado Amo*, p.23). The power to give new life is the only power held by women. César feels that he is humiliated by the lack of control over his personal life. This is one of the few points in the novel where a second, presumably female, narrative voice describes César huddled in foetal position under the sheets (*Amado Amo* p.23). The power of the female voice over the male is a theme deployed by Montero in her recently published short story, *La asesina de insectos*, where the husband spends his days trying to escape the lashing tongue of his wife (Montero, 1998:107). She describes him as a 'worm', a shapeless, worthless pre-being.

In addition, as we have seen, there are no female executives and this means that the established norm is the male executive and his wife. In a novelistic world, where failure to conform is seen to be severely punished, both Matías and César are losers. Paula can never break through the established stereotypes either and is, for this reason, doomed never to be admitted to the 'executives' table'.

The injustice, which Montero delineates as women's lot in the world of work, includes the classification of women as sexual objects. Paula represents the sexual side of working relationships since, on the one hand she is César's girlfriend, and on the other, César suspects that she is two-timing him with his rival in the company, Nacho. The narrator recounts how Paula had been César's lover for many years without earning the right to bring any of her belongings to his flat: 'in the five years that they had been together Paula had only earned the right to bring her toothbrush' (*Amado Amo*, p.116). It should be concluded that Paula's lack of power at work is replicated by her lack of power in her personal relationships. César, moreover, treats her with selfish coldness. He phones her only when he is lonely and when he feels in need of some female company (*Amado Amo*, p.31). It is only when César phones her and finds that she has gone out that he realises that he should pay her a little more attention: 'If Paula were to leave him, there would be no-one at all in the world who would bother with him' (*Amado Amo*, p.117). He does not wish to lose her, not because he values her company, but because he does not wish to be left on his own.

The sexual element which accompanies Paula is brought out again in the scene where she wants to take charge of her own destiny. It is significant that when Paula comes to César's home, concerned about a work-related issue, the narrator sees the events in sexual terms. She declines to make love to him because she is on her errand to pass details of the Golden Line contractual agreement to the Press. The scene is visually presented. Paula is seen 'striding about the bedroom with her burning gaze' (*Amado Amo*, p.173), whilst all that César can think of is the satisfaction of his sexual needs. He pleads with Paula: '"Forget all that business and come into bed"' (*Amado Amo*, p.172). César interprets everything that occurs as having sexual significance; he is offended that she does not respond to his advances and decides that the reason for her refusal is that she no longer loves him.

In his paranoia, his suspicion is confirmed that Paula has transferred her affections to Nacho. He accuses Paula of being Nacho's lover and Paula bursts out laughing. During a party at Nacho's house, César had been keeping a close eye on Paula and had read his own interpretation into a silence which fell on their conversation: 'Nacho and Paula had fallen silent' (*Amado Amo*, p.65). César's jealousy causes him to interpret the silence and the exchange of looks. He exclaims: 'People should not be allowed to look at each other so shamelessly in front of everyone' (*Amado Amo*, p.65). The narrator provides an interpretation of the actions of the two partygoers, a distorted mirror through which a glance can be taken as evidence of a sexual relationship.

Nacho's party provided César with an opportunity for reflection on the underhand methods, employed by Nacho in order to ruin César, and in these activities the innocent Paula now becomes implicated. It is significant that this putative crime serves in the end to bring about the dismissal of Paula from Golden Line. César, convinced that Paula was Nacho's mistress by the exchange of looks, betrays her, secure in the knowledge that she had betrayed him with Nacho. From César's point of view, it is a logical step to inform on Paula to Morton. The impression given by the actions of Paula and Nacho is confirmed when César rings Paula in the night and finds that she is out. Her betrayal is finally confirmed, in César's reasoning, by Paula's demonstrable unwillingness to make love, when she calls at César's flat for a copy of the document outlining the norms and conditions of employment, with which she intends to prove discrimination against herself by Golden Line. The last words of the novel recall the pivotal scene in Nacho's house: 'After all, Paula betrayed me first' (*Amado Amo*, p.204).

Montero is touching on one of the most serious problems facing women at work, the casting of a sexual interpretation on any innocent action. The male narrator represents the typical masculine reaction to Paula's refusal to make love. Once again it is clear that Montero seeks to go beyond feminist polemic, a feature of *Chronicle of Unlove* and, instead, allows the existence of sexualisation to be narrated, without comment, as one of the axes of the novel.[5]

The final theme to be dealt with is the woman as victim. The scene in which Paula visits César to obtain a copy of the conditions of employment shows that Paula is taking control of her destiny at work. Montero reveals her liberation, the fact that she is seeking justice, by allowing her voice to be heard directly. She cries: "'Leave me alone. You never take me seriously when it comes to talking about my work'" (*Amado Amo*, p.172).

Unfortunately, when Paula initiates the steps to expose the company for its abuse of power, she brings about her own downfall. She plans to inform the press about the way Golden Line operates and is betrayed on two levels. First of all, the journalist she approaches is hand-in-glove with Morton, and, secondly, César himself is prevailed upon to betray her. He feels justified, even though in doing so he succumbs to the bribe offered by Morton, an invitation to the annual executive convention. He also, whether knowingly or not, takes on the role of company informer and sneak, a role waiting to be filled following Matías' suicide. However, Montero makes it clear that, although César is duped or allows himself to be so, it is Paula who is the main loser, since she is the one who loses her job. The system and its manipulators, whether at the level of Morton, or beyond, from the shadows of the parent company, are the winners.

This novel requires careful reading. From what has been said, it should be recognised that although the perspective offered in the novel is distorted and requires careful reconstruction by the reader, within it the reader can find themes such as lack of opportunity for promotion, lack of opportunity to be heard and discriminatory workplace practices operating against women. A conclusion can be reached as to why Montero designs her novel in this form. Through it, the masculine narrator demonstrates his compliance with discriminatory practice. It is woman's struggle to be heard which the novel presents.

This novel can, then, be termed a study of subversion. The reader is called upon to reflect and recreate a system other than that presented in the novel. The system which the reader is left to create would be one based on solidarity, justice and recognition of merit. In *Amado Amo*, the reader has an active role in reconstructing the true meaning of events and in decoding the feminine voice. The act of creating a female voice itself develops solidarity among readers of *Amado Amo*. Moreover, the role of the novel in heightening awareness of the lack of justice in the workplace, particularly for women, its presentation of the workplace as Machiavellian in its intrigue, together with its revelation of unconscious and deliberate policy to discriminate against female workers, has a positive function. Ultimately, there is hope that through their awareness, and through solidarity, women can ensure that the new legislation is applied and can take advantage of the new opportunities which democratic Spain offers.

## Notes

[1] *Amado Amo* is a play on words meaning *Beloved Boss*, but, at the same time, it means *I Love, when I am Loved*. References to the book will be given in parenthesis in the text.

[2] Translations of all Spanish texts are the work of the author of the chapter.

[3] The Political, Professional and Labour Rights Law of 15th July 1961 reiterated the need for husbands to grant their permission for their wives to work; this was termed the '*licencia marital*'.

[4] *La educación en España. Bases para una política educativa*, Ministerio de Educación (Madrid: 1968). This reference is cited in Alberdi (1986:71).

[5] Sexual relationships between male and female staff, with the male in a dominant executive role and the female in a subservient role, are also a feature of *Chronicle*, in which Ana has unsatisfactory sexual relations with Soto Amon, her boss. Once again Montero uses wordplay: 'Amon' meaning Big Boss.

# 9 Female Labour Migration to Japan: Myth and Reality

NICOLA PIPER

## Introduction

Migratory movements have always involved the participation of women (Zlotnik, 1995), both internal and international.[1] Despite this fact, however, some commentators have criticised the lack of attention given to the active participation of women in previous works on global migration processes which have tended to focus on male migrants (Morokvasic, 1983 and 1984). Women have mainly been viewed as 'dependants' (that is, wives and mothers), but, as has rightly been argued, they must be acknowledged as *both* passive and active participants in migratory movements (Gulati, 1994). It is the latter which serves as the focus for this chapter: the increasing role of 'independent' female workers in recent years in international migration. The number of female migrants has increased globally (OECD, 1993) and in some instances even outnumbers male migrants. Major exporters of female labour are located in Asia (Gulati, 1994) with the Philippines 'exporting' most, followed by Thailand, Sri Lanka and Indonesia.[2]

Migration from the Asian periphery to Japan has become the focus of considerable interest and controversy during the last decade. The current migration of female labour is by no means a new phenomenon. The import and export of female labour has been an integral part of Japan's modernisation process. Female textile workers, for example, composed the first widespread category of wage employment in Japan, and remained a major part of the industrial workforce until the 1930s (Tsurumi, 1994; Bernstein, 1991). The majority of these workers were the daughters of poor farming families sent to work to help family finances for a few years before returning to their village to marry. Their jobs, predominantly unskilled, were characterised by extremely poor working conditions and exceedingly low wages. During the period 1910 to 1945 considerable numbers of Korean women from the colonial periphery entered Japan voluntarily or involuntarily as low grade industrial labour (Weiner, 1989). The plight of the so-called 'military comfort women' is another example of the 'use' of female labour in Japan's modern history (Howard, 1995).   Nonetheless, female labour migration has historically been distinguished from male, either legally, in the sense that they are not regarded as 'workers', or in terms of super-exploitation, with regard to poor pay and working conditions.   Japan has, therefore, experienced similar patterns of female labour exploitation as other industrialised countries, but as for the contemporary context, there are differences in its socio-economic stages of development.

This chapter is largely based on ongoing research and offers a preliminary analysis of female labour migration to Japan set within the broader context of genderised labour migration in Pacific Asia.   Japan's current experience of labour immigration is characterised by the overwhelming presence of migrant women in the sex and entertainment industry.   The situation of Thai and Filipino women is central to the discussion as they constitute the bulk of workers employed in these industries. In their capacity as entertainers and 'sex workers', these women are also likelier to encounter more problems and obstacles than male migrant workers. This is due to their marginal status within the labour market and to the nature of the labour they sell, and because in many cases their jobs are not socially recognised as 'work' (Ito, 1992).   The starting point for this analysis is, therefore, the general characteristics of the Japanese entertainment and sex industry, as well as the specific role and position of Filipino and Thai women employed therein.   These issues will then be contextualised in the dominant gender ideology of Japan.   I argue, however, that exploitative practices in regard to female migrant workers from Asia are not only based on 'gender', but also 'race'.   Therefore, a racial component will be added to this discussion and then finally I will discuss the socio-legal recognition of female migrant workers.[3]

## Characteristics of the Japanese Entertainment and Sex Industry

*General Background*

There is a long cultural tradition linking entertainment and prostitution[4] in Japan.   Today's western-style bar hostessing is rooted in the geisha tradition and is, in some respects, a modern version of that more artful manner of entertaining men.[5]   The geisha system emerged during the middle of the Edo period (1600-1868),[6] and by the mid-18th century it was confined to government-licensed brothel quarters.   Despite the fact that the geisha were legally distinguished[7] from the courtesans and prostitutes who provided sexual services, the distinction was often blurred (Kodansha Encyclopedia of Japan, 1983:15). The flirtatious roles which had traditionally been played by the geisha now belong to the hostess, a profession which first emerged in the 1920s with so-called café-girls (*jokyu*) (Greenfeld, 1994). Where the geisha embodies stereotypical images of the 'old' Japan with rigorous training in traditional arts, such as the playing of shamisen and fan dancing, the hostess is modern with no special training required, but karaoke singing, pouring drinks and flattering men's egos (Allison, 1994). Since the 1920s, the hostess industry has flourished at the expense of the traditional geisha.[8] Sex is not necessarily part of the hostess service, depending on the type of club and the individual woman involved.

An officially sanctioned public prostitution system was established in 1528 (Gulati, 1994) and was not abolished until 1956 under the Prostitution Prevention Law which rendered prostitution an illegal activity. The introduction of this law, however, was followed by a marked growth in the number of 'massage parlours' (Japan Anti-Prostitution Association [JAPA], 1995). The sex industry was, thus, merely moved to public bath houses (Asian Women's Association [AWA], 1988), and prostitution survives today under a variety of guises, such as the so-called 'Soaplands' (Ida, 1986). This has led the JAPA to speak of a 'modern version of the state-regulated prostitution system' (1995:8) as the Government has taken virtually no action to control these places. The general tolerance of prostitution is not only embedded in the historical and cultural importance of the entertainment and sex industry in Japanese society, but also in its high profitability. The *Weekend Keizai* (The Weekly Economic Forecast) published by *Asahi Shimbun* (6 April 1991), for instance, has been quoted as estimating the gross earnings of the sex-related industry to be Yen 4.2 trillion (£260 million) (Matsuda, 1992). According to the same source, earnings from prostitution alone are estimated to be about Yen five billion (£33 million).

There are instances of the 'use' of sexual labour provided by *foreign* women in Japanese pre- and post-war history. The plight of the 'military comfort women', mainly Korean, constitutes a well-known example. Korea was again the main destiny during the post-war period, this time of packaged sex tours dating from the early 1970s which attracted many Japanese men.[9] Due to successful demonstrations against sex tours in Korea and elsewhere, however, the percentage of male 'sex tour' (1995) travellers has decreased. According to the JAPA this also indicates that fewer tours are being organised. Instead, however, the number of Asian women entering Japan as 'entertainers' has been on the increase.[10]

The presence of migrant women intending to work in the sex-related industries, led to the creation of a new term: *Japayuki-san* (Yamatani Tetsuo, 1989) which translates as 'Miss Going-to-Japan'. This constitutes a historical continuum to the *Karayuki-san* ('Miss-Going-Abroad') phenomenon, which occurred earlier in this century. During this period, poverty forced many young Japanese women from rural areas to go abroad to Southeast Asian and other countries to work as prostitutes (Iyori, 1987). Today, the traffic in human bodies has reversed direction. Because of increased economic power, Japan now imports women from countries such as the Philippines, Thailand, Taiwan, South Korea, Latin America and most recently even from Russia and Eastern Europe (Sellek, 1996).

*Specific Context of Filipino and Thai Female Migrants*

Migrant female workers from the Philippines enter Japan on a working visa which covers all kinds of show business-related employment, such as singers or dancers. But most end up working in the entertainment and sex industry as hostesses, strippers, or even prostitutes (Iyori, 1987). A new category called 'entertainers' visa' was introduced in the early 1980s by the Japanese Embassy in the Philippines as a response to protests against sex tourism. In this way, the need for Japanese men to go abroad for certain pleasures was reduced by easing the import of sexual labour. This visa is valid for two months renewable up to a maximum of six months. Women from the Philippines make up the majority of these visa-holders. In this capacity, their working conditions are better than those of Thai women. Due to their legal status, Filipinas are less likely than Thai women to find themselves in situations of extreme sexual exploitation or suffer infringements of human rights.[11] They also tend to have higher educational levels,[12] possess a working knowledge of the English language, and are able to read Roman letters. According to the Philippine Desk, a support organisation whose activities are confined to Tokyo, despite varieties in educational backgrounds, there is also a tendency for more professional Filipinas, nurses and teachers, for example, to come to Japan as undocumented workers.

By contrast, Thai women enter Japan on tourist visas without even the minimal contractual and legal advantages of the entertainers' visa. As current Japanese immigration law only permits the entry of skilled workers, apart from exceptional cases, Thai women enter Japan via second and third countries with the help of networks and intermediaries in Thailand, Japan and elsewhere. This sometimes requires multiple sets of false documents arranged by brokers which in turn increases risks and costs. Upon arrival, their travel and identification documents are usually confiscated by their employers to prevent escape.   Wages are often withheld until they have worked off the 'debts' deriving from fees only for their travel arrangements.   These debts are estimated on average to amount to Yen four million (£29,000) (Migrant Women Worker's Research & Action Committee [MWWRAC], 1995).

There are two main groups of Thai women: those who have already been engaged in the sex industry in Thailand before coming to Japan, but who are led to believe that their earnings in Japan will be far higher; and those, often from rural areas, who were lured to the country by recruiters on the grounds of false promises.   Instead of working at jobs ranging from waitressing or factory work to modelling, they end up working in bars and clubs (Stalker, 1994).   A women's support organisation in Tokyo, SALAA, estimates that 80-85 per cent of all Thai women are smuggled into Japan and forced into prostitution by criminal gangs.   Although some of the Thai women know very well before arriving in Japan that they will work as prostitutes, their working and living conditions have been described as extremely severe.   This has led several NGOs to condemn the situation as sexual slavery (MWWRAC, 1995). As a result, Thai women are likely to experience the most serious human rights violations among all foreign migrants.   Moreover, they have the fewest support resources available to them in Japan for a number of reasons:

- Almost all Thais are Buddhist and cannot seek help from the Catholic Church in the same way as their Filippina counterparts (MWWRAC, 1995).

- Not only is their educational background lower, but virtually all are illiterate in Japanese and English; some of them are barely teenagers.

- They are sent to Japan by well organised recruiting agencies often connected with underground mafia type of organisations, so they are subject to high levels of coercive control.

- As large-scale migration of Thais to Japan was at the time still a recent phenomenon, there is no significant history of international migration between the two countries, as opposed to the Philippines which has a longer immigration history to Japan: therefore, the Thai community in Japan is relatively small and fragmented.

- Thai government agencies have been reluctant to assist female migrants due to their illegal status and their employment in the sex industry; this would damage Thailand's image as well as the relationship with the

Japanese government which is an important contributor in terms of ODA and direct investment.

The most common work-related problems encountered by female migrant workers are: contract violation, non-payment of wages, verbal and physical assaults, forced prostitution, rape and forced use of drugs, illegal confinement and the confiscation of documents. There are a number of organisations trying to support these women, such as Labour Relations Offices set up by local councils. One of the main problems, however, is that the employer can only be sued for forcing or organising prostitution if the names of customers are provided before the case is brought to trial. Customers do not usually reveal their names and even if they do, Japanese names can be hard to remember for foreigners unfamiliar with the Japanese language (AWA, 1988). Not only do these migrant women usually not know the names of their customers, but are also kept deliberately ignorant of the names of their employers, or owners of their workplaces. This is aggravated by the fact that they are often moved from one place to another within short periods of time.

The Immigration Bureau has been trying to prosecute unlawful brokers and traders, check out unauthorised entrants and deport them back to their countries of origin. This has not, however, been very successful as the JAPA informs us that

> the effect of the measures taken by the Immigration Bureau only results in the deporting of women workers and leaves brokers or traders unquestioned. It should be the criminal syndicates rather than women workers that receive legal discipline (1995:18).

As elsewhere, the employment of immigrant women in highly industrialised countries occurs particularly, but not exclusively, in metropolitan areas which have undergone a major shift from secondary to tertiary industries and have a rapidly expanding service sector (Sassen, 1991). The major areas of employment for foreign entertainers are Tokyo, Osaka and Nagoya, but according to Komai (1995:76), in 1991, undocumented female workers were apprehended in *all* 46 prefectures, with the single exception of Saga prefecture. As a considerable proportion of these women are entertainers, this suggests that they can be found in smaller provincial cities too.

**Dominant Gender Ideology in Japan**

The engagement of female migrant workers mainly in the Japanese entertainment and sex industry reflects both the dominant gender ideology and notions of sexuality in modern Japan (Bernstein, 1991). Contemporary forms of discrimination against women derive from the ideals of Neo-Confucianism which provided much of the ideological basis to traditional elite family life and the status of women. The androcentric values of the Samurai code were institutionalised by the Meiji system (1868-1912) during which the Japanese centralised nation-state was created. This resulted in a social structure which generally lowered the position of women. Up until today, men have been expected to be the main breadwinners, women to be 'good wives and wise mothers' (*ryoosai kenbo*):[13] a concept which in the contemporary context signifies a full-time housewife who takes care of children at home as opposed to an increasing number of married women who have joined the labour force (Fujita, 1989). In a country where people work comparatively long hours, this leads to the belief that men are entitled to well-deserved relaxation in karaoke and hostess bars with little opposition from the conventional Japanese wife (Allison, 1994).

A further ideological element is provided by the institution of the male-dominated family system (*ie seido*) which emphasises lineal continuity. Under this system, one of the most important tasks that women must fulfil is childbirth. Although legally abolished in 1947 under the externally imposed postwar constitution, practices derived from the *ie* system persist (Hendry, 1981). Placing women in the domestic sphere creates a paradox: there have historically always been numerous examples of women performing social functions in the public domain (Bernstein, 1991). Many of these women have been and still are working in the entertainment and sex industry, professions which are based on sexualised femininity (Allison, 1994).

As the main historical function of the wife is to bear an heir for the continuity of the household, the role of the wife as an 'object' of romantic and sexual attraction for her husband is weak. This represents a further denial of the wife's own subjective sexuality (Coleman, 1983). Japanese gender ideology has encouraged men to have affairs with women of the entertainment quarters (Bernstein, 1991). By contrast, women are divided into 'good women', or housewives, and 'bad women', or prostitutes, and this dichotomy has been carried over into the present day (AWA, 1991). The Japanese gender ideology, and attitudes and actions associated therein, are directly related to the migratory movement of Filipino and Thai women to Japan. Generally, women are seldom considered workers as such, with the exception of the geisha who was/is considered a professional, and while a certain aspect of the entertainment business is referred to as the 'sex industry', those women who work in it are not granted a workers' status, but are normally treated only as sex objects (Ito, 1992).

The expansion of the entertainment industry needs to be seen in the wider social context as 'an inseparable part of Japan's economic system' reflecting the situation of women and men in Japan (AWA, 1988:9). The rigid gender division of labour, of which the sex industry is both a cause and a consequence, has been described as a relationship between the corporate 'warrior', the 'professional housewife' and the 'entertainers' (Matsui, 1991; Kanai, 1995). Japanese men are forced to work an average of 2,100 hours per year, compared to 1,600-1,700 hours in Europe and the United States (US). with very few holidays. Entertainment has become a subsidised form of compensation for intense work patterns (Allison, 1994). The increasing demand for *foreign* women in the sex industry derives from two factors: firstly, Japanese women possess higher levels of education and seek employment which offers high status, greater remuneration, and the opportunity to meet prospective marriage partners (Gulati, 1994); and secondly, the expansion of the service industry during the 'bubble' economy. It has also been driven by campaigns against sex tourism of the late 1980s conducted by women in Japan and elsewhere in Asia.

**Racial Dimension**

The current structure of the Japanese sex-related industry is but the latest phase in an historical continuum which extends from licensed prostitution of the Edo period through to the crimes committed by the Japanese government against the 'military comfort women', mainly conscripted from regions under colonial control who were, according to Howard (1995) mainly Korean, during the Pacific War (Matsuda, 1992). The same ideology of 'race' which fuelled imperial expansion between 1895 and 1945 also served to legitimise the exploitation of labour, both female and male, in Korea, China, and Taiwan. In the contemporary context, too, a racial hierarchy is apparent in the sex industry which distinguishes between Japanese entertainers and those from other Asian countries. Japanese and western hostesses, for example, tend to be mainly employed in first-class clubs or bars where higher wages are paid and where prostitution is far more the 'choice' of the individual women than in lower class establishments (Allison, 1994).

This history of sexual labour provided by Asian women continues in the postwar period. A number of commentators have mentioned 'the legacy of US military bases' which has 'conditioned the demand for prostitutes' and facilitated the initial infrastructural development by 'creating a conducive climate for entrepreneurs to organise prostitution' (Thanh-Dam, 1983:537). Following the American withdrawal, entertainment centres upon military bases have been maintained mainly in Thailand and the Philippines and 'now serve the needs of a different category of visitor, the tourist' (1983:537). Lee (1991) suggests, in a piece on *Prostitution and Tourism in South East Asia*, that previous studies have given the impression that prostitution is a reflection of specifically Asian practices and attitudes. She does, however, argue that the purchase of sexual services is less about buying sexuality than it is about exercising power over another human being, in this case over a foreign (Asian) woman. This in turn suggests an element of racialisation, a concept which requires the examination of the conditions under which specific processes of racialisation have taken place rather than the acceptance of the idea of 'race' as a biological given (Miles, 1989; Small, 1994). In the context of organised sex tours, for instance, this is reflected in the promotion campaigns of travel agencies. According to Lee, these agencies 'offer often a deeply *racist* mythology of Asian women to European or Japanese men when they speak of them as "without desire for emancipation but full of warm sensuality"' (1991:91, my emphasis). In the same context, Robinson has observed that 'Asian is a site of fantasy for men in an era when they feel that "traditional" values of male pre-eminence in the family are being undermined' (1996:53). Discourses centre upon Asian women as truly feminine while depicting the East as the source of traditional family values. Virtually identical racist stereotypes of Asian women also exist in the Japanese context. Since Japanese women have lately begun to reject masculine claims of their natural superiority, Japanese men, too, 'are finding increasing recourse in the idea of the more submissive "Asian" women to fill traditional sexual and maternal roles' (Pollack, 1993:708), even if the Asian woman has 'to be forced into recognising and fulfilling her essential nature', as Pollack rightly remarks. Sano notes that 'there is a racial and nationalistic arrogance, a tendency to sexualise a hierarchical relationship that these Japanese assume exists between their country and other Asian nations' (quoted by Allison, 1994:139-40). Underlying this is a Japanese sense of superiority, itself rooted in Japan's history as an aggressive colonising Asian power, a fact which partly explains Korea's popularity as a tourist destination for Japanese 'sex tourists' and high proportion of Japanese-Korean women employees in the sex industry 'at home'.

This racialisation of foreign prostitutes confirms Glenn's (1992) argument that sexual *and* racial stereotypes have been historically institutionalised within labour markets. Therefore, assumptions about gender are not only informed by sexism, but also by racism (Whitworth, 1994). According to Tyner (1994), these stereotypes are already at work in the pre-migration process: gendered and racial assumptions are manifest within labour recruitment processes channelling women migrants into domestic services and sex-related industries before their arrival in the 'host' countries. The combined impact of sexism and racism on the labour market also informs the recognition, or non-recognition, of female migrants as workers.

**Socio-legal Recognition of Female Migrant Workers**

Many female migrant workers tend to take on employment in a narrow range of industries, as domestic workers and in semi-skilled or unskilled service occupations, and thus find themselves in the domain of sex-affective services, care-taking and social maintenance of labour. This type of work has been described as reproductive labour (Brochmann, 1991).

It might be useful at this point to reflect on the meaning of 'work'. According to Grint, work tends to be

> an activity that transforms nature and is usually undertaken in social situations, but exactly what counts as work is dependent on the specific social circumstances under which such activities are undertaken, and, critically, how these circumstances and activities are interpreted by those involved (1991:7).

From this, past and present definitions of work act as cultural symbols or as mirrors of power. In other words, work is socially constructed and there is no permanent or objective activity called 'work'. Thus, the very model of work has been criticised as the reflection of androcentric or patriarchal systems in which the division between work and home is not free from ideological notions. In Japan, too, work is considered a 'male realm' (Allison, 1994:91). Despite a larger proportion of women entering salaried employment outside the home,

> work is still considered, ideologically and culturally, an activity that is more important for men and that identifies the male more than it does the female. A woman may work, but her social status and place in society is not defined primarily as worker (Allison, 1994:91).

The non-recognition of women as workers also applies to the case of female labour migrants, as summarised by Morokvasic: 'The work of native women and migrant women does not always fit in the reigning ideology of work and is... not always recognised as an economic activity at all' (1984:887).

Tyner (1994) and Singhanetra-Renard and Prabhudhanitisarn (1992) have argued that migrant women have, if compared with their male counterparts, less employment opportunities in the general labour market. Female workers from Thailand and the Philippines have few employment alternatives at home and abroad, due to their limited education, as in the case of Thailand, or to genderised channelling into specific roles. When they are prevented from obtaining higher education, or even vocational training, they are practically excluded from higher skilled and higher paying occupations. In Thailand, for example, the son's education is regarded as more important than the daughter's and 'it is common to find that a son's education is supported not by parents but by a daughter who has migrated to the city' (Singhanetra-Renard and Prabhudhanitisarn, 1992:163). It should be noted that both men and women opt for overseas migration because of lack of employment opportunities in their home country, but women are more likely to be channelled into gender specific jobs. Therefore, as Tryner (1994) rightly argues, female employment in either service sector jobs or entertainment and sex-related work represents an absence of choice. Not only in Thailand, but also in the Philippines, the lack of opportunities 'coupled with limited opportunities based on subservience and sexuality, reflects an institutionalised system of oppression' (Tryner, 1994:607).

In the Japanese context, between 1979 and 1985, women occupied about 90 per cent of the total number of foreign workers, 80 per cent of whom worked in the sex industry (MWWRAC, 1995). Female migrants had, therefore, been entering Japan in fairly large numbers before any significant inflows of male migrants took place. However, 'it was not until the latter began to arrive that the "migrant invasion" generated any public response' (Tyner, 1994:608). It seems, therefore, to be a general tendency in Japan to deny these women the status of 'workers'. This is also reflected on an institutional level in the Japanese Immigration Law and labour-related laws.

*Immigration Law*

In practice, Japan's immigration policy restricts employment opportunities for Asian women to one area: entertainment. Under current laws, employment visas are only granted for jobs that cannot be done by Japanese, such as professors, teachers, chefs and entertainers. This does not, however, reflect the real need of the Japanese economy which is one of the reasons for the high number of undocumented workers of whom there are now more men than women (Sellek, 1996). For women, classification as an 'entertainer' is simply a matter of convenience to obtain a visa which allows them to enter Japan, since they are actually engaged in work as hostesses and other jobs related to the sex industry (MWWRAC, 1995). In other words, they enter legally but engage in activities which their status of residence does not actually permit, or continue to work after their visas have expired. In this way, their status becomes 'illegal'. Thus, a significant proportion of all foreign workers in Japan are undocumented or unauthorised as the result of the government's visa and entry policy.

*Labour Laws*[14]

Female migrant workers have been subject to a number of violations of the Labour Standards Law or other labour-related laws:

- Workers from Asian neighbour countries applying for visas under such job titles as 'entertainers' are supposed to work officially under contract, but in reality they are 'dispatched' which is illegal in Japan. The government, thus, ignores, or tacitly approves of, the violation of the Manpower Dispatching Business Act of 1985 which forbids the involvement of subcontracting agencies or brokers in dispatching unskilled workers. In addition, practices such as 'skimming', where a portion of wages is confiscated by a mediating agent, infringes on the Labour Standards Law. Charging fees for assistance in finding work constitutes a breach of the Employment Security Act.

- The entertainment visa is issued for a maximum of six months. It is a regular practice for wages to be withheld until this six month period of employment has been completed, and to be paid to the women at the airport when they are about to leave. This practice has been adopted in order to prevent entertainers from running away from their employers. This is, however, a violation of Article 24 of the Labour Standards Law which regulates the payment of wages and stipulates that wages should be given to employees at least once per month.

- The salaries paid to Asian female 'entertainers' are commonly lower than those of their Japanese or western counterparts. This is a violation of Article 28 of the Labour Standards Law which regulates minimum wages.

- Another problem area is that of penalties. Hostesses are fined for failing to satisfy *Dohan*, requiring entertainers to attract and invite more customers to the club during off-club hours, for being absent from work without notice, or coming late. These penalties are prohibited by Articles 16 and 91. The former forbids contracts that specify compensation to the employer, the latter states that each subtraction of fines from employees' wages may not exceed one half the amount of the daily wage or one tenth the amount of the total paycheck. This article also renders the introduction of penalties for absence an illegal act.

- A further serious problem is the imposition of work not specified in the contract. Article 5 of the Labour Standards Law prohibits this conduct. However, in many cases entertainers/hostesses are coerced into performing as topless dancers or engaging in prostitution.

- Last but not least, the confiscation of travel documents and passports is illegal as it violates Article 5 which forbids forced labour.

Furthermore, regarding labour rights, 'entertainers' are excluded from worker's accident compensation insurance and health insurance. The national health insurance scheme can only be entered after a residential period of one year, but the entertainer visa is limited to a maximum of six months. In addition, there are no restrictions on overtime pay and on working hours.

As a result, it can be said that the content of the work of women who come to Japan under the category of 'entertainer' is far from the actual meaning of 'entertainer' as defined by Japanese Immigration Law. Similarly, they remain largely unprotected by current labour laws. As the entertainment visa is, however, more or less the only visa available to Asian women, this means if Asian female workers want to work legally in Japan, they must abandon their rights as 'labour', as stipulated in the Labour Standards Law.

## Concluding Remarks

This chapter demonstrates that until the mid-1980s there was little official recognition of international labour migration in Japan despite the presence of a considerable number of female migrants. One of the reasons for this is that female migrants have not been recognised as 'workers', either institutionally or socially. As opposed to their male counterparts, the bulk of female migrants to Japan experience super-exploitation on the basis of 'race', 'gender' and the commercialisation of the female body. This exploitation is rooted in the sexual division of labour reinforced by public policy as reflected in the entertainment visa system.

The issue of employment in the entertainment and sex industry is related to problems which are fundamental to women's role in the global workforce and to problems which are specifically rooted in Japanese socio-historical circumstances. Women's lack of economic and educational opportunities, resulting in prostitution becoming an important means of survival in a male-dominated society is related to the former. As for the latter, the long history of feminised types of entertainment and the use of prostitution, 'at home' and 'abroad', involving Japanese and foreign women, combined with a gender ideology based on the slogan of 'good wife, wise mother' have led to employment opportunities being socially constructed on the basis of 'gender' and 'race'.

The question of international migration involves more than immigration control: it must include the protection of foreign migrants. The Japanese state's passivity in confronting the reality of trade and trafficking in Asian women, however, expresses its androcentric and racialised character. The official recognition of these women as workers would be an important step towards the improvement of their socio-legal position. At the same time, entry into other types of employment should be legalised so that women would have the opportunity to work in areas other than the entertainment and sex-related industries. This would be one step towards improving migrant women's position as 'workers' and as 'Asians' in Japan.

## Notes

[1] A world-wide analysis of census data for the period 1970 to 1986 found that about 77 million people lived outside their country of origin of whom 48 per cent were women (Stalker, 1994:106).

[2] The ILO estimates that some 800,000 Asian women leave their countries of origin for jobs abroad each year (*Migration News*, vol. 3(6), 1996).

[3] A considerable amount of information contained in this chapter was obtained from various NGOs directly engaged with foreign migrant workers during a one-month visit to Tokyo during March 1996.

[4] 'Prostitution' is here understood in its conventional sense as 'the provision of sexual services against payment' (Thanh-Dam, 1983:535).

[5] Geisha were 'women entertainers of a traditional type, who provide singing, dancing, conversation, games, and companionship to customers in certain restaurants' (Kodansha Encyclopedia of Japan, 1983:14).

[6] The very first geisha were male entertainers and only gradually did such entertaining

become a primarily female occupation (Kodansha Encyclopedia of Japan, 1983:15).

[7] And not only legally: in Eastern societies, brothels and concubinage have also had a distinct class connotation. According to Thanh-Dam, '[c]ourtesanery was widely practised in monarchist circles, and concubinage was common among powerful lords whose accumulation of wives mirrored their accumulation of power.... On the other hand, brothels served commoners.... Women working in brothels were usually bought as slaves...' (1983:535).

[8] The Kodansha Encyclopedia of Japan informs that the total number of geisha in the 1920s was about 80,000 reduced to around 17,000 in the late 1970s (1983:14).

[9] Thanh-Dam mentions a figure of 'more than one million Japanese tourists' who visited Thailand, the Philippines, South Korea, Taiwan and Hong Kong on such tours in 1982 (1983:533).

[10] The number of registered foreign entertainers in 1993 was 28,500 (Japan Immigration Bureau, Ministry of Justice). This figure represents only a small portion of the women employed in the entertainment and sex industry as many of them are not registered. Komai, therefore, suggests a figure of more than 80,000 foreign women working in this particular industry (1995:72).

[11] This is confirmed by the number of Thai women seeking assistance and support in shelters such as HELP in Tokyo where the number of Thais has surpassed the number of Filipino women since 1990.

[12] A general survey of Filipinas trying to find employment abroad found that 60 per cent of them were college students compared to 30 per cent for male migrants (Stalker, 1994:107).

[13] This slogan derives from the Meiji period. The influence of this ideology on contemporary Japanese society has been noted by a number of commentators (Smith, 1987; Uno, 1993).

[14] The information in this section largely derives from two informal talks with a representative of the Labour Relations Office of a particular part of Tokyo.

# 10 Conclusion: That 2020 Vision?

MAIREAD OWEN

## Introduction

In this final chapter, I draw together some of the constant themes that have emerged throughout the contributions in relation to 'women and work' and ask, are we indeed entering into an age of post-feminism where women's work experience will take on a new and unexpected character, both at the individual and social level. If these trends continue and are projected into the coming years, does a consistent picture emerge? What sort of experience of work will women throughout the world, of different classes, ages, ethnic backgrounds, physical abilities and sexual orientations, encounter in this immediate cliché, the New Millennium? What sort of relationship will their labour bear to capitalism and to patriarchy?

## Changing Patterns

Many writers have written over the last 20 years or so of the changes in the nature of work in our society. Increasingly, we are witnessing the death throes of the heavy industries which were the core of the Industrial Revolution. The pits are grassed over or have become industrial museums, the shipyards are closed, the roar of the furnaces in the steelworks is dying down.

Service industries are growing and multiplying but the work within these industries differs from that of the heavy industries which grew in the nineteenth century. It is this new pattern which is coming to be the template of modern work organisation. Dual labour market theories (Barron and Norris, 1976: Beechey, 1986; Dex, 1985; Doeringer and Piore, 1971: Hartmann, 1981; Walby, 1986) point to the fact that the monolithic work forces of the large multinational, transnational and national companies are more and more becoming divided into a core and periphery: a small core of workers with essential skills and experience together with a growing army of peripheral workers brought in on short-time contracts, on part-time hours, as temporary workers, as outworkers. As described in so many of the chapters of this book, flexibility is the mantra. Globalisation and capitalism's inexorable drive to maximise profits, encouraged by the shifts to New Right, free market, laissez-faire policies in some of the biggest producing industrialised nations, lead to the movement to minimise the cost of that most recalcitrant of the forces of production, people.

Joanne Cook's chapter points out the importance of critically deconstructing 'flexibility' and shows how universally the ideology of flexibility as a good has been accepted. One does not need to be a die-hard Marxist to see a ruling ideology neatly selling the idea that it is to the employee's benefit that s/he should stay at home to work, thus saving the employer the costs of several factors of production.

Part-time working and temporary contracts are increasing. As Jill Rubery (1996) has suggested, for a huge number of occupations in Britain the security and stability once associated with her examples of the civil service, health professionals and banking, are disappearing. Privatisation, the introduction of private sector management techniques to the public service sector and the crucial use of information technology in banking and similar services have led to a situation of

> the dismantling of the tried and tested, and well-known employment systems associated with the job, with the result that job and career choice is inhibited not only by the number of jobs available but also by lack of information on what responsibilities, rewards and security are likely to be associated with a particular career or training decision (Rubery, 1996:25).

The chapters from Hilary Rollin and Jean Burrell and from Catherine Fletcher bear out the increasing instability in areas of work traditionally entered by women.

The pattern of part-time working is repeated throughout the developed industrial nations, though it is essential to bear in mind that this is for different reasons and with different results within the social organisation of different countries. As Janice Monk and Maria Dolors Garcia-Ramon suggest, 'the reasons why women are working part-time, which women are involved and the implications of that work for their daily lives and for career advancement differ markedly (1996:20). In Britain, overwhelmingly, part-time work is chosen by women to fit in with domestic commitments (Gallie, 1996; Gregory, 1999; Witz, 1993). As Jeanne Gregory suggests,

> part-time work could therefore be regarded as a trap for women, which marginalises their position in the labour market, reduces their chances of

economic independence and lets men 'off the hook' as far as domestic responsibilities are concerned (1999:394).

This point is forcibly made in the chapter by Linda Walsh and Liz James in their ironic suggestion that women *choose* part-time work, short term contracts and 'flexible working': 'Women choose low pay!' In Britain the growth of part-time employment may have more than a little to do with the lack of protection hitherto for part-time workers. This may change depending on the strength of European Union initiatives (ch.2; Gregory and O'Reilly, 1996; Rees, 1999), the effects of new legislation and how far there is a real commitment to equality in employment. A further factor in Britain has also been a social acceptance that mothers, rather than parents, should bear the ultimate responsibility for children and since childcare facilities, especially from the state, are poor, the only alternative is part-time working built around school hours. However, it is often overlooked that, as Monk and Garcia-Ramon (1996) point out, it is not just mothers who work part-time. In Eastern Europe many older women work part-time as this is seen as a transition to retirement. Equally many women in agricultural areas work part-time both in day-to-day terms and also seasonally, often combining agricultural work with involvement in tourism. While Rollin and Burrell (ch.3) reiterate this point, that the definitions of part-time work and its apprehension as 'good' or 'bad' for women differ in different societies, they suggest that in general part-time work is not beneficial and believe this and other 'atypical' work patterns are set to continue:

> The increase in 'atypical' work, the economic downturn, increased competition and employment crises have exposed (women) to unemployment, part-time work that is imposed rather than chosen, (particularly among young women) and reduction in pay brought by attempts to redistribute work in the name of solidarity (p.51).

The contracting out of services by many governmental organisations and larger companies as part of the 'downsizing' of the 1980s and early 1990s has also led to less secure employment. As John Allen and Nick Henry (1996) observe,

> Our argument in brief is that what is new about the growth of these industries is not so much the absolute increase in job numbers but rather the transformation of the employment relations experienced by those who have been pushed out of secure employment or who are entering the bottom end of the labour market for the first time. More significantly, we argue that this transformation is part of a

wider political and economic shift in the nature of employment relations in the UK, a shift which could be said to be leading towards a new employment based upon *precarious employment* (1996:66, emphasis in original).

More and more people are becoming self-employed.   As Granger et al. (1995:499) point out, the rise in the category of the self-employed has been the subject of much interest to social scientists and politicians alike in recent years.  Throughout the long years of the Industrial Revolution there had been a decline in the importance of self-employment as rural workers and the artisans of the towns alike were drawn into the new factory culture.  However this two-century old decline has been halted in most countries of the developed world, particularly in Britain (OECD, 1986).  Especially with the rise of the New Right in the earlier years of the Thatcher administration, the rise in the numbers of self-employed was hailed as the 'crank wheel' for a new prosperity and, indeed, the necessary replacement for the old heavy industries. This, of course, underlies such projects as the Prince's Trust and many other British start-up agencies.  However, it has been increasingly realised that while the number of small new businesses starting up is growing, so also are the number of bankruptcies one or two years down the line.

> More recently, however, the perception of the resurgence of the self-employed as a measure of positive economic development has been challenged by research linking the growth of self-employment to the employment policies of large firms and the condition of the labour market during periods of recession (Granger et al., 1995:499).

Employment in organisations can be equally uncertain.  It is not just at the individual level that work is changing.  At the other end of the employment scale from the 'small is beautiful' is the globalisation of industry and commerce.  Increasingly the multinationals bestride this narrow world.  Their mastery of the money markets and the ever-increasing efficiency and penetration of information technology lead to the situation where they are much more powerful than many of the nation states.  An unusual concomitant of size is flexibility.  Just as individuals are expected to be flexible, so too are companies.  Diane Elson and Ruth Pearson (1989) have remarked on the capacity of the multi-nationals for international relocation of activities.

> Multinationals have no specific commitment to any location... a multinational engages in frequent comparisons of the profitability of different locations across national boundaries.  Multinational activities are in a constant state of flux -

closing plant at some locations; opening plant at other locations; buying up other firms; selling off divisions that no longer fit its corporate strategy (1989:2).

They go on to comment on one of the strongest features of present-day strategy by the multinationals, the imperative to locate to areas of low cost labour. This mobility is a further contribution to employment uncertainty.

An aspect of 'flexibility' is working at a distance, teleworking or telecommuting as it has been variously described. Heather Hamblin (1995) argues that

> working at a distance (that is, work done in the home at a physical distance from the employer, using information-based electronic equipment for some parts of the job) will become an increasingly significant phenomenon towards the twenty-first century (1995:73).

Equally homeworking, where people make or process raw materials delivered to their homes, has a long history. And, increasingly, reports detail the very low pay of workers in such occupations as finishing textile goods, making up such objects as Christmas crackers, and knitting, both in this country and in the developing world. As Greer (1999) points out, most outworkers are female and, in Britain, 'the average outworker has children, works over 30 hours a week and can earn as little as £56 for her weekly toil' (Greer, 1999:126). The struggle of such low-paid workers to maintain themselves and their families is repeated but in far worse conditions in Third World countries. So that alongside outworkers utilising the new technology can be ranged those who practise skills with a long history. As Lydia Morris (1991) points out, the wide definition of homeworker used in official statistics leads to the fact that the poverty of most women homeworkers is obscured.

> For example, the majority of homeworkers (71 per cent) are women while the majority of people working from home as a base (71 per cent) are men. ...they are among the highest paid workers in Britain (one-fifth with hourly earnings in the top 10 per cent) and among the lowest paid (one-third with hourly earnings in the lowest 10 per cent, however the great majority of workers in the former category are men and in the latter category women; three quarters of homeworkers are satisfied with their pay, but ironically women are more satisfied than men (Morris, 1991:84).

We therefore have, increasingly, a majority of work that is relatively uncertain, paid at low rates, temporary. There has been a growth in short-term contracts, a growth in part-time work. Even for core workers, shorter contracts are becoming the norm.  As the Equal Opportunities Review (1999) points out, the fastest growth in jobs over the past ten years has come in 'non-standard' employment.

## Women and The Changing Nature of Work

These changes in the pattern of work have had particular impact on the work of women.  As has been well documented we are seeing an increase in female employment and a decrease in male employment.  Social Trends 29 comments on the situation in the United Kingdom (1999),

> One of the most striking overall features of the labour market is that women are taking an increasingly important role.  In 1971, just over half of women in the 25 to 44 age group were economically active, that is, either in work or seeking work: this rose to over three-quarters by 1997.  As the proportion of economically active women has increased, the proportion of economically active men has declined.... Projections for Great Britain indicate a further narrowing of the gender gap (Social Trends 29, 1999:73).

This trend is becoming established and seems to represent a change which will continue in the twenty-first century.  Anne Harrop and Peter Moss suggest the effect this will have on employers,

> The number of women in the labour force will increase.  Two-thirds of labour force growth between 1983 and 1987 was made up of married women, and by 1995 the projected increase in the size of the female labour force is some three-quarters of a million, over 80% of the total.... (Employers) will need women employees, and must recognise both their career ambitions and domestic responsibilities (1995:421).

The changes in the general patterns of employment are ones that overwhelmingly favour the employment of women, those 'preferred workers', to whom Liz Sperling (p.2) refers.  The reduction in heavy industry, which appeared to call for physical strength, and the rise of service industries, which seems to call for social skills, caring and physical attractiveness, exemplify the sexual stereotypes of a patriarchal society so that there appears a fall in masculine work and a rise in feminine work.  Crompton et al. (1996) quote the statistic that from 1971 to 1993 service employment has grown from 53 per cent to a staggering 73 per cent (1996:3).  Allied with this is the, albeit limited, success of feminism and equal opportunities policies which has allowed women to infiltrate employment previously thought of as masculine spheres and, incidentally, men into previously female spheres. The success of high profile women in the media mentioned by Sperling (p.2) is reported more often than the continuing and steady success of men in commanding the positions of authority in traditional women's work such as nursing and teaching. It would seem that both these trends are also set to continue. Again, although women are increasingly taking fewer career breaks, in the industrialised world, taking less and less time off for maternity leave (Equal Opportunities Review, 1997b), for example, the picture of women as available as a reserve army of labour still persists. In fact, because of the increasing lack of permanent, secure jobs, this becomes more and more a realistic picture. It is women who, because of domestic commitments, childcare and increasingly elder care (Nissel and Bonnerjea, 1982; Lewis and Meredith, 1988), accept homeworking, telecommuting, part-time work, and short-term contracts. It has to be said that for some professional women, these circumstances have brought opportunity. Granger et al. (1995) have mentioned, for example, women workers in publishing. Nevertheless, these women form a minority. Even professional women have had to come to terms with the short-term contracts so prevalent in, for example, academic work or scientific research. Walsh and James have drawn on the work of Sara Arber and Jay Ginn (1995) on the significance of caring, for women, pointing out how rarely those responsibilities now lead to withdrawal from the labour market, instead merely adding to women's workload. For most carers, this results in extremely long hours of work and Arber and Ginn speculate that, 'It is likely that the health of these carers and their career opportunities suffer in consequence, particularly if such dual demands continue over a long period of time (1995:445). Both New Right policies and, increasingly, New Left policies continue to endorse Care in the Community combined with family values and if this persists then it seems that, in the UK at least, the difficulties experienced by women at work will endure.

**Which Women?**

The tendency to treat all women's experience as homogenous, however, has to be avoided. Class, race, age, physical ability and sexual orientation are factors which cannot be ignored in considering the trends which are shaping women's employment. Anne Witz (1993) has stressed the importance of being alert to:

the differences between white women, Asian women and Afro-Caribbean women in Britain not only in relation to homeworking but also in relation to part-time and full-time employment and the kinds of job done (1993:279).

In relation to home working, Anne Phizacklea and Carol Wolkowitz (1995) point to the increasing polarisation between skilled professional women working in relatively well-paid jobs at home and women homeworkers from ethnic minority families forced to work long hours for extremely low pay.

Working class women still find difficulties in infiltrating traditional male areas of employment. Jill Rubery and Colette Fagan (1995) have noted the 'low share of women in production and manual jobs' right across the European Union (EU) countries, only exceeding 20 per cent in Denmark and Portugal (Rubery and Fagan, 1995:219,222). In the professions, nevertheless, there 'is an upward trend in the female share observable in all countries (making it thus the most consistent occupational sector for increasing female shares in the 1980s)' (Rubery and Fagan, 1995:223). There persists the usual pattern where women are concentrated in the caring professions, health associated professions and teaching, though with a preponderance of men in the managerial and higher positions. Again, within these lower strata come short-term contracts, part-time, job-sharing, shift work (particularly in the health sphere). Nevertheless, as Susan McRae, for the Policy Studies Institute, writes,

> the evolving structure of the labour market means that there is likely to be more room for women at the top of the occupational hierarchy. It is highly probable that the marked postwar increase in higher-level and professional occupations will continue well into the next decade and beyond (1990:1).

Lesbian women have argued that movements towards equal opportunities for women have consistently ignored them. This is a particularly salient topic in a book on women and work and is ironic since, as Gill Valentine has pointed out, because lesbian women are not able to marry legally, they do not even conform to the female stereotype of dependent wife and mother covered by a male breadwinner's 'family wage'. They are dependent completely on their own earning power (1996:112). Women earn consistently less than men, therefore the necessity for legislation and practice to support women's equal rights is doubly apparent, but is not forthcoming. It would seem that in the future lesbian women will need to mobilise around this issue. How far will mainstream gender equality movements support them? Gillian Dunne's research suggests that lesbian women may be showing the way to a different set of values. However, Dunne's sample were professionals and when we are talking about subsistence, equality of pay and a decent minimum wage must be the essential priority.

Similarly age as a factor in equality and employment varies in different countries and the attitudes towards the older woman arise out of different cultural perspectives. In a world in which there is an increasing proportion of older people, which actually means older women since women have a longer life expectancy, in the more developed nations, the 'problem' of this growing non-productive group is leading to something of a moral panic (Hutton, 1995; Vincent, 1995; Bytheway, 1989; Owen, 1999) The poverty of the older woman has concerned the EU (Denman, 1997). This poverty is a direct result of women's interrupted employment patterns at low paid work. A few lone voices have called for a more flexible retirement age so that those who wish to do so could continue to work, but for women who are engaged in demanding physical work or who have merely spent many years in unrewarding work, this may be problematic. Nevertheless, moves to end age discrimination for all would surely benefit women.

The growing population of the very elderly also affects women in mid-life and the 'young-old'; women in these groups can find themselves caring for frail and disabled dependants. It is also the case that very elderly women (and men) care for equally elderly partners. In Britain, it is argued,

> The state, alarmed by the phenomenon of an ageing population and the growing burden of the cost of caring for the infirm elderly has tried to thrust the burden of care back on to the community and the family. (Bradley, 1996:18).

Feminists have been quick to point out that in this scenario the community and the family overwhelmingly equate to women. Sally Baldwin and Julia Twigg (1991) have described the reception of Janet Finch and Dulcie Groves' paper on this debate.

> Finch and Groves' paper transformed the existing debate on community care in two ways. It cut through the euphemistic language of 'community' and 'family' to argue that community care was essentially about the care provided by women; and it discussed the effects of caring on women's life chances in terms of equality of opportunities with men (Baldwin and Twigg, 1991:118).

The debate on the feminist approach to the future care of the elderly dependent is far from being resolved. The 'problem' of the demographic increase in the elderly, but more essentially the social construction of a moral panic around the burden of the elderly, is a trend that will continue throughout the developed world.

There seems a glimmer of hope in regard to women and disability in the industrialised nations. Helen Collins (1992) has described the HELIOS programme of the EU which had the aim of enabling and integrating into society those people with disabilities. While the programme came to an end in 1996, the aim is now to mainstream these concerns, so that no legislation is implemented without taking disability into account. The 1995 Disability Discrimination Act suggests that the British Government has at last recognised the case put forward by the disability lobby, after blocking previous bills. Mike Oliver (1991) argues that in spite of these initiatives, advances will depend on the disabled themselves:

> there are limited grounds for optimism in the rise of new technologies which are being developed within present-day, post-capitalist society and that this optimism is dependent upon the extent to which disabled people themselves can advance their own claim for full participation in society, including the work process (1991:146).

The move to mainstreaming both gender and disability issues by the European Union (Rees, 1999) raises concern that what seems like an advance in social thinking will merely enable these issues to disappear into general issues and be subverted by economic constraints. Certainly, in the less developed world, equality for women with disabilities will continue to be hampered by poverty.

Racism cannot be separated out from issues of gender and class. An extreme example of discrimination is reflected in Nicola Piper's picture of sex workers in Japan. The sex industry too has been subject to globalisation and flexibility. Unless the countries of the west forsake their Fortress Europe or Fortress United States approach, there will continue to exist a cynical exporting of the ugliest faces of patriarchy and capitalism. Piper's chapter paints a picture reflected across the world:

> Women's lack of economic and educational opportunities resulting in prostitution becoming an important means of survival in a male-dominated society is related to [...] problems which are fundamental to women's role in the global workforce... (p.162).

It is part of that continuing tradition of imperialism which seems an integral part of both capitalism and patriarchy, part of that long western obsession with the Orient most overtly displayed in art. For example, Jo Anna Isaak (1996) is describing the paintings of Henri Matisse when she talks of 'a fashionable colonial discourse in which the erotic management of human subjects in cultural production thinly disguises a collective assertion of control over human subjects, territory, and property (1996:59). That 'assertion of control' assumes no disguise when sex tourism is the issue.   Added to prejudice between those of different 'races', an intensification of ethnicity in regard to religion, nationality, and culture seems to be emerging.   As Harriet Bradley remarks,

> The interest in the idea of ethnicity has ... been encouraged by the events in Europe and Asia which followed the collapse of Russian communism and the break up of the Soviet Union and its empire. The emergence of long suppressed ethnic loyalties and conflicts and the formation of new nations have drawn our attention to the force of national and ethnic identities as a base of social conflict and have contributed greatly to the notion that social fragmentation is on the increase (1996:17).

However, for all women, whatever their differences, their status as 'the second sex' persists into the workforce.   The endemic, subtle and persistent culture of discrimination is clearly portrayed in the chapter on the novel, *Amado Amo*. The situation in Spain regarding working women discussed by Lesley Twomey is interesting to compare with Rollin and Burrell's picture of contemporary Spain and reinforces their comment that 'legislation can rarely do more than provide a framework for remedying inequalities' (p.51) The two snapshots, taken at different times, the one close-up, the other with wide-angle lens, underline the comment that,

> It is predictable and inevitable that social changes, involving fundamental changes in attitudes, expectations and values of both employers and employees, can be brought about only gradually (Rollin and Burrell, p.51).

## Legislation and Practice

In many of the societies which have been discussed in the book, legislation around equality of gender, as well as in regard to discrimination in other areas, has been put into place.   In the UK the key pieces of legislation have been the Equal Pay Act 1970, The Sex Discrimination Act 1975, the Race Relations Act 1976, and the Disability Discrimination Act 1995.   Each one of these was preceded by a long drawn-out battle to get them on to the statute books and their shortcomings are acknowledged.   The situation is similar in many of the developed countries.   Nevertheless as the Equal Opportunities Commission suggests in regard to equal pay in Britain,

> Over the twenty years since it was introduced, the Equal Pay Act has not been without effect.   There have also been improvements in women's access to education and training and to managerial and professional occupations.   Despite this, the pay gap remains a persistent feature of many women's lives (EOC, 1996: 1).

It needs to be said that there has been improvement in women's participation and achievement in education and employment in countries where there is no Equal Pay Act, or indeed Equal Opportunities Commission, and the impact of legislation is a long-running debate.   The quote, though, neatly encapsulates the persistence of a gradual putting into place of equality legislation alongside the difficulty in ensuring that the *spirit* of equality accompanies it.   The battle to establish equal rights for women and men and perhaps especially for those of ethnic minorities, different sexual orientation, differing physical and mental abilities and those of different ages, has been a constant theme of the book. Catherine Fletcher's qualitative research into the way that same spirit of equality is frustrated by the culture in regard to training in the French and British insurance industries again adds to the picture and describes the same culture as the very different work environment of the Northshire Fire Service described by Andrea Lee.   As far as gender issues are concerned, EU laws do seem to have played a part in policing any reluctant national governments, not least that of Britain.   It is a long war of attrition, however, and, as Cook has discussed, legal rights are of little use without knowledge of the laws and the power and opportunity to access these.   It is apparent that the battle to establish legal equal opportunities is never won even with the most well-intentioned legislature.   When swathes of opinion from neo-liberal to New Right believe in free markets or the return of women to the home, or to the 'geisha' trades, it is clear that the future implies permanent struggle.

**The Future is Female?**

The twin movements of globalisation and flexibility which have been described, each in its own way throws a long shadow forward.   From the trends discussed in this book it seems that there is one constant: there has been, and continues to be, a change in the structure of employment.   More and more jobs are geared to the perceived qualities, skills and abilities of women.   More and more jobs are calling for workers to display the traditional work pattern of women, low-paid, uncertain, in that the work is temporary, part-time, perhaps done from home or 'hot-desk' office, or production shift in the factory. In addition, significantly there has been a return of domestic service, with working-class women often employed by that smaller class of women who do break into the professions or management (Gregson and Lowe, 1994). Increasingly, therefore, we see that women are working and men are unemployed, certainly in Britain where Government figures project into the next century 'a further narrowing of the gender gap' (*Social Trends* 29, 1999: 73). Suzanne Moore (1995) commented on a 'Panorama' programme on British television that,

> At 15 the children interviewed had already decided for themselves that girls have a more positive attitude towards education, that boys need to be pressurised into doing any work at all and that in the future women would get all the best jobs (Moore, 1995:5).

Are we really seeing the most major change in the lives of people of working age? Women are able to get jobs and men are not, unless they accept 'women's' jobs and women's low pay and acquire women's skills. And when employers can get women workers already trained in the skills and socialised in the acceptance of the poor working conditions, why should they take men? This is a time when declared feminists can announce that they have 'recanted' and now worry about the inequalities suffered by men (Coward, 1999). 'Post-feminists' point to 'girl-power' and the present threat to men and masculinity. Truly a paradigm shift.

It has been long argued that capitalism and patriarchy go hand in hand. The debate has been how far that interdependence goes. Are they essentially one system or merely so intertwined as to be practically indistinguishable? Heidi Hartmann (1981:21-22) has suggested that the two are a partnership and espoused dual system theories, in which the interests of both have coincided in the exploitation of women's subordinate position; whereas writers like Christine Delphy (1984) have seen patriarchy as a mode of production in itself. Certainly in the later nineteenth century and in the twentieth century the interests of patriarchy and capitalism have coincided in direct and observable ways. Perhaps it is important here to be especially aware of the meaning of 'patriarchy', the rule of the father, that is, rule by a broad cohort of powerful men who are able to impose their needs and advantage on, not only women, but also children and less powerful men. Even where the trade unions became more powerful and supported the family wage and, concomitantly, the exclusion of women in a scene of predominantly heavy industry, healthy, relatively better paid men with supporting women bringing up the workers of the future seemed a profitable deal. With the change to high technology where strength is not important, where dexterity is, and where the 'feminine' skills at relationships are also saleable, has the partnership between patriarchy and capitalism at last been dissolved? Is capitalism now better served by that reserve army of female labour? Is it even the case that the interests of capitalism and patriarchy are becoming opposed? Certainly it does not seem in the interests of capitalism to have women, who have already been socialised into the patterns required, serving men at home, when they could be serving capitalism directly at work. This does not suppose that in the future capitalism will necessarily advance the position of women beyond that of men. It seems to me that the logic of capitalism merely demands a proletariat. There is no reason why in the future men should not develop the necessary skills demanded by post-Fordism.

Nevertheless, women have a head start and I would suggest that we may be entering a very interesting transition period. Whether this transition will benefit women has been an underlying source of unease throughout the contributions of the book. Can women really 'feminise' the workplace? Can it be made a more democratic place, where decisions are arrived at co-operatively and where aggressive competition between workers is seen as self-defeating, where a real balance is struck between a stimulating and rewarding work environment and home and other interests, as Dunne has advocated? Or on a more sinister note, could we be entering a phase of an uneasy alliance between feminism and capitalism? Surely not! Theoretically, there seems no reason why capitalism does really need patriarchy. Politically, surely it is only a very limited liberal feminism that could co-exist with the global and flexible capitalism forecast in this book?

It has always been a weakness of the pure Marxist approach that it neglected the issue of gender and/or that certainly it has never been easy to incorporate gender into the Marxist dialectic. Are we viewing, perhaps, in experiential terms rather than philosophical terms, the insistent intrusion of 'the woman question' into analyses of the world of work? It is an irony that perhaps the old master would have appreciated that the world is changing while the philosophers have not quite caught up with their understanding.

# Bibliography

Actualidad Política (1997), *Valoración del Tercer Plan de Igualdad de Oportunidades entre Hombres y Mujeres*, http://www.psoe.es/actpol/valplanig/htm.

Adkins, L. (1995), *Gendered Work: Sexuality, Family and the Labour Market*, Buckingham: Open University Press.

Afshar, H. and Maynard, M. (eds) (1994), *The Dynamics of 'Race' and Gender: Some Feminist Interventions*, London: Taylor & Francis.

Alberdi, I. (1986), 'La educación de la mujer en España', in C. Borreguero (ed.).

Alborg, C. (1988), 'Metaficción y feminismos en Rosa Montero', *Revista de Estudios Hispánicos*, 22 (1) pp.67-76.

Allen, J. and Henry, N. (1996), 'Fragments of industry and employment: contract service work and the shift towards precarious employment', in R. Crompton, D. Gallie and K. Purcell (eds).

Allison, A. (1994), *Sexuality, Pleasure and Corporate Masculinity in a Tokyo Hostess Club*, London: University of Chicago Press.

Almond, P. and Rubery, J. (1998), 'The gender impact of recent European trends in wage determination', *Work, Employment and Society*, 12 (4) pp.675-693.

Alvira Martín, F., Torres Ruis, M., Blanco Moreno, F. and Cruz Chust, A. M. (1994), *La Empresa del Futuro y el Acceso de la Mujer a Puestos Directivos: Informe Realizado Para el Instituto de la Mujer*, Madrid: Instituto de la Mujer.

Amin, A. (ed.) (1994), *Post-Fordism: A Reader*, Oxford: Blackwell.

Appadurai, A. (1990), 'Disjuncture and difference in the global cultural economy', *Public Culture*, 2 (2) pp.1-24.

Arber, S. and Ginn, J. (1995), 'Gender differences in the relationship between paid employment and informal care', *Work, Employment and Society*, 9 (3) pp.445-471.

Arribas, I. (1991), 'Poder y feminismo en *Amado Amo* de Rosa Montero', *Romance Languages Annual*, 3 pp.348-353.

Ashburner, L (1992), 'Just inside the counting house: women in finance', in A. Coyle and J. Skinner (eds), *Women and Work: Positive Action for Change*, London: Macmillan.

Asian Women's Association (1988), *Women from Across the Seas: Migrant Workers in Japan*, Tokyo: Asian Women's Association.

Aulagnon, M. (1998a), 'L'allocation parentale d'éducation a incité plus de 200 000 femmes à quitter leur emploi', *Le Monde*, 28 February.

Aulagnon, M. (1998b), 'Les femmes ne se reconnaissent pas dans les lois qui sont votées', *Le Monde*, 8 June.

Ayllón, M. D. (1995), 'Integración de la mujer en la vida laboral en la actual coyuntura socioeconómico', in M. José Carrasco, A. García Mina, J. Labrdor and C. Alemany Briz (eds).

Bachrach, P. and Baratz, M. (1963), 'Decisions and non-decisions: an analytical framework', *American Political Science Review*, 57 pp.632-642.

Baldwin, S. and Twigg, J. (1991), 'Women and community care', in M. McLean and D. Groves (eds), *Women's Issues in Social Policy*, London: Routledge.

Barbalet, J. M. (1988), *Citizenship*, Milton Keynes: Open University Press.

Barling, J. and Gallagher, D. (1996), 'Part-time employment', in C. Cooper and I. Robertson (eds), *International Review of Industrial and Organizational Psychology*, Chichester: Wiley.

Barron, R. D. and Norris, G. M. (1976), 'Sexual division and the dual labour market', in Leonard Barker, D. and Allen, S. (eds), *Dependence and Exploitation in Work and Marriage*, London: Longman.

Bazen, S. and Martin J. P. (1991), 'The impact of the minimum wage on earnings and employment in France', *OECD Economic Studies*, 16 pp.199-221.

Becker, G. (1975), *Human Capital: A Theoretical and Empirical Analysis*, Chicago: University of Chicago Press.

Beechey, V. (1986), 'Introduction', in V. Beechey and E. Whitelegg (eds), *Women in Britain Today*, Milton Keynes: Open University.

Beechy, V and Perkins, T. (1987), *A Matter of Hours: Women, Part-time Work and the Labour Market*, Cambridge: Polity.

Benokraitis, N. and Feagin, J. (1986), *Modern Sexism: Blatant, Subtle and Covert Discrimination*, Engelwood Cliffs, NJ: Prentice Hall.

Berk, S. F. (1985), *The Gender Factory: The Apportionment of Work in American Households*, New York: Plenum.

Bernstein, G. (1991), *Recreating Japanese Women 1600-1945*, London: Routledge.

Bird, D. and Corcoran, L. (1994), 'Trade union membership and density 1992-93', *Employment Gazette*, June, pp.189-197.

Bisault, L., Bloch-London, C., Lagarde, S. and Le Corre, V. (1996), 'Le développement du travail à temps partiel', *Données Sociales*, INSEE.

Blanco Corrujo, O. and Morant Deusa, I. (1995), *El Largo Camino Hacia la Igualdad: Feminismo en España 1975-1995*, Madrid: Ministerio de Asuntos Sociales and Instituto de la Mujer.

Blumberg, R. L. (1995), 'Introduction: engendering wealth and well-being in an era of economic transformation', in R. L. Blumberg, C. A. Rakowski, I. Tinker and M. Monteon (eds).

Blumberg, R. L., Rakowski, C. A., Tinker, I. and Monteon, M. (eds), *Engendering Wealth and Well-Being: Empowerment for Global Change*, Oxford: Westview Press.

Blumstein, P. and Schwartz, P. (1985), *American Couples*, New York: Pocket Books.

Borreguero, C. (ed.), *La Mujer Española: de la Tradición a la Modernidad (1960-1980)*, Semilla y Surco, Serie Sociología, Madrid: Tecnos.

Bowles, M. (1990), 'Recognising deep structures in organisations', *Organisation Studies*, 11/12 pp.395-412.

Bradley, H. (1989), *Men's Work, Women's Work*, Cambridge: Polity.

Bradley, H. (1996), *Fractured Identities: Changing Patterns of Inequality*, Cambridge: Polity.

Bradley, H. (1999), *Gender and Power in the Workplace*, Basingstoke: Macmillan.

Brah, A. (1994), '"Race" and "Culture" in the gendering of labour markets: South Asian young Muslim women in the labour market', in H. Afshar and M. Maynard (eds).

Brannen, J. and Moss, P. (1991), *Managing Mothers: Dual Earner Households after Maternity Leave*, London: Unwin Hyman.

Bretherton, C. and Sperling, L. (1996), 'Women's networks and the European Union: towards an inclusive approach?', *Journal of Common Market Studies*, 34 (4) pp.487-508.

Brochmann, G. (1991), 'The significance of gender relations in international migration', *Forum For Utviklingsstudier - Norsk Ukenrikspolitisk Institutt (Oslo)*, no.1 pp.113-124.

Brondel, D., Guillemot, D. and Marioni, P. (1996), 'La population active: facteurs d'évolution et perspectives', *Données Sociales*, INSEE.

Brooksbank Jones, A. (1997), *Women in Contemporary Spain*, Manchester: Manchester University Press.

Brown, P. and Scase, R. (eds), *Poor Work: Disadvantage and the Division of Labour*, Buckingham: Open University Press.

Bruegel, I. (1989), 'Sex and race in the labour market', *Feminist Review*, 32 pp.49-68.

Bruegel, I. (1994), 'Labour market prospects for women from ethnic minorities', in R. Lindley (ed.), *Labour Market Structures and Prospects for Women*, Manchester: Equal Opportunities Commission.

Bruegel, I. (1996), 'Whose myths are they anyway?: a comment', *British Journal of Sociology*, 47 (1) pp.175-177.

Burchell, B., Dale, A. and Joshi, H. (1997), 'Part-time work among British women', in H-P. Blossfield and C. Hakim (eds), *Between Equalization and Marginalization: Women Working Part-time in Europe and the USA*, Oxford: Oxford University Press.

Burrell, G. (1984), 'Sex and organisational analysis', *Organisational Studies*, 5 (2) pp.97-118.

Burrows, R. and Loader, B. (eds), *Towards a Post-Fordist Welfare State*, London: Routledge.

Bytheway, W. (ed.) (1989), *Becoming and Being Old: Sociological Approaches to Later Life*, London: Sage.

Calero Fernández, M. Á. (1996), 'La imagen de la mujer en la literatura', *Scriptura*, 12, Lerida: Universitat de Lleida.

Camps, V. (1998), *El Siglo de las Mujeres*, Feminismos, Madrid: Cátedra.

Cappuccini, G. (1996), *Role Division and Gender Role Attitudes: Couples Adjusting to the Arrival of their First Baby*, unpublished PhD Thesis: University of Birmingham.

Card, D. and Krueger, A. (1995), *Myth and Measurement: the New Economics of the*

*Minimum Wage*, Princeton NJ: Princeton University Press.

Carvel, J. (1966), 'Schools urged to focus on low achieving boys', *The Guardian*, 11 July.

Cash, T. (1998), 'Lessons from the international experience of statutory minimum wages', *Labour Market Trends*, September, pp.463-467.

CEDAW (1999), *Fourth Report of the United Kingdom of Great Britain and Northern Ireland United Nations Convention on the Elimination of all forms of Discrimination against Women*, http://www.womens-unit.gov.uk/199/cedaw.pdf.

Chambers, D. (1986), 'The constraints of work and domestic schedules on women's leisure', *Leisure Studies*, 5 pp.309-325.

Close, P. (1995), *Citizenship, Europe and Change*, Basingstoke: Macmillan.

Cockburn, C. (1981), 'The material of male power', *Feminist Review*, 9 pp.41-48.

Cockburn, C. (1983), *Brothers: Male Dominance and Technological Change*, London: Pluto.

Cockburn, C. (1991), *In the Way of Women: Men's Resistance to Sex Equality in Organisations*, Basingstoke: Macmillan.

Cockburn, C. (1996), 'Strategies for gender democracy', *The European Journal of Women's Studies*, vol.3 pp.7-26.

Coleman, S. (1983), *Family Planning in Japanese Society: Traditional Birth Control in a Modern Urban Culture*, Princeton NJ: Princeton University Press.

Collins, H. (1992), *The Equal Opportunities Handbook*, Oxford: Blackwell.

Collinson, D. L., Knights, D. and Collinson, M. (1990), *Managing to Discriminate*, London: Routledge.

Commission of the European Communities (1993), *White Paper on Growth, Competitiveness: The Challenges and Ways Forward into the 21st Century*, Brussels.

Commission of the European Communities (1995), *Flexibility in Working Time and Security for Workers*, Brussels.

Conde, R. and Carballal, T. (1986), 'La familia española: continuidad y cambio', in C. Borreguero (ed.).

Conseil Supérieur de l'Egalité Professionnelle (1995), *Quelle Action pour l'Egalité Professionnelle dans les Branches Professionnelles, les Entreprises et les Etablissements?*, Report of Working Party 3.

Cook, J. (1997), 'Restructuring social rights: does a flexible employment and benefits regime entrench exclusion and inequality?', in M. Roach and R. Van Berkel (eds), *European Citizenship and Social Exclusion*, Aldershot: Ashgate.

Cook, J. (1998), 'Flexible employment: implications for gender and citizenship in the new European Union', *New Political Economy*, 3 (2).

Cook, J. (1999), 'Flexible employment: implications for a gendered political economy of citizenship', in J. Cook, J. Roberts and G. Waylen (eds).

Cook, J., Roberts, J. and Waylen, G. (eds), *Towards a Gendered Political Economy*, Basingstoke: Macmillan.

Cousins, C. (1994), 'A comparison of the labour market position of women in Spain and the UK with reference to the flexible specialisation debate', *Work, Employment and Society*, 8 (1) pp.45-62.

Coward, R. (1999), *Sacred Cows: Is Feminism Relevant to the New Millenium?* London: HarperCollins.

Crompton, R. (1994), 'Occupational trends and women's employment patterns', in R. Lindley (ed.).

Crompton, R. and Sanderson, K. (1990), *Gendered Jobs and Social Change*, London: Unwin Hyman.

Crompton, R. and Le Feuvre, N. (1992), 'Women in finance in Britain and France', in M. Savage and A. Witz (eds), *Gender and Bureaucracy*, Oxford: Blackwell.

Crompton, R. and Sanderson, K. (1994), 'Gendered restructuring of employment in the finance sector', in A. MacEwen Scott (ed.).

Crompton, R., Gallie, D. and Purcell, K. (1996), *Changing Forms of Employment: Organisations, Skills and Gender*, London: Routledge.

Crompton, R. and Harris, F. (1998), 'Gender relations and employment: the impact of occupation', *Work, Employment and Society*, 12 (2) pp.297-315.

Cross, M. (1997), 'Feminism', in C. Flood and L. Bell (eds), *Political Ideologies in Contemporary France*, London: Pinter.

Crouch, C (1995), 'Exit or voice: two paradigms for European industrial relations after the Keynesian Welfare State', *European Journal of Industrial Relations*, 1 (1) pp.63-81.

David, M. (1986), 'The family in the New Right', in R. Levitas (ed.), *The Ideology of the New Right*, Cambridge: Polity.

Davies, C. (1992-3), 'Entrevista a Rosa Montero (Madrid, 22 de enero de 1993)', *Journal of Hispanic Research*, 1 pp.383-387.

Davies, C. (1994), *Contemporary Feminist Fiction in Spain: The Work of Montserrat Roig and Rosa Montero*, Oxford: Berg.

del Campo, S. (1994), *Tendencias Sociales en España (1960-1990)*, Madrid: Fundación BBV.

Delphy, C. (1984), *Close to Home: a Materialist Analysis of Women's Oppression*, London: Hutchinson.

Delphy, C. and Leonard, D. (1992), *Familiar Exploitation: A New Analysis of Marriage in Contemporary Western Societies*, Cambridge: Polity.

Delsen, L. (1994), *International Quantitative Comparison of Part-time and Temporary Employment*, Paper for International Industrial Relations Association.

Denman, M. (1997), 'Age becomes her: older women in the European Union', *Women of Europe Dossier*, May-June-July, no. 45.

Dex, S. (1985), *The Sexual Division of Work*, Brighton: Wheatsheaf.

Dex, S. and Walters, P. (1990), 'Women's working experience in France and Britain', in S. Macrae (ed.), *Keeping Women In*, London: Policy Studies Institute.

Dex, S., Lissenburgh, S. and Taylor, M. (1994), *Women and Low Pay: Identifying the Issues*, Equal Opportunities Commission Research Discussion Series no. 9, Manchester: Equal Opportunities Commission.

Dex, S. and McCulloch, A. (1995), *Flexible Employment in Britain: A Statistical Analysis*, Equal Opportunities Research Discussion Series no. 15, Manchester: Equal Opportunities Commission.

Directorate-General for Employment, Industrial Relations and Social Affairs (1991), *Third Medium-Term Community Action Programme on Equal Opportunities for Women and Men (1991-1995)*, Brussels.

Directorate-General for Employment, Industrial Relations and Social Affairs (1995), *Fourth Medium-Term Community Action Programme on Equal Opportunities for Women and Men (1996-2000)*, Brussels.

Directorate-General for Employment, Industrial Relations and Social Affairs (1996), *Employment in Europe 1996*, Luxembourg.

Directorate-General for Employment, Industrial Relations and Social Affairs (1997), 'Women and men in Europe and equal opportunities: results of an opinion poll', *Eurobarometer*, 44 (3).

Doeringer, P. and Piore, M. (1971), *Internal Labour Markets and Manpower Analysis*, Lexington, Mass: D. C. Heath.

Doucet, A. (1995), 'Encouraging voices: towards more creative methods for collecting data on gender and household labour', in L. Morris and S. Lyon (eds.), *Gender Relations in the Public and the Private*, London: Macmillan.

Doucet, A. and Dunne, G. A. (1999), 'Who essentially cares? Towards a reformulation of the gender dynamics of care giving', in A. O'Reilly and S. Abbey (eds), *International Perspectives on Mothers and Daughters*, Toronto: Rowman & Littlefield.

Duchen, C. (1994), *Women's Rights and Women's Lives in France 1944-1968*, London: Routledge.

Duncan, S. (1991), 'The geography of gender divisions of labour in Britain', *Transactions of the Institute of British Geographers*, 5 (4) pp.263-284.

Dunne, G. A. (1997a), *Lesbian Lifestyles: Women's Work and the Politics of Sexuality*, Basingstoke: Macmillan and University of Toronto Press.

Dunne, G. A. (1997b), 'Why can't a man be more like a woman? In search of balanced domestic and employment lives', *LSE Gender Institute Discussion Paper Series*, 3.

Dunne, G. A. (1998a), 'Pioneers behind our own front doors: new models for the organization of work in partnerships', *Work Employment and Society*, 12 (2) pp.273-295.

Dunne, G. A. (1998b), 'A passion for "sameness": sexuality and gender accountability', in E. Silva and C. Smart (eds), *The 'New' Family?* London: Sage.

Dunne, G. A. (1998c), 'Add sexuality and stir: towards a broader understanding of the gender dynamics of work and family life', *The Journal of Lesbian Studies*, 2 (4).

Dunne, G. A. (ed.) (1998d), *Living 'Difference': Lesbian Perspectives on Work and Family Life*, Binghamton, NY: The Harrington Park Press.

Dunne, G. A. (1999a), 'What difference does difference make? Lesbian experience of work and family life', in J. Seymour and P. Bagguley (eds), *Relating Intimacies: Power and Resistance*, Basingstoke: Macmillan and The BSA.

Dunne, G. A. (1999b), 'Opting into motherhood: lesbians blurring the boundaries and re-defining the meaning of parenting', *Gender and Society*, 13 (6).

Dunsire, A. (1978), *Implementation in a Bureaucracy*, Oxford: Martin Robertson.

Duru-Bellat, M. (1990), *L'Ecole des Filles: Quelle Formation pour Quels Roles Sociaux?*, Paris: L'Harmattan.

Dworkin, A. (1981), *Pornography: Men Possessing Women*, London: Women's Press.

Edgeworth, F. Y. (1922), 'Equal pay to men and women for equal work', *Economic Journal*, http:www.socsci.mcmaster.ca.

Elson, D. and Pearson, R. (1989), 'Introduction: nimble fingers and foreign investments', in D. Elson and R. Pearson (eds.), *Women's Employment and Multinationals in Europe*, Basingstoke: Macmillan.

Encuesta de Población Activa and Instituto Nacional de Empleo (1998), in *Anuario El País 1998*, Madrid.

Enloe, C. (1989), *Bananas, Beaches and Bases: Making Feminist Sense of International Politics*, London: Pandora.

Equal Opportunities Commission (1994), *Some Facts about Women 1994*, Manchester: Equal Opportunities Commission.

Equal Opportunities Commission (1995), *The Gender Impact of CCT in Local Government*, Manchester: Equal Opportunities Commission.

Equal Opportunities Commission (1996), *Briefings on Women and Men in Britain: Pay*, Manchester: Equal Opportunities Commission.

Equal Opportunities Commission (1997), *Job-sharing and Flexible Working Hours – A Summary of Case Law*, Manchester: Equal Opportunities Commission.

Equal Opportunities Commission (1998), *Facts about Women and Men in Great Britain 1998*, Manchester: Equal Opportunities Commission.

Equal Opportunities Review (1996a), 'Parental and family leave in Europe', *Equal Opportunities Review*, no. 6.

Equal Opportunities Review (1996b), 'EC Fourth Equality Action Programme', *Equal Opportunities Review*, no. 67.

Equal Opportunities Review (1997a), 'Parental leave and part-time rights for UK workers', *Equal Opportunities Review*, no. 74.

Equal Opportunities Review (1997b), 'Increase in women returning after maternity', *Equal Opportunities Review*, no. 75.

Equal Opportunities Review (1998a), 'Dismissal due to pregnancy-related illness is discriminatory', *Equal Opportunities Review*, no. 81.

Equal Opportunities Review (1998b), 'Reshuffle responsibilities', *Equal Opportunities Review*, no. 81.

Equal Opportunities Review (1999), 'Part-time work is a "first-rate option"', *Equal Opportunities Review*, no. 85.

Esping-Andersen, G. (1990), *Three Worlds of Welfare Capitalism*, Cambridge: Polity.

European Commission (1993), *Social Europe*, 2/93, Brussels: European Commission.

European Commission (1995), *Mid-term Report on the Third Community Action Programme on Equal Opportunities for Men and Women*, Brussels.

European Commission Network on Childcare and other Measures to Reconcile Employment and Family Responsibilities (1996), *The EC Childcare Network: A Decade of Achievements 1986-96 Final Report*, Brussels.

*European Industrial Relations Review* (1997, 1998), 'Sexual harassment at the workplace', vols. 287, 288, 289.

Eurostat (1997), *Continuing Vocational Training Survey in Enterprises: Results*, Luxembourg: Office for Official Publications of the European Communities.

Eyre, P. (1996), *Mujeres, Veinte Años Después*, Barcelona: Plaza y Janés.

Ferguson, K. (1984), *The Feminist Case Against Bureaucracy*, Philadelphia PA: Temple University Press.

Ferreira, V. (1996), 'Mujer y trabajo. La división sexual del trabajo en el análisis sociológico: de natural a socialmente construida', in M. A. García de León, M. García de Cortázar and F. Ortega (eds), *Sociología de la Mujer Española*, Madrid: Editorial Complutense.

Ferri, E and Smith, K. (1996), *Parenting in the 1990s*, London: Family Policy Studies Centre.

Fletcher, C. (1995), 'Continuing vocational training in Europe', *European Business Review*, 95 (1).

Folbre, N. (1994), *Who Pays for the Kids?*, London: Routledge.

Freidenberg, J., Imperiale, G. and Skovron, M.L. (1988), 'Migrant careers and well-being of women', *International Migration Review*, 22 (2) pp.208-225.

Fujita, M. (1989), '"It's all mother's fault": childcare and the socialization of working mothers in Japan', *Journal of Japanese Studies*, 15 (1) pp.67-92.

Gadrey, N. (1992), *Hommes et Femmes au Travail: Inégalité, Différences, Identités, Logiques Sociales*, Paris: L'Harmattan.

Gallie, D. (1996), 'Skill, gender and the quality of employment', in R. Crompton, D. Gallie and K. Purcell (eds).

García de León, M. A. (1994), *Elites Discriminadas: Sobre el Poder de las Mujeres*, Madrid: Anthropos.

Garcia de Leon, M. A., García de Cortázar, M. and Ortega, F. (eds) (1996), *Sociología de la Mujer Española*, Madrid: Editorial Complutense.

García de Sola, P. (1998), 'Contra la discriminación laboral de las mujeres', *El País, Negocios*, 13 December, Madrid.

García Sanz, B. (1997), *Mujeres y Empleo (1976-1996)*, Madrid: Ministerio de Trabajo y Asuntos Sociales.

Garcia-Ramon, M. D. and Monk, J. (eds.), *Women of the European Union: the Politics of Work and Daily Life*, London: Routledge.

Garrido González, E., Folguera Crespo, P., Ortega López, M. and Segura Graiño, C. (eds) (1997), *Historia de las Mujeres en España*, Madrid: Síntesis.

Garrido, L. (1992), *Las Dos Biografías de la Mujer en España*, Madrid: Instituto de la Mujer.

Giddens, A. (1984), *The Constitution of Society*, Cambridge: Polity.

Ginn, J. and Arber, S. (1994), 'Midlife women's employment and pension rights in relation to coresident adult children', *Journal of Marriage and the Family*, November, pp.813-819.

Ginn, J., Arber, S., Brannen, J., Dale, A., Dex, S., Elias, P., Moss, P., Pahl, J., Roberts, C., and Rubery, J. (1996), 'Feminist fallacies: a reply to Hakim on women's employment', *British Journal of Sociology*, 47 (1) pp.167-174.

Ginn, J. and Sandall, J. (1997), 'Balancing home and employment: stress reported by Social Services staff', *Work, Employment and Society*, 11 (3) pp.413-434.

Glenn, E. N. (1992), 'From servitude to work: historical continuities in the racial division of paid productive labor', *Culture and Society*, 18 (1) pp.1-43.

Graham, H. and Labanyi, J. (eds), *Spanish Cultural Studies: An Introduction. The Struggle for Modernity*, Oxford: Oxford University Press.

Grahl, J. and Teague, P. (1995), 'Is the European Social Model Fragmenting?', paper presented to Euroconference *Social Policy in an Environment of Insecurity*, New University of Lisbon, Portugal.

Granger, B., Stanworth, J. and Stanworth, C. (1995), 'Self-employment career dynamics: the case of "unemployment push" in U.K. book publishing', *Work Employment and Society*, 9 (3) pp.499-516.

Greenfeld, K. T. (1994), *Speed Tribes: Children of the Japanese Bubble*, London: Boxtree.

Greer, G. (1999), *The Whole Woman*, London: Doubleday.

Gregory, A. and O'Reilly, J. (1996) 'Checking out and cashing up: the prospects and paradoxes of regulating part-time work in Europe', in R. Crompton, D. Gallie and K. Purcell (eds).

Gregory, J. (1999) 'Gendered labour markets and political action', *Work, Employment and Society*, 13 (2) pp.389-398.

Gregson, N. and Lowe, M. (1994), *Servicing the Middle-Classes: Class, Gender and Waged Domestic Labour*, London: Routledge.

Grint, K. (1991), *The Sociology of Work: An Introduction*, Cambridge: Polity.

Guillaumin, C. (1995), *Racism, Sexism, Power and Ideology*, London: Routledge.

Gulati, L. (1994), 'Women in international migration', *Social Development Issues*, 16 (1) pp.75-97.

Hakim, C. (1979), *Occupational Segregation: a Comparative Study of the Degree and Pattern of Differentiation Between Men and Women's Work in Britain, the US and Other Countries*, Department of Employment Research Paper no.9, London: HMSO.

Hakim, C. (1993), 'The myth of rising female employment', *Work, Employment and Society*, 7 (1) pp.97-120.

Hakim, C. (1995), 'Five feminist myths about women's work', *British Journal of Sociology*, 46 (3) pp.429-45.

Hakim, C. (1996a), 'The sexual division of labour and women's heterogeneity', *British Journal of Sociology*, 47 (1) pp.178-188.

Hakim, C. (1996b), *Key Issues in Women's Work: Female Heterogeneity and the Polarisation of Women's Employment*, London: Athlone.

Hakim, C. (1998), 'Developing a sociology for the twenty-first century: Preference Theory', *British Journal of Sociology*, 49 (1) pp.137-143.

Halford, Susan (1989), 'Local authority women's initiatives, 1982-1988: the extent, origins and efficacy of positive policies for women in British local government', University of Sussex, Working Paper no. 69.

Hamblin, H. (1995), 'Employees' perspectives on one dimension of labour flexibility: working at a distance', *Work, Employment and Society*, 9 (3) pp.473-498.

Hantrais, L. and Letablier, M-T. (1995), 'La relation emploi-famille et ses modes de construction dans les pays de l'Union Européenne', *Dossiers du Centre d'Etudes de l'Emploi*, 6.

Hantrais, L. and Letablier, M-T. (1996), *Families and Family Policies in Europe*, Harlow: Longman.

Harman, H. (1993), *20th Century Man, 21st Century Woman: How Both Sexes can Bridge the Century Gap*, London: Vermilion.

Harrop, A. and Moss, P. (1995), 'Trends in parental employment', *Work, Employment and Society*, 9 (3) pp.421-444.

Hartman, H. (1976), 'Capitalism, patriarchy and job segregation by sex', *Signs*, 1 (3) pp.137-169.

Hartman, H. (1981), 'The unhappy marriage of Marxism and feminism: towards a more progressive union', in L. Sargent (ed.), *The Unhappy Marriage of Marxism and Feminism: A Debate on Class and Patriarchy*, London: Pluto.

Hayek, F.A. (1979), *The Road to Serfdom*, London: Routledge & Kegan Paul.

Hendry, J. (1981), *Marriage in Changing Japan*, London: Croom Helm.

Hewitt, P. (1993), *About Time: The Revolution in Work and Family Life*, London: Rivers Oram Press.

HM Treasury (1997), *Employment Opportunity in a Changing Labour Market*, London: HM Treasury.

HM Treasury (1998), *The Modernisation of Britain's Tax and Benefit System: the Working Families Tax Credit*, London: HM Treasury.

HMSO (1999), *Employment Relations Bill*, Session 1998/99, London: HMSO.

Hochschild, A. R. (1989), *The Second Shift*, New York: Avon Books.

Hogwood, B. and Gunn, L. (1984), *Policy Analysis For The Real World*, Oxford: Oxford University Press.

Holdsworth, C. and Dale, A. (1997), 'Ethnic differences in women's employment', *Work, Employment and Society*, 11 (3) pp. 435-457.

*Hombres y Mujeres*, http://www.psoe.es/actpol/valplanig/htm.

hooks, b. (1984), *Feminist Theory: From Margin to Centre*, Boston: South End Press.

Hoskyns, C. (1996), *Integrating Gender: Women, Law and Politics in the European Union*, London: Verso.

Howard, K. (ed.) (1995), *True Stories of the Korean Comfort Women*, London: Cassell.

Hutton, W. (1995), 'Forget austerity era - Britain's rich', *Guardian*, 16th October.

Huws, U. (1994), *Home Truths: Key Results from a National Survey of Homeworkers*,

*Report No. 2*. Leeds: National Group on Homeworking.

Huws, U (1997), *Flexibility and Security: Towards a New European Balance*, Citizen's Income Trust, Discussion Paper no. 3.

Ida, K. (1986), 'Revision of the prostitution law: a menace to human rights', *AMPO: Japan-Asia Quarterly Review*, 18 (2-3) pp.77-80.

IFF Research Ltd. (1993), *Employer Provided Training in the UK*, London: IFF.

Instituto de la Mujer and Ministerio de Asuntos Sociales (1987), *Plan Para la Igualdad de Oportunidades (1988-1990)*, Madrid.

Instituto de la Mujer and Ministerio de Asuntos Sociales (1993), *II Plan Para la Igualdad de Oportunidades (1993-1995)*, Madrid.

Instituto de la Mujer and Ministerio de Asuntos Sociales (1994), *La Mujer en Cifras: Una Década, 1982-1992*, Madrid.

Instituto de la Mujer and Ministerio de Trabajo y Asuntos Sociales (1997a), *Tercer Plan de Igualdad de Oportunidades entre Hombres y Mujeres 1997-2000*, Madrid.

Instituto de la Mujer and Ministerio de Asuntos Sociales (1997b), *Las Mujeres en Cifras: 1997*, Madrid.

Instituto Nacional de Estícas (1996), *Encuesta de la Población Activa*, no. 11 http://www.mtas.es.

International Labour Office (1995), *Gender Equality at Work: Strategies Towards the 21st Century*, Geneva: ILO.

International Labour Office (1999), *The Role of Employment and Work in Poverty Eradication: the Empowerment and Advancement of Women*, http://spider.oneworld.org/search97cgi/s9.

International Labour Office and United Nations Research and Training Institute for the Advancement of Women (1985), *Women in Economic Activity: A Global Statistical Survey (1950-2000)*, Santo Domingo: INSTRAW.

Irazusta, M. (1996), 'El Perfil Laboral de las Españolas', *Su Dinero 20*, http://w3.el-mundo.es/su-dinero/noticias/act-20-3.html.

Isaak, J. A. (1996), *Feminism and Contemporary Art*, London: Routledge.

Ito, R. (1992), '"Japayuki-san" genshoo saikoo' [Re-examination of the Japayuki-san phenomenon], in T. Iyotani and T. Kajita (eds), *Global Approach: Gaikokujin Roodoosharon* [*Global Approach: Theories on Foreign Migrant Workers*], Tokyo: Kobundo.

Iyori, N. (1987), 'The traffic in Japayuki-san', *Japan Quarterly*, 34 (1) pp.84-88.

Janis, I. (1972), *Victims of Group Think*, Boston: Houghton Mifflin.

Japan Anti-Prostitution Association (1995), *Against Prostitution and Sexual Exploitation Activities in Japan*, Tokyo: Kobundo.

Jeffreys, S. (1995), 'European industrial relations and welfare states', *European Journal of Industrial Relations*, 1 (3) pp.317-337.

Jenkins, R. (1996), *Social Identity*, London: Routledge.

Jessop, B (1994), 'The transition to post-Fordism and the Schumpeterian workfare state', in R. Burrows and B. Loader (eds), *Towards a Post-Fordist Welfare State*, London: Routledge.

Joekes, S. (1987), *Women in the World Economy*, INSTRAW: Oxford University Press.

José Carrasco, M., García Mina, A., Labrador, J. and Alemany Briz, C. (eds), *Mujer, Trabajo y Maternidad*, Madrid: UPCO.

Joshi, H., Dale, A. Ward, C., Davies, H. (1995), *Dependence and Independence in the Finances of Women aged 33*, Family Policy.

Kanai, Y. (1995), 'Overview: Issues for Japanese Feminism', *AMPO: Japan-Asia Quarterly Review*, 25 (4) and 26 (1).

*Kodansha Encyclopedia of Japan* (1983), Tokyo: Kodansha.

Komai, H. (1995), *Migrant Workers in Japan*, London: Kegan Paul International.

Land, H. and Rose, H. (1985), 'Compulsory altruism for some or an altruistic society for all?', in P. Bean, J. Ferris and D. Whynes (eds), *In Defence of Welfare*, London: Tavistock.

Laufer, J. (1992), *L'Entreprise et l'Egalité des Chances*, Documentation Française.

Lebaube, A. (1998), 'Les inégalités hommes-femmes s'accentuent de nouveau. Le monde des initiatives emploi', *Le Monde*, 25 February.

Lee, W. (1991), 'Prostitution and tourism in South-East Asia', in N. Redclift and M. T. Sinclair (eds), *Working Women: International Perspectives on Labour and Gender Ideology*, London: Routledge.

Leibfried, S. and Pierson, P. (eds) (1995), *European Social Policy*, Brookings Institute.

Letablier, M-T. (1995), 'Women's labour force participation in France: the paradoxes of the 1990s', *Journal of Area Studies*, no. 6.

Levitas, R. (ed.) (1986), *The Ideology of the New Right*, Cambridge: Polity.

Lewin, E. (1993), *Lesbian Mothers*, Cornell: Cornell University Press.

Lewis, C. and O'Brien, M. (eds) (1987), *Reassessing Fatherhood: New Observations on Fathers and the Modern Family*, London: Sage.

Lewis, J. and Meredith, B. (1988), *Daughters Who Care: Daughters Caring for Mothers at Home*, London: Routledge.

Lindley, R. (ed.) (1994), *Labour Market Structures and Prospects for Women*, Manchester: Equal Opportunities Commission.

Lipsey, R. and Chrystal, K. (1999), *Principles of Economics* (9th edn), Oxford: Oxford University Press.

Lister, R. (1995), 'Dilemmas in engendering citizenship', *Economy and Society*, 24 (1) pp.1-40.

Lister, R. (1997), *Citizenship: Feminist Perspectives*, Basingstoke: Macmillan.

Low Pay Commission (1998), *The National Minimum Wage: First Report of the Low Pay Commission*, London: HMSO.

Lukes, S. (1974), *Power: a Radical View*, Basingstoke: Macmillan.

Macías Sistiaga, C. (1996), *Las Actitudes del Empresario ante la Contratación de Mujeres*, Getafe Servicio de Comunicación/ Ayuntamiento de Getafe.

MacEwen Scott, A. (ed.), *Gender Segregation and Social Change*, Oxford: Oxford University Press.

MacKinnon, C. (1989), *Towards a Feminist Theory of the State*, Cambridge, Mass: Harvard University Press.

Marcone, R. M. (1998), 'Voices of protest in Rosa Montero's *Crónica del Desamor*', *Neophilologus*, 82 (1) pp.63-70.

Martínez Quintana, M. (1992), *Mujer, Trabajo y Maternidad. Problemas y Alternativas de las Madres que Trabajan*, Madrid: Instituto de la Mujer.

Maruani, M. (1989), *Au Labeur des Dames: Métiers Masculins, Emplois Féminins*, Paris: Syros.

Matsuda, M. (1992), 'Women from Thailand', *AMPO: Japan-Asia Quarterly Review*, 23 (4) pp.16-19.

Matsui, Y. (1991), 'Asian migrant women working in Japan's sex industry: victims of international trafficking', *Asian Women's Liberation*, 4 (8) pp.5-11.

Mazey, S. and Richardson, J. (eds) (1993), *Lobbying in the European Community*, Oxford: Oxford University Press.

Mazur, A. (1992), 'Symbolic reform in France: égalité professionnelle during the Mitterrand years', *West European Politics*, 15 (4).

Mazur, A. (1995), *Gender Bias and the State: Symbolic Reform at Work in the Fifth Republic of France*, Pittsburgh: University of Pittsburgh Press.

McElroy, W. (1992), 'Preferential treatment of women in employment', in C. Quest (ed.).

McRae, S. (1990), *Keeping Women In: Strategies to Facilitate the Continuing Employment of Women in Higher Level Occupations*, London: Policy Studies Institute.

Meehan, E. (1993), *Citizenship and the European Community*, London: Sage.

Melhuish, E. and Moss, P. (eds) (1991), *Day Care for Young Children: International Perspectives*, London: Routledge & Kegan Paul.

Metcalf, D. (1999), 'The Low Pay Commission and the national minimum wage', *The Economic Journal*, 109 (453) pp.46-66.

Mies, M. (1998), *Patriarchy and Accumulation on a World Scale: Women in the International Division of Labour*, London: Zed Books.

Migrant Women Workers' Research and Action Committee (1995), *NGO's Report on the Situation of Foreign Migrant Women in Japan and Strategies for Improvement*, Tokyo: The Forum on Asian Immigrant Workers.

Migration News (1996), 3 (12)
http://www.usc.edu/isd/elecresources/gateways/ migration.html.

Miles, R. (1989), *Racism*, London: Routledge.

Miles, R. (1989), *The Women's History of the World*, London: Paladin.

Mills, A. and Murgatroyd, S. (1991), *Organisational Rules: a Framework for Understanding Organisational Action*, Milton Keynes: Open University Press.

Mills, A. (1989), 'Gender, sexuality, and organisational theory', in J. Hearn, P. Tancred-Sheriff and G. Burrell (eds), *The Sexuality of Organisations*, London: Sage.

Ministerio de Educación y Ciencia (1995), *Desarrollo de la L.O.G.S.E., Educación Infantil*, Madrid.

Miranda, M. J. (1987), *Crónicas del Desconcierto: Actitudes Básicas y Demandas Políticas de las Españolas*, Serie Estudios: 8, Madrid Ministerio de Cultura and Instituto de la Mujer.

Mitter, S. (1986), *Common Fate Common Bond: Women in the Global Economy*, London: Pluto Press.

Moghadan, V. M. (1995), 'Gender dynamics of restructuring in the semiperiphery', in R. L. Blumberg, C. A. Rakowski, I. Tinker and M. Monteon (eds).

Monk, J. and Garcia-Ramon, M. D. (1996), 'Placing women of the European Union', in M. D. Garcia-Ramon and J. Monk (eds).

Montero, R. (1979), *Crónica del Desamor*, Madrid: Debate.

Montero, R. (1995a), *Amado Amo* (9th edn), Madrid: Debate.

Montero, R. (1995b), 'Political transition and cultural democracy: coping with the speed of change', in H. Graham and J. Labanyi (eds).

Montero, R. (1995c), 'The silent revolution: the cultural and social advance of women in democratic Spain', in H. Graham and J. Labanyi (eds).

Montero, R. (1998), 'La asesina de insectos', *Relatos de Fin de Milenio*, pp.107-117.

Moore, S. (1995), 'Girls on top of the learning curve', *Guardian*, 19 October.

Morgan, G. (1986), *Images of Organisation*, London: Sage.

Morokvasic, M. (1983), 'Women in migration: beyond the reductionist outlook', in A. Phizacklea (ed.), *One Way Ticket: Migration and Female Labour*, London: Routledge & Kegan Paul.

Morokvasic, M. (1984), 'Birds of passage are also women...' *International Migration Review*, 18 (4) pp.886-907.

Morris, L. (1990), *The Workings of the Household*, Cambridge: Polity.

Morris, L. (1991), 'Women's poor work', in P. Brown and R. Scase (eds).

Morris, L. (1993), 'Domestic labour and employment status among married couples: a case study in Hartlepool', *Capital and Class*, 49 pp.37-52.

Moser, C. and Young, K. (1981), 'Women of the working poor', *IDS Bulletin*, 12 (3) pp.54-62.

Moss Kanter, R. (1977), *Men and Women of The Corporation*, New York: Basic Books.

Neathey, F. and Hurstfield, J. (1995), *Flexibility in Practice: Women's Employment and Pay in Retail and Finance*, Equal Opportunities Commission Research Discussion Series no.16, Manchester: Equal Opportunities Commission.

Newell, S. (1993), 'The Superwoman Syndrome: gender differences in attitudes towards equal opportunities at work and towards domestic responsibilities at home', *Work, Employment and Society*, 7 (2) pp.275-289.

Nichol, C. (1998), 'Patterns of pay: results of the 1998 New Earnings Survey', *Labour Market Trends*, December, pp.623-634.

Nissel, M. and Bonnerjea, L. (1982), *Family Care of the Elderly: Who Pays?* London: Policy Studies Institute.

OECD (1986), 'Self-employment in OECD countries', *Employment Outlook*, Paris: OECD.

OECD (1993), *Trends in International Migration*, Paris: OECD.

OECD (1994), *Women and Structural Change: New Perspectives*, Paris: OECD.

OECD (1996), *Employment Outlook 1996*, Paris: OECD.

OECD (1998), 'Making the most of the minimum: statutory minimum wages, employment and poverty' in *Employment Outlook*, Paris: OECD.

Office for Official Publications of the European Committees (1992), *Treaty on European Union*, Brussels: European Commission.

Oliver, M. (1991), 'Disability and participation in the labour market', in P. Brown and R. Scase (eds).

*Omnibus Time Use Survey* (1995), London: Office of National Statistics.

Ostner, I. and Lewis, J. (1995), 'Gender and the evolution of European social policies', in S. Leibfried and P. Pierson (eds).

Owen, M. (1999) '"Sere and yellow women": colonialist theories and the social construction of older women', paper given at 'White? Women' Conference, University of York, 17 April.

Papps, I. (1992), 'Women, work and well-being', in C. Quest (ed), *Equal Opportunities: A Feminist Fallacy*, London: Institute of Economic Affairs.

Pateman, C. (1988a), *The Sexual Contract*, Cambridge: Polity.

Pateman, C. (1988b), 'The fraternal contract', in J. Keane (ed.), *Civil Society and the State*, London: Verso.

Peace, H. F. (1993), 'The pretended family: a study of the divisions of domestic labour in lesbian families', *Leicester University Discussion Papers in Sociology*, no. S93/3.

Pedraza, S. (1991), 'Women and migration: The social consequences of gender', *Annual Review of Sociology*, 17 pp.303-325.

Pereda, C., Actis, W. and Ángel de Prada, M. (1996), *Tiempo Social Contra Reloj: Las Mujeres y la Transformación en los Usos del Tiempo*, Serie Estudios, 48, Madrid: Ministerio de Asuntos Sociales and Instituto de la Mujer.

Pérez del Río, T. (1990), *Igualdad de Oportunidades*, Comisiones Obreras.

Pérez, J. (1992), 'España queda sin niños y las parejas entran en crisis', *Cambio*, 16, 14 de diciembre, pp.44-50.

Pettman, J. J. (1996), *Worlding Women: A Feminist International Politics*, London: Routledge.

Phillips, A. (1991), 'Citizenship and feminist theory', in G. Andrews (ed.), *Citizenship*, London: Lawrence & Wishart.

Phillips, A. (1993), *Democracy and Difference*, Cambridge: Polity.

Phillips, A. and Taylor, B. (1986), 'Sex and skill: notes towards a feminist economics', in Feminist Review Collective (eds), *Waged Work: A Reader*, London: Virago.

Phizacklea, A. (1994), 'A single or segregated market? gendered and racialized divisions', in H. Afshar and M. Maynard (eds).

Phizacklea, A. and Wolkowitz, C. (1995), *Homeworking Women: Gender, Racism and Class at Work*, London: Sage.

Pixley, J. (1993), *Citizenship and Employment: Investigating Post-Industrial Options*, Cambridge: Cambridge University Press.

Pollack, D. (1993), 'The revenge of the illegal Asians: aliens, gangsters, and myth in Kon Satoshi's "World Apartment Horror"', *Positions: East Asia Cultures Critique*, 1 (3) pp.677-714.

Pollert, A. (1988), 'Dismantling flexibility', *Capital and Class*, 34 pp.42-75.

Pringle, R. (1988), *Secretaries Talk: Sexuality, Power and Work*, London: Verso.

Pujol Algans, C. (1992), *Código de la Mujer*, Madrid: Ministerio de Asuntos Sociales and Instituto de la Mujer.

Quest, C. (ed.) (1992), *Equal Opportunities: A Feminist Fallacy*, London: Institute of Economic Affairs.

Rees, T. (1992), *Women and the Labour Market*, London: Routledge.

Rees, T. (1999), 'Mainstreaming equality,' in S. Watson and L. Doyal (eds), *Engendering Social Policy*, Buckingham: Open University.

Regàs, R. (1999), 'Por una libertad económica', *El Mundo*, 8 de marzo, http:www.el-mundo.es,.

Rhodes, M. (1995), 'Subversive Liberalism: market integration, globalisation and the European welfare state', *Journal of European Public Policy*, 2 (3) pp.384-406.

Rich, A. (1980), 'Compulsory heterosexuality and lesbian existence', in A. Snitow, C. Stansell, and S. Thompson (eds), *Desire: The Politics of Sexuality*, London: Virago.

Riddell, P. (1991), *The Thatcher Era and its Legacy*, Oxford: Blackwell.

Robinson, K. (1996), 'Of mail-order brides and "Boys' Own Tales"', *Feminist Review*, 52 pp.53-68.

Roche, M. (1992), *Rethinking Citizenship*, Cambridge: Polity.

Rollin, H. (1995), 'Women, employment and society in Spain: an equal opportunity?', *Journal of the Association for Contemporary Iberian Studies*, 8 (2) pp.45-59.

Rollin, H. (1996), 'The hazards of cross-national research', paper given at Women's/Gender Research Forum, Oxford Brookes University, 21 October.

Roper, M. (1996), 'Seduction and succession: circuits of homosocial desire in management', in D. Collinson and J. Hearn (eds), *Men as Managers, Managers as Men*, London: Sage.

Rubery, J. (1996), 'The labour market outlook and the outlook for labour market analysis', in R. Crompton, D. Gallie and K. Purcell (eds.).

Rubery, J. and Fagan, C. (1993), 'Occupational segregation of women and men in the European Community', *Social Europe*, Supplement 3/93.

Rubery, J., Horrell, S. and Burchell, B. (1994), 'Part-time work and gender inequality in the labour market', in A. MacEwen Scott (ed.).

Rubery, J. and Fagan, C. (1995), 'Gender segregation in societal context', *Work, Employment and Society*, 9 (2) pp.213-240.

Rubin, G. (1975), 'The traffic in women: notes on the "political economy" of sex', in R. R. Reiter (ed.), *Towards an Anthropology of Women*, London: Monthly Review Press.

Saint-Saëns, A. (1996), *Historia Silenciada de la Mujer: La Mujer Española Desde la Epoca Medieval hasta la Contemporánea*, Madrid: Editorial Complutense.

Salaman, G. (1986), *Working*, Tavistock: Ellis Horwood.

Sánchez-Rivera Peiró, J. M. (1995), 'Interrogantes interculturales sobre la mujer en el mundo de hoy', in M. José Carrasco, A. García Mina, J. Labrador and C. Alemany Briz (eds).

Sassen, S. (1991), *The Global City: New York, London, Tokyo*, Princeton, NJ: Princeton University Press.

Schroedel, J. (1985), *Alone in a Crowd*, Philadelphia, Penn: Temple University Press.

Seager, J. (1997), *The State of Women in the World Atlas* (2nd edn), London: Penguin.

Secrétariat d'état aux droits des femmes and INSEE (1991), *Les Femmes*.

Sellek, Y. (1996), 'Female migrant workers in Japan: working for the Yen', EARC Research Papers 96.7, Sheffield: University of Sheffield East Asia Research Centre.

Seymour, J. (1992), 'Women's time as a household resource', *Women's Studies International Forum*, 15 (2) pp.187-192.

Siltanen, J. (1994), *Locating Gender: Occupational Segregation, Wages and Domestic Responsibilities*, London: UCL Press.

Singhanetra-Renard, A. and Prabhudhanitisarn, N. (1992), 'Changing socio-economic roles of Thai women and their migration', in S. Chant (ed.) *Gender and Migration in Developing Countries*, London: Belhaven Press.

Sloman, J. (1998), *The Essentials of Economics*, London: Prentice Hall.

Sly, F. (1996), 'Women in the labour market: results from the Spring 1995 Labour Force Survey', *Labour Market Trends*, March, pp.91-113.

Small, S. (1994), *Racialised Barriers*, London: Routledge.

Smith, R. J. (1987), 'Gender inequality in contemporary Japan', *Journal of Japanese Studies*, 13 (1) pp.1-26.

Smith, S.W. (1994), *Labour Economics*, London: Routledge.

Social Trends 28 (1998), London: HMSO.

Social Trends 29 (1999), London: HMSO.

Spain, D. (1992), *Gendered Spaces*, London: Chapel Hill and University of North Carolina Press.

Speakman, S. and Marchington, M. (1999), 'Ambivalent patriarchs: shiftworkers, "breadwinners" and housework', *Work, Employment and Society*, 13 (1) pp.83-105.

Stalker, P. (1994), *The Work of Strangers: A Survey of International Labour Migration*, Geneva: International Labour Office.

Steans, J. (1998), *Gender and International Relations: An Introduction*, Cambridge: Polity.

Steiner, J. (1992), 'From direct effect to Francovich: shifting means of enforcement of Community Law', *European Law Review*, vol.18 pp. 3-22.

Steiner, J. and Woods, L. (1996), *Textbook on EC Law* (5th edn), Aldham: Blackstone.

Streeck, W. (1995), 'From Market Making to State Building? Reflections on the Political Economy of European Social Policy', in S. Leibfried and P. Pierson (eds), *European Social Policy*, Brookings Insitute.

Tasker, F. and Golombok, S (1998), 'The role of co-mothers in planned lesbian-led families', *The Journal of Lesbian Studies*, 2 (4).

Telo, M. (1986), 'La evolución de los derechos de la mujer', in C. Borreguero (ed.).

Thair, T. and Risdon, A. (1999), 'Women in the labour market: results from the Spring 1998 Labour Force Survey', *Labour Market Trends*, March, pp.103-128.

Thanh-Dam, T. (1983), 'The dynamics of sex tourism: the case of Southeast Asia', *Development and Change*, no.14 pp.533-553.

Thornley, C. and Coffey, D. (1999), 'The Low Pay Commission in context', *Work, Employment and Society*, 13 (3) pp.525-538.

Tickner, J. A. (1991), 'On the fringes of the world economy: a feminist perspective', in C. N. Murphy and R. Tooze (eds), *The New International Political Economy*, Boulder: Lynne Rienner Publishers.

Tocino, I. (1999), 'El machismo y la política', *El Mundo*, 23 de enero, p.8.

Tono, H. (1986), 'The Japanese sex industry: a heightening appetite for Asian women', *AMPO: Japan-Asia Quarterly Review*, 18 (2-3) pp.70-76.

Toutain, G. (1992), *L'Emploi au Féminin: pour Une Méthode de la Mixité Professionnelle*, Paris: Secrétariat Chargé des Droits des Femmes.

Tsurumi, E. P. (1994), 'Yet to be heard: the voices of Meiji factory women', *Bulletin of Concerned Scholars*, 26 (4) pp.18-28.

TUC (1995), *The New Divide*, London: TUC .

Tusell, J. (1997), 'La transición española: la recuperación de las libertades', *Historia*, 16, Madrid: Temas de Hoy.

Tyner, J. A. (1994), 'The social construction of gendered migration from the Philippines', *Asian and Pacific Migration Journal*, 3 (4) pp.589-617.

Unión General de Trabajadores de Andalucía (1992), *Guia de Asesoramiento a Mujeres en Materia de Empleo*, Seville.

United Nations (1991), *The World's Women 1970-1990: Trends and Statistics*, New York: United Nations.

United Nations (1995a), *Women in a Changing Global Economy: 1994 World Survey on the Role of Women in Development*, New York: United Nations.

United Nations (1995b), *From Nairobi to Beijing: Second Review and Appraisal of the Implementation of the Nairobi Forward-Looking Strategies for the Advancement of Women*, New York: United Nations.

United Nations (1995c), *Women: Looking Beyond 2000*, New York: United Nations.

United Nations (1996), *The Beijing Declaration and the Platform for Action: Fourth World Conference on Women*, New York: United Nations.

Uno, K. (1993), 'The death of "Good Wife, Wise Mother"?', in A. Gordon (ed.), *Postwar Japan as History*, Oxford: University of California Press.

USDAW (1994), *Problems of Flexible Working: USDAW Evidence to the Commission on Social Justice*, Manchester: USDAW.

Valentine, G. (1996), 'An equal place to work? Anti-lesbian discrimination and sexual citizenship in the European Union', in M. D. Garcia-Ramon and J. Monk (eds).

Valenzuela, E. (1994a), 'Cristina Alberdi: las reglas del juego de la política son masculinas' *Cambio* 16, 19 de diciembre, p.24.

Valenzuela, E. (1994b), 'Asalto al poder', *Cambio* 16, 19 de diciembre, pp. 21-3.

Vallance, E. and Davies, E. (1986), *Women of Europe: Women MEPs and Equality Policy*, Cambridge: Cambridge University Press.

Van Eeckhout, L. (1998), 'La crise ravive les vieux démons discriminatoires. Le monde des initiatives emploi', *Le Monde*, 25 February.

van Soest, A. (1994), 'Youth minimum wage rates: the Dutch experience', *International Journal of Manpower*, 15 (2/3) pp.100-117.

Van Every, J., (1995), *Heterosexual Women Changing the Family: Refusing to be a 'Wife'*, London: Taylor Francis.

Vincent, J. (1995), *Inequality and Old Age*, London: UCL Press.

Wacjman, J. (1996), 'Women and men managers: careers and equal opportunities', in R. Crompton, D. Gallie and K. Purcell (eds).

Walby, S. (1986), *Patriarchy at Work: Patriarchal and Capitalist Relations in Employment*, Cambridge: Polity.

Walby, S. (1988), *Gender Segregation at Work*, Buckingham: Open University Press.

Walby, S. (1990), *Theorizing Patriarchy*, Oxford: Blackwell.

Walby, S. (1994), 'Is citizenship gendered?', *British Journal of Sociology*, 28 (2) pp.379-396.

Walby, S. (1997), *Gender Transformations*, London: Routledge.

Walby, S. (1999), 'The restructuring of the gendered political economy: transformations in women's employment', in J. Cook, J. Roberts and G. Waylen (eds).

Walsh, J. (1999), 'Myths and counter-myths: an analysis of part-time female employees and their orientations to work and working hours', *Work, Employment and Society*, 13 (2) pp.179-203.

Weiner, M. (1989), *The Origins of The Korean Community in Japan, 1910-1923*, Atlantic Highlands, NJ: Humanities Press International.

West Midlands Low Pay Unit (1992), *Minimum Wages: EC Practice and UK Attitudes*, Briefing Paper 23, Birmingham: LPU.

Weston, K. (1991), *Families We Choose*, New York: Columbia University Press.

White, G. (1999), 'Pay structures of the low-paid and the national minimum wage', *Labour Market Trends*, March, pp.129-135.

Whitworth, S. (1994), 'Gender, international relations and the case of the ILO', *Review of International Studies*, 20 (4) pp.389-405.

Williams, F. (1994), 'Social relations, welfare and the post-Fordism debate', in R. Burrows and B. Loader (eds).

Witz, A. (1993), 'Women at work', in D. Richardson and V. Robinson (eds.), *Introducing Women's Studies*, Basingstoke: Macmillan.

Witz, A. and Savage, M. (1992), *Gender and Bureaucracy*, Oxford: Blackwell.

*Women of Europe Newsletter*, (1977) March, no. 68, Brussels.

Yamatani, T. (1989), *Japayuki-san* [Miss-Going-to-Japan], Tokyo: Joohoosentaa.

Young, K. (1977), 'Values in the policy process', *Policy and Politics*, 5 (3) pp.1-22.

Young, K. and Mills, L. (1980), *Public Policy Research: A Review of Qualitative Methods*,

Social Science Research Council.

Younger, M. and Warrington, M. (1996), 'Differential achievement of girls and boys at GCSE: some observations from the perspective of one school', *British Journal of the Sociology of Education*, 17 (3) pp.299-314.

Yuval-Davies, N. (1992), 'Women as citizens', in A. Ward, J. Gregory and N. Yuval-Davies (eds), *Women and Citizenship in Europe: Borders, Rights and Duties*, London: Trentham Books and EFSF.

Zatlin, P. (1987), 'Women novelists in democratic Spain: freedom to express the female perspective', *Anales de Literatura Española Contemporánea*, 12 pp. 29-44.

Zlotnik, H. (1995), 'The South-to-North migration of women', *International Migration Review*, 29 (1) pp.229-254.

# Index